FRAMING RISKY CHOICES

Framing Risky Choices

Brexit and the Dynamics of High-Stakes Referendums

ECE ÖZLEM ATIKCAN, RICHARD NADEAU, and ÉRIC BÉLANGER

McGill-Queen's University Press
Montreal & Kingston • London • Chicago

© McGill-Queen's University Press 2020

ISBN 978-0-2280-0079-2 (cloth)
ISBN 978-0-2280-0080-8 (paper)
ISBN 978-0-2280-0224-6 (ePDF)
ISBN 978-0-2280-0225-3 (ePUB)

Legal deposit second quarter 2020
Bibliothèque nationale du Québec

Printed in Canada on acid-free paper that is 100% ancient forest free (100% post-consumer recycled), processed chlorine free

This book has been published with the help of a grant from the Canadian Federation for the Humanities and Social Sciences, through the Awards to Scholarly Publications Program, using funds provided by the Social Sciences and Humanities Research Council of Canada.

We acknowledge the support of the Canada Council for the Arts.

Nous remercions le Conseil des arts du Canada de son soutien.

Library and Archives Canada Cataloguing in Publication

Title: Framing risky choices: Brexit and the dynamics of high-stakes referendums / Ece Özlem Atikcan, Richard Nadeau, and Éric Bélanger.

Names: Atikcan, Ece Özlem, 1982– author. | Nadeau, Richard, 1956– author. | Bélanger, Éric, author.

Description: Includes bibliographical references and index.

Identifiers: Canadiana (print) 20200171690 | Canadiana (ebook) 20200171720 | ISBN 9780228000808 (paper) | ISBN 9780228000792 (cloth) | ISBN 9780228002246 (ePDF) | ISBN 9780228002253 (ePUB)

Subjects: LCSH: European Union—Great Britain. | LCSH: Referendum—Great Britain.

Classification: LCC JF497.G7 A85 2020 | DDC 341.242/20941—dc23

This book was typeset by Marquis Interscript in 10.5/13 Sabon.

Contents

Figures and Tables   vii

Acknowledgments   xi

1   The Brexit Conundrum   3

2   The Brexit Campaign in Comparative Perspective   34

3   Preparing and Executing the Brexit Campaign   71

4   How Did the Scapegoating of the European Union Affect the Vote Choice?   95

5   How Did the Perceptions of Risk Affect the Vote Choice?   124

6   Why Do Some Remain Voters Accept the Outcome and Some Do Not?   151

7   Arguing for and against Borders   168

APPENDICES
1   Interviews   187
2   Data and Variables   195
3   Tables   200

Notes   203

Bibliography   217

Index   237

Figures and Tables

FIGURES

1.1 Three patterns of opinion change in referendums   12
1.2 Difference between support for Yes in pre-referendum polls and support in the vote in percentages   14
1.3 Selection of posters for Britain Stronger in Europe campaign   22–3
1.4 Selection of posters for Vote Leave campaign   24–5
1.5 Vote Leave leaflet strategically imitating a government leaflet   26
2.1 Selection of posters for Yes Scotland campaign   57
2.2 Selection of posters for Better Together campaign   58
3.1 Media coverage on economy versus immigration in percentages   93
4.1 Trends in 'free choice' European identity, 1996–2015   98
4.2 Attitudes toward the UK's relationship with the EU, 1992–2015   99
4.3 Logistic regression model of the Leave vote including socioeconomic variables (baseline model)   116
4.4 Logistic regression model of the Leave vote including socioeconomic variables and attitudes toward the EU   117
4.5 Pseudo-R-squared with different models among all respondents   120
4.6 Pseudo-R-squared with different models among early deciders   120
4.7 Pseudo-R-squared with different models among late deciders   120

viii Figures and Tables

5.1 Logistic regression model of the Leave vote including socioeconomic variables, attitudes toward the EU, and opinions on campaign arguments 139

5.2 Logistic regression model of the Leave vote including socioeconomic variables, attitudes toward the EU, opinions on campaign arguments and leader images 142

5.3 Logistic regression model of the Leave vote including socioeconomic variables, attitudes toward the EU, opinions on campaign arguments, leader images, and emotions 144

5.4 Pseudo-R-squared with different models among all respondents 145

5.5 Pseudo-R-squared with different models among early deciders 145

5.6 Pseudo-R-squared with different models among late deciders 145

5.7 Logistic regression model of the Leave vote including socioeconomic variables, attitudes toward the EU, opinions on campaign arguments, and risk attitudes 148

6.1 Linear regression models for satisfaction with democracy in the UK (losers and winners) 161

6.2 Linear regression models for satisfaction with democracy in the UK (sore losers, graceful losers, and winners) 162

6.3 Average marginal effects of anchor variables, attitudes toward the EU, information, timing of decision, and emotions: model of winners, sore losers, and graceful losers 165

TABLES

2.1 Strategies in EU referendums 40
2.2 Keywords in interview data 41
2.3 Brexit referendum strategies in a comparative perspective 69
3.1 Strategies in the Brexit referendum campaign 72
3.2 Issue balance in the media coverage of the referendum in percentages 91
4.1 Relationship between age and the referendum vote 102
4.2 Relationship between gender and the referendum vote 102
4.3 Relationship between education and the referendum vote 103

Figures and Tables

4.4	Relationship between wealth and the referendum vote 104
4.5	Feelings of attachment toward the UK and the EU 106
4.6	Opinion on the degree of EU intervention 106
4.7	Evaluation of the benefits of British membership in the EU 107
4.8	Opinion about the European integration project on free trade and immigration 108
4.9	Performance of the EU in dealing with various issues 109
4.10	Support for Leave and feelings of attachment toward the UK 111
4.11	Support for Leave and feelings of attachment toward · the EU 111
4.12	Support for Leave and opinion on the degree of EU intervention 112
4.13	Support for Leave and evaluation of the benefits of British membership in the EU 113
4.14	Support for Leave and opinion about the European integration project on free trade 114
4.15	Support for Leave and opinion about the European integration project on immigration 114
5.1	Opinions about David Cameron's deal and the vote 127
5.2	Evaluations of campaign success in 'putting forward a clear vision of the UK it wants' 128
5.3	Leaders' performance during the Brexit campaign 130
5.4	Leaders' persuasiveness during the Brexit campaign 130
5.5	Time of decision and the vote in the Brexit referendum 130
5.6	Perceptions of the consequences of a Leave vote 132
5.7	Opinions about the level of migration in the UK 134
5.8	Arguments mentioned by Leave voters 135
5.9	Arguments mentioned by Remain voters 135
5.10	Relationship between support for three campaign arguments and the vote 138
5.11	Leaders' ratings 141
5.12	Relationship between supportive emotions toward the Leave victory and the vote choice 143
6.1	Reactions to the Brexit referendum result 158
6.2	Satisfaction with UK democracy and the Leave vote: Losers versus winners 158

6.3	Satisfaction with UK democracy and the Leave vote: Sore/graceful losers versus winners 159
6.4	Descriptive statistics for winners, graceful losers and sore losers 164
A2.1	Variables 195
A3.1	Logistic regression models for a vote in favour of leaving the EU 200
A3.2	Linear regression models for satisfaction with democracy in the UK 201
A3.3	Multinomial regression model of winners, sore losers, and graceful losers 202

Acknowledgments

The Brexit referendum and its outcome puzzled the academic world. Many studies sought to explain the factors behind this critical decision, ranging from long-standing Euroscepticism to misinformation disseminated during the campaign. Our starting point was different. The core idea behind this project was to understand how unique this referendum was. Instead of taking it as a single case, we wanted to go beyond and contextualize this puzzling referendum by looking closely into what we know about referendums elsewhere in the world and understand whether Brexit was similar to these previous cases and where it differed from them. This comparative angle was essential to reveal the role played by referendum politics. Referendums generate peculiar dynamics, necessitating specific strategies and providing unequal opportunities to the two sides. A comparison of the Brexit referendum strategies to those used in previous referendums provides a better understanding of which arguments on European integration and political autonomy gained more traction than others. This project therefore offers a much-needed comparative, multi-method analysis of the Brexit vote by paying special attention to referendum politics and framing strategies.

It is a great pleasure to express our gratitude to those who supported our research and writing. Our editor at McGill-Queen's University Press, Richard Baggaley, was extraordinarily supportive from the moment he saw the manuscript. His encouragements have been invaluable in navigating the review and the publication processes. Special thanks go to our anonymous reviewers who gave highly constructive comments that made the manuscript much stronger. We would also like to extend our warmest thanks to Sara Hobolt, Catherine De Vries,

John Curtice, Richard Rose, Julie Smith, Ben Seyd, Robert Thomson, Zachary Greene, Heinz Brandenburg, and Neil McGarvey, who all provided us with sharp questions, thought-provoking viewpoints, and key contacts at the EPOP, APSA, ECPR, and EPSA conferences and at the University of Strathclyde, where we presented our work in progress. We also appreciate receiving permission to reprint material from an earlier article published in the *Journal of Elections, Public Opinion and Parties* (12 April 2019, copyright EPOP, available online at http://www.tandfonline.com/doi/full/10.1080/17457289.2019.16 04528). Chapter 6 presents a revised version of this article.

We gratefully acknowledge the contributions of the Quebec Research Council/Fonds de recherche du Québec–Société et culture (FRQSC) and the Department of Politics and International Studies at the University of Warwick. We are especially indebted to all of our interviewees who took time from their busy schedules to answer all of our questions. The amazing team at Survation – Chris Hopkins, Frederick Alloh, and Marius Mosoreanu – helped us in building the survey and did not hesitate to check time after time to make sure everything was exactly as we wanted. We also thank El Hadj Touré for his diligent research assistance and Emma Hall for her patience and wonderful editorial skills. We are particularly grateful to Maureen Garvie for reading every word with such attention in her diligent copy-editing.

It goes without saying that none of this would have been possible without the endless support and patience of our families. Without them, we would not be where we are today, professionally and personally.

Ece Özlem Atikcan
Leamington Spa, United Kingdom

Richard Nadeau
Éric Bélanger
Montreal, Canada

FRAMING RISKY CHOICES

1

The Brexit Conundrum

There are two 'truisms' in all elections, the iron law of politics: firstly, the economy trumps everything at the ballot box; secondly, if people are undecided, at the last minute they will stick with the status quo. Both were proven wrong in this referendum.[1]

James McGrory

David Cameron offered the British people a direct say in arguably the most important political decision of a generation. Should Britain remain a member of the European Union (EU)? The vote would mark the future of British politics and economy. Its impact would not be limited to Britain: it could derail European integration, change the map of the EU, and have implications for the Euro and Britain's role in the international economy. Given the strong tradition of Euroscepticism in the UK, proposing the referendum was a considerable gamble for a prime minister who sought to deliver a Remain vote. After an intense campaign full of emotions and drastically contradicting claims from the two sides, on 23 June 2016, 52 per cent of the public voted to leave the EU. The result split the country along generational, geographical, and class lines, bringing about a change more significant than any in living memory.

Interestingly, a great majority of policy-makers, stakeholders, and academics as well as the general public had expected the British public to vote to remain in the EU. The British Political Studies Association carried out an expert survey of journalists, academics, and pollsters about their predictions of the outcome (Jennings and Fisher 2016).[2] The results, based on the expectations of 596 experts in total, demonstrated that 87 per cent thought the UK would stay in the EU, with only 5 per cent believing that Brexit would be the most likely outcome. This expectation was based on what McGrory put as the 'truisms' of elections – the well-established idea that voters resent change. Voters prefer the status quo to uncertainty and tend to avoid economic costs (Samuelson and Zeckhauser 1988). Why, then, did these 'truisms' not work for everyone? Why did a critical group of the British public defy these apparent rules and vote to take a major economic risk?

Political scientists have been baffled by the Brexit result. However, it looks less surprising when four crucial but neglected factors are drawn upon in the analysis. Most studies treat the Brexit referendum as a single case, overlooking the peculiar dynamics of referendum politics, ignoring the power of certain kinds of political arguments, and lacking a systematic analysis with a multi-method approach. In this book, we take a comparative perspective, locating the Brexit vote within the bigger picture of EU and independence referendums and paying special attention to campaign dynamics in referendums.

The way that an issue is presented or 'framed' can produce dramatic differences in public opinion, and this happens more often in referendums than in regular elections. Moreover, strong arguments are not necessarily those that rely on evidence. They are strong in their *appeal*. Catchy, emotional, and negative arguments that resonate with existing voter concerns move public opinion more than dull and technical statements. Through their campaign rhetoric, politicians redefined what Brexit would mean for the public and whether remaining or leaving would be riskier. Despite contradicting 'the experts', the Leave side prevailed in this battle and made this historic decision possible. We make this argument by adopting a much-needed multi-method approach, showing how the campaign contributed to the outcome via three kinds of data: interviews with the campaigners, media content analysis of the news media, and a detailed post-referendum survey. Through this data, we build our argument step by step. We track the impact of the campaign, beginning from how it was planned, relying on interviews, then move on to how it was portrayed in the media, using content analysis, and conclude with how it contributed to the vote choice, using survey data.

Adopting a comparative perspective does not immediately shed light on the puzzle. At first glance, the outcome of the Brexit referendum cannot be understood within existing explanations of referendums elsewhere in the world. In previous EU referendums, whenever an anti-EU vote was presented as having drastic economic consequences or potentially leading to an exit from the EU, a majority tended to vote in favour of European integration (Atikcan 2015b, 2018; Hobolt

2006b). Notable examples of such behaviour can be seen in the votes on the Fiscal Treaty and in the repeated votes on the Maastricht, Nice, and Lisbon treaties. In independence referendums as well, economic costs consistently trump national identity, as a majority of voters worry about the economic costs of a departure from the host state (Meadwell 1995; Nadeau, Martin, and Blais 1999; Scott 2016). But a closer look at campaigns, and a comparison of the strategies used in the Brexit referendum with those used on previous occasions, help us understand why the Brexit result departed from typical voting behaviour in these previous referendums. To achieve a systematic analysis of the campaign, we draw on an extensive bank of strategies used by pro-EU/anti-EU and pro-independence/anti-independence campaigners, involving over 150 in-depth, face-to-face interviews with campaigners in Scotland and England and across Europe. These interviews not only allow comparisons but also reveal the rationale behind the key campaign decisions. We also use media content analysis and a detailed post-referendum survey including survey experiments.

Our core argument is as follows. The opinion polls showed a critically split public in the run-up to the referendum, and the main expectation was that the status quo bias would motivate enough voters for a tight result in favour of remaining in the EU. However, the opposite happened. We argue that knowing how the Brexit referendum compares to previous referendums is crucial in understanding this unusual, anti-status-quo outcome. In the Brexit vote, as in any referendum, the risk assessment depended primarily on the campaign strategies of the Remain and Leave campaigns. These strategies helped voters understand the risks involved in the choice. Voting against the status quo for an uncertain future outside the EU was made easier for a critical section of the society because the pro-Leave arguments strongly suggested that remaining in the EU would be at least as risky as leaving it. These voters chose to 'Take Back Control' of their country. Strikingly, the Leave campaign's strategy also had an impact on the degree to which Remain voters accepted the referendum result. By effectively de-risking the Brexit decision, the pro-Leave arguments convinced a group of moderate Remain voters that the concept of Brexit could potentially be palatable.

This chapter is organized into three sections. The first two provide the book's theoretical foundations, and the third presents its core argument and methodology. In the first section, we discuss why existing studies of the Brexit vote cannot adequately account for this phenomenon. In the second, we take a step back to explore referendum politics, focusing on factors that increase or decrease volatility in public opinion and paying particular attention to the status quo bias and campaign framing. The chapter's final section serves as an entry point to the book, presenting the main actors and arguments of the Brexit campaign and detailing the book's key argument, methodology, and road map.

UNDERSTANDING THE BREXIT REFERENDUM: WHAT DO WE ALREADY KNOW?

The referendum result was a seismic upheaval for British and European politics, but attempts to explain the public opinion dynamics of this political earthquake have thus far been found wanting. Most works on the topic seek to discuss the negotiation process and the reasons behind holding the referendum in the first place (Glencross 2016), to provide an insider but anecdotal view of the Brexit referendum (e.g., Banks 2016; Bennett 2016; Mosbacher and Wiseman 2016; Oliver 2016; Shipman 2016) or to study the Brexit vote in detail but as a single case study (e.g., Becker, Fetzer, and Novy 2017; Clarke, Goodwin, and Whiteley 2017; Colantone and Stanig 2018; Goodwin and Heath 2016; Hobolt 2016; Matti and Zhou 2017; Swales 2016).

In explaining the result, these studies mostly highlight long-term trends in British public opinion, such as the importance of sociodemographic factors like age and education, people's attitudes toward immigration, their past support for the United Kingdom Independence Party (UKIP), their feelings of national identity, and their attitudes toward European integration. For instance, Goodwin and Heath (2016) find in an aggregate-level analysis of the Brexit vote that public support for Leave was very similar to past support for UKIP. In other words, the local districts that supported UKIP in the 2014 European elections also supported Brexit in 2016, and those districts that were younger and better educated tended to vote Remain, underlining the importance of education and age in explaining the outcome. The authors link this voting pattern to socioeconomic changes over the years, which created a category of 'left-behind' voters – older, working-class, white voters with few qualifications and low income – who were having difficulty adapting to a post-industrial economy. Other studies, similarly examining the impact of long-term factors on the Brexit result, confirm the presence of significant electoral divides based on age, gender, education, and income (e.g., Becker, Fetzer, and Novy 2017; Matti and Zhou 2017; Swales 2016).

Clarke, Goodwin, and Whiteley (2017) present an in-depth analysis of the Brexit vote that combines these long-term factors with some short-term ones, such as the leadership roles of the campaigners and emotions. The authors' core argument is that Brexit was caused by a complex and crosscutting mix of calculations, emotions, and cues. People's long-term attitudes toward immigration and their feelings of national identity existed long before the campaign began, but immediate forces such as risk assessments, emotional reactions to the EU, and the images of party leaders had an impact as well.

Hobolt (2016) similarly provides an explanation that focuses on both long-term and short-term factors. She bases her explanation on the existing Euroscepticism in the UK but argues that these feelings were activated in an intense campaign. Her work speaks directly to the EU referendums literature, which has been traditionally divided between 'second-order' and 'issue-voting' schools in explaining the referendum results, essentially attributing the results to either domestic or European factors. The 'second-order' school argues that EU referendum results do not reflect voters' opinions on integration issues and that national factors, such as the level of satisfaction with the government and voter identification with the parties holding office, are decisive (Franklin Eijk, and Marsh 1995; Reif and Schmitt 1980). Hobolt belongs to the second school, arguing instead that the Brexit vote was in line with British citizens' underlying broad attitudes toward European integration (Siune, Svensson, and Tonsgaard 1994). Although this factor is essentially a long-term one, Hobolt (2009) argues that such feelings become activated only when voters are exposed to intense campaigns and detailed campaign information. Accordingly, she finds that, in the intense Brexit campaign, Leavers voted on the basis of their EU attitudes, which were motivated by anti-immigration and anti-establishment feelings. The vote thus reflected the divide between those feeling left behind by the globalization process and those who welcomed it. Focusing on the implications of the Brexit vote for electoral studies (Clarke, Goodwin, and Whiteley 2017) or for the EU referendum literature (Hobolt 2016), these studies tell us that the Brexit outcome was due to a combination of long-term socioeconomic changes and attitudes toward European integration, as well as to an intense campaign that gave cues to the voting public.

From the beginning, the polls were quite close, and the campaign unquestionably had an impact on the narrow outcome. That is why, instead of simply underlining the importance of campaign cues or campaign information, we provide a comprehensive and nuanced understanding of how the Brexit campaign differed from previous referendum campaigns and how these differences likely contributed to the unexpected outcome. To achieve this understanding, we address four overlooked aspects. First, we compare the Brexit referendum to other referendums. Without a *comparative* perspective, it is impossible to understand whether the Brexit referendum was unique. Second, we adopt a multi-method approach. Without such a *systematic* analysis, it is impossible to know in what ways the campaign contributed to the outcome. Third, we focus on the political dynamics of referendums, because they generate *a specific type of campaign*. Why does the Brexit vote not fit the existing explanations of referendum outcomes? Why did a critical group of British voters choose to vote for departure from the EU despite a resourceful Remain campaign that activated the status quo bias and spelled out the drastic consequences of such a departure? Finally, we pay special attention to campaign arguments. *Not every argument is equally effective* in shaping individual minds. How did the Brexit campaign cues or campaign information compare to such cues provided in other referendums? Which strategies did the campaigners adopt? What kind of campaign information did the public receive, and what information was more likely to shift their views on the topic?

On the last point, only two studies so far have examined the importance of campaign framing. Using a survey experiment conducted before the campaign began in autumn 2015, Goodwin et al. (2018) explore the potential impact of various pro- and anti-EU arguments. While underlining the potential of pro-EU arguments, they find that the impact of these arguments was mitigated by pro-Leave arguments. These results predate the Brexit campaign but lend support to our core argument, signalling the difficulty that pro-EU arguments would face when contrasted with anti-EU arguments.[3] In another experimental study, Morisi (2018) compares how risk attitudes mattered in the Scottish independence and Brexit referendums and finds that subjecting individuals to information, particularly to pro and con arguments, dampens the impact of risk attitudes on the vote choice. This finding also parallels our core argument that the information disseminated during the Brexit campaign, which included pro and con arguments on the economic risks of departure, helped 'de-risk' the decision for some critical voters. We carry these studies further by analysing the battle of arguments in the actual campaign, beginning with interview data detailing the rationale behind the choice of the campaign arguments, then observing how those arguments were conveyed in the news media, and finally exploring their likely impact by using our post-referendum survey.

In this book, to provide a comprehensive and nuanced answer to the Brexit puzzle, we first study various kinds of referendums to extract the most commonly used referendum campaign strategies. We also build a thorough understanding of campaign communications by combining the findings of literatures on political campaigns, framing theory, and social movements. We then position the Brexit referendum campaign within this analytical framework to understand what the Leave side did differently. Next, to explain how the Brexit campaign strategies might have contributed to the outcome, we rely on our three-step methodology. Further, by showing that the strength of an argument is not about its empirical validity but about its public appeal, we explore the core mechanism behind post-truth politics.

REFERENDUM POLITICS AND FRAMING

How do voters and campaigners behave in referendums?

Much has been said about the role of campaigns in politics. Those who argue that campaigns exert a significant and growing influence on voter behaviour are generally at odds with those who believe that an election's outcome is mostly influenced by long-term factors, such as voters' partisan identification and ideological positioning, or even the political and economic juncture a few months before the election (e.g., Erikson and Wlezien 2012; Vavreck 2009; Nadeau and Lewis-Beck 2012; Nadeau et al. 2019).

By their nature, however, referendums are very different from elections and have been studied as a distinct field in political science (e.g., Altman 2010; Butler and Ranney 1994; Closa 2007; Morel and Qvortrup 2018; Oppermann 2013; Qvortrup 2013). The main difference is the specific nature of the referendum question, which can range from a proposal with which the public is highly familiar to one that is complex and technical. Emphasizing that opinion formation is an interaction of information and predisposition, LeDuc (2002) suggests that voting behaviour in referendum campaigns exhibits greater volatility than in regular elections (e.g., Darcy and Laver 1990; de Vreese 2007; de Vreese and Semetko 2004; Hobolt 2005; McAllister 2001; Zaller 1992). Depending on the nature of the proposal and the circumstances of the referendum, these campaigns take different forms (e.g., Clarke, Goodwin, and Whiteley 2017; Martin and Nadeau 2001; Liñeira, Henderson, and Delaney 2017).

When a referendum question concerns an issue in a long-standing debate, and the positions of the political parties on the issue are well known, voting behaviour conforms to predictable patterns and resembles election campaigns. However, when ideological alignments are unclear and parties line up in a non-traditional way, referendum campaigns are more influential than regular election campaigns (LeDuc 2002). This is particularly the case in referendums on complex international treaties or large packages of constitutional provisions, as voters do not have well-formed opinions (Johnston et al. 1996; LeDuc 2002). Consequently, public opinion shows greater movement during these campaigns, culminating in outcomes that pre-campaign polls are unable to predict. Campaign materials give voters cues that serve as shortcuts to help them make sense of conflicting information.

Accordingly, there are three types of referendum campaigns: opinion formation, opinion reversal, and uphill struggle (LeDuc 2002). Volatility in public opinion is highest in the first type because the proposal is unfamiliar and the partisan or ideological cues are limited. This circumstance results in a gradual opinion-formation period. The Canadian constitutional referendum in 1992, or the referendums on the European Constitutional Treaty in France and the Netherlands in 2005, present important examples of this type, where voters had little knowledge on the complex and unfamiliar proposals and public opinion shifted significantly over the course of the campaigns (e.g., Atikcan 2015a; Hobolt 2009; Johnston et al. 1996). Second, opinion-reversal campaigns can bring a new dimension to a fairly well known issue and thereby decrease the impact of previous beliefs. The results of the 1986 Irish referendum on divorce or the 1999 Australian referendum on the monarchy contradicted the pre-campaign predictions, proving that campaigns are able to change existing attitudes (e.g., Darcy and Laver 1990; Highley and McAllister 2002). In the third type, uphill struggle campaigns, volatility is the lowest. Public opinion is highly stable with pre-existing beliefs anchoring the outcome. This stability occurs because one of the two things results in strong partisan or ideological cues: the nature of the issue itself or the circumstances of the referendum (LeDuc 2002, 728). The 1993 referendum in New Zealand on the electoral system, the 1997 devolution referendum in Scotland, and the 1995 sovereignty referendum in Quebec were instances in which an important part of the voters were already mobilized on the basis of available and familiar cues (e.g., Aimer and Miller 2002; Denver 2002; Pammett and LeDuc 2001). As figure 1.1 demonstrates, there is no drastic shift over the course of the campaign because the referendum reinforces predispositions based on partisanship or ideology. The nature of the question and the way it is presented to the public are thus crucial to understanding referendum voting behaviour. Campaigners often have a key role in defining the meaning of the referendum proposal.

What kinds of strategies do referendum campaigners use to frame the vote choice? Although the political actors participating in a referendum campaign are very similar to those participating in an election campaign, their goal is somewhat different. They need *to reach the winning majority of 50 per cent*, as opposed to mobilizing a more limited and familiar voter base, and need to do so on a specific question. Referendum campaigners must therefore pay specific attention to swing voters (Usherwood and Wright 2017). LeDuc (2002) argues that especially in the third type of campaign, where there is a tight race, campaigners' attention is directed toward wavering or undecided voters, because the result could well depend on a few percentage points. In the Swedish referendum on EU membership in 1994, or in the Quebec sovereignty referendum in 1995, campaigners resorted to this particular strategy. In the latter case, the Parti québécois government knew that it could count on the support of the most committed hard-core *sovereignist* voters, but it also needed the votes of the moderate 'soft nationalists' in order to secure a majority for its proposal (LeDuc 2002).

Campaigners in referendums also pay close attention to *controlling the status quo bias*. Numerous studies show that in making decisions, individuals weigh losses more heavily than gains (e.g., Ehrlich and Maestas 2010; Kahneman 2011; Kahneman and Tversky 1979, 1984; Kam and Simas 2010; Nadeau, Martin, and Blais 1999; Samuelson and Zeckhauser 1988; Steenbergen and Siczek 2017; Thaler 1980). In other words, individuals disproportionately choose the status quo over the alternatives, because they weigh the potential losses from switching as larger than potential gains. The existence of status quo

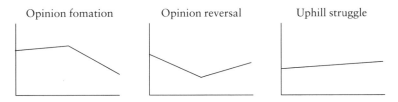

Figure 1.1 Three patterns of opinion change in referendums

Source: LeDuc 2002.

bias in referendum voting has been indicated many times in the literature (e.g., Bowler and Donovan 1998; Goldsmith 2005; Magleby 1984; Magleby and Patterson 1998).[4] Samuelson and Zeckhauser (1988, 36) argue that the status quo bias depends directly on the 'framing' of gains and losses. Nadeau, Martin, and Blais (1999, 526) similarly suggest that individuals seek to avoid the potentially regrettable consequences attached to a given option, especially 'when those consequences are extreme and widely discussed'. This tendency, in turn, offers politicians an incentive to exploit and emphasize the worst-case scenarios.

Interestingly, in the framing of the status quo bias by political actors in the campaign, the two sides are not on equal footing. The No side in a referendum campaign has certain political advantages (Atikcan 2015a; Atikcan 2018; LeDuc 2005; Nadeau, Martin, and Blais 1999). The No campaigners do not necessarily need to make a coherent and persuasive case against a proposal. They need only to raise doubts in the minds of voters, play upon known fears, or link the proposal to other less popular issues or personalities. The No side can prevail if it conducts careful research on which parts of the issue the voters would not like, makes effective commercials appealing to such themes, and generates sufficient money for advertising. For example, LeDuc (2005) explores the debate in the 2000 Danish and 2003 Swedish referendums on the common currency Euro and argues that the No side benefitted from this advantage by broadening the subject to contentious issues such as enlargement, social welfare, and national sovereignty. Similarly, Jerit (2004), in her research on the framing of the Canada-US free trade agreement in the 1988 Canadian federal election, emphasizes that the proponents of the policy had the burden of explaining why the agreement was worth supporting, while the opponents could appeal to anger or fear.

Empirically, to assess whether this status quo bias holds in referendums, Fisher and Renwick (2016) look at all 268 national referendums held in democracies since 1990, finding that the public in fact supports change at a rate that falls between 40 and 69 per cent of referendums.[5] But their data also show an average swing to the status quo by 1.5 per cent following the final polls.[6] In other words, people do vote for change in certain cases, but the overall tendency is in line with the expectation that supporters of the status quo, and thereby the Remain side, will win. The data also demonstrate that although voters often support the 'change option' at the start of the campaign, they increasingly prefer the less risky status quo option as the campaign progresses (LeDuc 2003; LeDuc and Pammett 1995; Renwick 2014). Thus, voters tend to choose in the end the 'the devil they know'. Based on data compiled by Renwick and LeDuc, figure 1.2 illustrates the difference in support for voting Yes in pre-referendum polls and the actual vote itself in percentages.

If the bar points up, it implies that the support for the Yes goes up; if it points down, support for the Yes option falls. The Yes vote almost always means the change option. Renwick (2014) observes that the support for change goes down more often than up, and that the drops in support for change are typically much bigger than the rises. Typical examples of such votes include the Canadian constitutional referendum in 1992, the British electoral reform referendum in 2011, the Irish referendum on the Senate in 2013, and the Scottish independence referendum in 2014. Where there are exceptions to this rule, Renwick (2014) explains them in light of how the campaign portrayed the vote choice.[7]

Campaign arguments are therefore extremely important in referendums, helping voters to find meaning in the often-unfamiliar choices they face. We argue that there are two key strategies available to referendum campaigners: swinging the critical 'undecided' voters and controlling the status quo bias. We next discuss how campaigners use their communications strategically to achieve these goals.

Framing the Choice in Referendum Campaigns

HOW DOES CAMPAIGN FRAMING AFFECT INDIVIDUALS?
In the study of campaign communications, there are three schools of thought on the influence of political communications on public opinion: pre-war theories of mass propaganda, postwar theories of

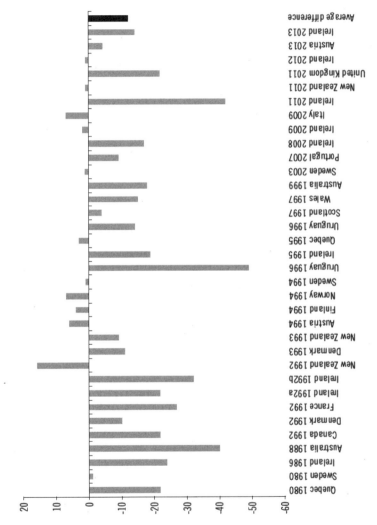

Figure 1.2 Difference between support for Yes in pre-referendum polls and support in the vote in percentages

Source: Renwick 2014

partisan reinforcement, and recent theories of cognitive, agenda-setting, and persuasion effects (Brady, Johnston, and Sides 2006; Norris et al. 1999). Because the first two approaches fail to explain election outcomes fully, attention has turned to the role of strategic communications, particularly agenda setting and persuasive effects.

Agenda-setting theories focus on the process in which competing political elites define their most important issues and present them to the public (Iyengar 1993; Riker 1993; Soroka 2002). The better they place their issues on the agenda, the more successful they are. Framing, in turn, is 'a process by which people develop a particular conceptualization of an issue or reorient their thinking about an issue' (Chong and Druckman 2007b, 104).[8] A framing effect occurs when, in describing an issue or event, a speaker's emphasis on a subset of potentially relevant considerations causes individuals to focus on these considerations when forming their opinions (Druckman 2001, 1042; Entman 2004, Nadeau, Pétry, and Bélanger 2010).

Research on this topic considers an attitude toward an issue as the weighted sum of evaluative beliefs. In other words, attitude is the combination of the *evaluation* of an issue's attributes and the *salience weight* associated with each of these attributes (Chong and Druckman 2007b, 105). For instance, a person's attitude toward a new housing project might consist of both positive and negative evaluations, based on different dimensions such as economic benefits (positive) and environmental harms (negative). The overall attitude would therefore depend on the relative weights assigned to these dimensions. Politicians attempt to mobilize voters behind their policies by encouraging them to think along particular lines, emphasizing certain features of these policies. The influence of these frames on the voter is known as the framing effect.

The way that an issue is framed can produce dramatic differences in public opinion. For example, in an American study, when answering whether they would favour or oppose allowing a hate group to hold a political rally, 85 per cent of respondents answered in favour if the question highlighted the importance of free speech, whereas only 45 per cent were in favour when the question emphasized public safety and the risk of violence (Sniderman and Theriault 2004). Also, approximately 20 per cent of the American public believed that too little was spent on 'welfare', while 65 per cent thought that too little was spent on 'assistance to the poor' (Rasinski 1989).

WHAT ARE THE INGREDIENTS OF A STRONG FRAME?

Most research on political campaigns treats campaign 'cues' or 'information' as a uniform category, paying attention to the positioning of the political parties or the amount (intensity) of campaign information available to voters. But the *kind* of campaign information also matters. Not every argument is equally effective. Framing studies mostly focus on the psychological processes behind such effects. Research on political psychology shows that it is essentially the *availability*, *accessibility*, and *applicability* of frames that matter (Chong and Druckman 2007b). People draw their opinions from the set of *available and accessible* beliefs stored in their memory. In other words, they should be able to comprehend the content of the frame. Individuals may also consciously evaluate the *applicability* of the frames. Consideration of applicability comes into the picture when individuals are sufficiently motivated, which usually results from their being exposed to competing frames. As such, high personal motivation and competitive contexts encourage individuals to engage in conscious questioning of which frame is more applicable to the situation. Frames coming from credible sources and those that appeal to cultural values also enjoy higher applicability and strength (Druckman 2001; Petty and Cacioppo 1986).

The literature on social movements has generated strikingly similar findings on frame strength. The way that people interpret their grievances is shown to be critical to their participation in movements (Gamson 1988; Goffman 1974; Snow et al. 1986). Social movements are therefore deeply involved in the work of naming grievances, connecting them to other grievances, and constructing larger frames of meaning that will resonate with a population's predispositions (Tarrow 1998). Within this field, *frame resonance* is the key to assessing the mobilizing potential of frames, as it answers why some frames are effective – why they 'resonate' while others do not. Social-movement literature's exploration of frame resonance reveals findings on credibility and salience that parallel public-opinion literature's stress on availability, accessibility, and applicability of frames, as well as its finding that frames involving cultural values and those coming from credible sources resonate more. For the frame to be influential, the perceived fit between the frame and the local reality should be close.

While it is essentially the familiarity and applicability of frames that define their strength, public-opinion research adds a variety of other factors that impact effectiveness. For one, emotions are very important in shaping public opinion. Political events take their meaning from the language used to depict them, and this language can generate different types of emotions, such as fear, anxiety, sadness, or optimism (Edelman 1985; Pennebaker 1993; Pennebaker and Francis 1996). Voters are shown to be affected by their emotions in their decision-making (e.g., Brader and Marcus 2013; Huddy and Gunnthorsdottir 2000; Groenendyk 2011; Marcus, Neuman, and MacKuen 2000; Nadeau, Niemi, and Amato 1995; Neuman et al. 2007; Ridout and Franz 2011; Ridout and Searles 2011).[9] Emotionally interesting, concrete, or image-provoking news stories are more easily remembered than those that are not. For example, in the French referendum on the European Constitution, the French No campaign used images of the Turkish prime minister signing the European Constitution. Although all the candidate countries were part of the European Convention process that drafted the Constitution, the campaigners chose to use this image to imply misleadingly that the Constitution would advance Turkey's accession into the union. This concrete, vivid message tapped into the fears of the French public regarding immigration. In the end, many voters said they voted against the Constitution because of Turkey's accession into the EU (Atikcan 2015a; Brouard and Sauger 2005).

Politicians have strong incentives to use emotions (Jerit 2004). First, emotional memories can have lasting impact even when citizens are not conscious of them. Political elites who speak the language of emotion thus have a better chance of connecting with the electorate than those who do not. Second, emotional appeals project images that are universally valued since they can appeal to all, regardless of their socioeconomic status or political views. Thus, they can be used to mobilize the party's base as well as to attract the support of the uncommitted. These emotional appeals signal that the stakes are high, rousing citizens from inattention. Third, due to their preference for drama and excitement, the media are more likely to cover emotional appeals than sober factual formulations. Vivid information is more easily recalled than dull or pallid stimuli (Jerit and Barabas 2006; Nadeau and Niemi 1995). Elites can either use literal descriptions or adopt a thematic approach and invoke images to deliver their message. For example, in explaining a proposal, US politicians or policy-makers may state, 'The administration's plan uses the social security surplus to reduce the federal debt, saving billions in interest payments that would then be used to extend the life of the program.' As an alternative, they may use a thematic approach ('The vice president's plan provides security to millions of elderly Americans'), or they may invoke images such as a 'lock box' (Jerit and Barabas 2006, 280). All else being equal, emotional and vivid arguments, especially those evoking fear, anxiety, and anger, are expected to be more enduring than those that do not elicit an affective response.

People also pay more attention to negative information and are better able to recall it than positive information (Pfau and Kenski 1990; Soroka 2014). Psychological research shows that con arguments, opposing a policy initiative, usually prevail over pro arguments. Not only do people weigh negative information more heavily than positive but impressions formed on the basis of negative information are likely to last longer and be more resistant to change (Cobb and Kuklinski 1997). This bias results from two factors (Lau 1985). First, people tend to focus more on potential losses than potential gains, much in line with the status quo bias. Second, negative information stands out, because it is less common than positive. Overall, vivid, concrete, image-provoking, emotionally compelling frames that contain negative information are stronger and are thereby expected to be successful in affecting individuals' opinions by increasing the salience of the particular dimension they emphasize.

Importantly, the strength of a frame is not based on its intellectual or moral content. Its strength lies in its appeal to audiences (Chong and Druckman 2007b, 111). That is why what we call 'post-truth' politics is so prevalent today. The debate on Barack Obama's birthplace provides an interesting case in point. In 2008, the supporters of Hillary Clinton and subsequently Donald Trump questioned Obama's eligibility for presidency, claiming that he was not born in the United States. This was a strong frame that was not based on evidence. Although Obama repeatedly posted his birth certificate online, and the director of Hawaii's Department of Health confirmed in 2009 that Obama's birth records were on file, this evidence did not put an end to the debate. Initially 45 per cent of US citizens had doubts about Obama's birthplace. After the evidence was provided, the figure fell to 33 per cent, only to rise to 41 per cent once again in 2012 'in a startling rejection of facts' (d'Ancona 2017). This happened because whether or not a frame is strong does not depend on its accuracy, validity, or relation to scientific evidence (Chong and Druckman 2007a, 652; Hopkin and Rosamond 2017). To borrow a much-disputed term from Kellyanne

Conway, senior aide to Donald Trump, political actors sometimes offer 'alternative facts' (d'Ancona 2017). An effective argument can involve exaggeration or disinformation playing on the fears of the public. Strong frames often rest on symbols, endorsements, and links to ideology and may use heuristics rather than direct information on the substance of a policy.

The framing literature also shows that competitive contexts could give a further advantage to strong frames. Deliberation over opposing frames of sharply contrasting strengths may give rise to a counter-effect (Lecheler and de Vreese 2012). In other words, as Chong and Druckman (2007c, 111) argue, 'the weak frame may backfire especially among motivated individuals by causing their opinions to move in a direction opposite to the position advocated by the weak frame.' This effect is particularly interesting in relation to the use of fear-based arguments, as they can be perceived as lacking credibility when they are used at the same time as opposing frames and when they are exaggerated.[10] The backfiring aspect has also been studied in various fields of psychology, where studies demonstrate that strong fear appeals are more persuasive than weak ones, yet appealing to fear appears to be effective only when these fear-based frames tap into something *perceived* as a significant and relevant threat and when they outline effective responses that appear easy to implement (Witte and Allen 2000). This literature warns that appeals to fear should be used cautiously, as they may backfire if the public does not believe the proposed solutions will effectively avert a threat.

This large and eclectic body of research shows that in attempting to go beyond the 50 per cent threshold and to control the status quo bias, the referendum campaigners who have the closest fit between their arguments and the daily lives and feelings of the voters had the biggest impact on public opinion. Especially when they can use emotional language and negative information, and do so credibly, campaigners have a notably increased chance of moulding the vote choice.

THE ARGUMENT, THE METHODOLOGY, AND THE ROAD MAP

Below, we present the main actors and arguments of the Brexit campaign and then go on to detail the book's core argument, methodology, and road map.

Introducing the Brexit Campaign

In February 2016, Prime Minister David Cameron announced that the Brexit referendum would take place in June 2016. The Electoral Commission decided on which campaigns would have the official designation in April 2016. The campaigns were permitted to spend up to £7 million and to make use of a free mailing through the post, TV broadcasts, and £600,000 of public funds. Britain Stronger in Europe, chaired by Lord Rose, was the only group to apply for the Remain designation, whereas there was fierce competition between various campaign groups on the Leave side. Vote Leave, backed by Boris Johnson and Michael Gove, won the official designation but only after serious challenges from rival campaigns such as Grassroots Out (championed by Conservative MP Peter Bone and UKIP leader Nigel Farage) and Leave.EU (led by UKIP donor Aaron Banks), as well as applications from the Trade Union and Socialist Coalition.

On the Remain side, Britain Stronger in Europe focused on the economic costs of a departure from the EU. They presented a number of different themes in the early days of the campaign, and the argument was threefold: EU membership would be better for the UK's economy, security, and place in the world. However, as the campaign unfolded, their message became more and more focused on the economy. On the Leave side, the official Vote Leave campaign also started out with a threefold argument: the UK needed to 'Take Back Control' from the EU in policies on money, borders, and laws.

Figures 1.3–1.5 show sample posters from both sides of the campaign. Although the strength of a frame depends on its familiarity (the perceived fit between its content and the experience/existing feelings of the public), campaign posters can be used strategically to enhance the way the frame is presented. Posters can render arguments more vivid and emotional. As figure 1.3 demonstrates, the Remain campaign focused on economic figures to represent what it would mean to leave the EU. This emphasis on the drastic consequences of losing EU membership was widely criticized as 'Project Fear,' much as the Scottish Better Together campaign was only two years earlier.

The posters in figure 1.4 present the core messages of the Vote Leave campaign, which Conservative MEP Daniel Hannan articulated as 'Britain shackled to the corpse of Europe.'[11] The '£350 million' figure and the 'Take Back Control' slogan became very powerful in the debate, as the interview data discuss below.[12] The posters served not only to challenge the Remain side's economic figures but also to tell voters that there would be detrimental consequences if the UK remained in the EU. Figure 1.5 presents a Vote Leave campaign leaflet designed to look similar to a government information brochure to boost its credibility, which the chief executive of Vote Leave, Matthew Elliott, explained was extremely effective.[13] In addition, Nigel Farage used a poster carrying an openly anti-immigrant message, showing a queue of immigrants with the slogan 'Breaking Point: The EU has failed us all.'

Locating the Brexit Campaign: The Argument

As mentioned at the outset, 87 per cent of experts responding to the online survey conducted between 24 May and 2 June 2016 thought that the UK would vote to remain in the EU (Jennings and Fisher 2016). That belief was firmly rooted despite the drastically split public opinion polls signalling a possible victory for both sides. The expectation was thus that at the end of the day a critical segment of the public would vote against a costly change, leading to a slim majority voting to remain in the EU. This idea was strengthened by previous referendum experiences in the UK, with the status quo option consistently winning over the change option in the 1975 referendum on EU membership, the 2011 referendum on the electoral system, and again in the 2014 referendum on Scottish independence. In this case, the exact opposite happened.

On the aforementioned continuum developed by LeDuc (2002), the Brexit referendum would fall between the 'opinion formation' and 'uphill struggle' categories. The Brexit case, being an 'exit' referendum from the union, was not focused on a technical and lengthy EU treaty, which normally leads to opinion formation campaigns. The British public already had an idea of what EU membership meant to them, as shown by the clear split in opinion polls (Butler and Kitzinger 1976; Clarke, Goodwin, and Whiteley 2017; Evans and Norris 1999; Hobolt 2016; King 1977). Thus campaigners could easily employ simple heuristics and tap into feelings of attachment toward the UK and the EU, or into the perception that the EU's bureaucracy in Brussels was cumbersome, inefficient, and insensitive to the needs of British citizens (Clarke, Goodwin, and Whiteley 2017; Hobolt 2016; Kuklinski and Quirk 2000; Sniderman, Brody, and Tetlock 1991). But as the second and third chapters demonstrate in detail, the Brexit

Figure 1.3 Selection of posters for Britain Stronger in Europe campaign

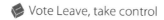

Vote Leave, take control

Let's give our **NHS** the
£350 million
the EU takes every week

Vote Leave, take control

Let's Take Back Control
- [X] **Our Money** – Give the NHS millions more every week
- [X] **Our Economy** – Create new jobs with new trade deals
- [X] **Our Borders** – A new points-based immigration system
- [X] **Our Security** – Deport dangerous foreign criminals
- [X] **Our Taxes** – Cut VAT on household energy bills

Vote Leave, take back control on 23 June

Save our NHS

Help protect your local hospital...

 Vote Leave, take control

Figure 1.4 Selection of posters for Vote Leave campaign

... the safer option

Which is safer - a vote to keep sending hundreds of millions to the EU every week, or a vote to put that money into our priorities like the NHS and the Cancer Drugs Fund?

Which is safer – letting unelected EU bureaucrats decide how our hospitals should be run, or a vote to take back control?

If we Vote Leave, we'll be able to invest more in local hospitals and improve our NHS.

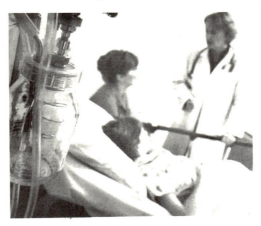

 Vote Leave, take control

voteleavetakecontrol.org

INFORMATION ABOUT THE REFERENDUM ON 23 JUNE 2016

The UK and the European Union:

THE FACTS

Figure 1.5 Vote Leave leaflet strategically imitating a government leaflet

THE UK AND THE EUROPEAN UNION: THE FACTS

On 23 June, there will be a vote to decide whether the UK should remain a member of the European Union, or leave and take back control. It's a big decision – and there may not be another chance to vote for years. Here are the facts:

- The UK joined the European Union in 1973. Back then, it was known as the Common Market. But over the past 43 years, the EU has taken control over more and more areas which don't have anything to do with trade – such as our borders, our public services, and whether prisoners have the right to vote.

- When we joined, there were just 9 member states. Now there are 28, the most recent being Romania, Bulgaria and Croatia. Five more countries are being considered for membership: Albania, Macedonia, Montenegro, Serbia, and Turkey. If they are let in, they will have the same rights as other member states.

- More than half of net migration to the UK comes from the EU. More than a quarter of a million people came to the UK from the EU in the 12 months to September 2015 – the equivalent of a city the size of Plymouth or Newcastle in just one year.

- While we're in the EU, the UK can't make trade deals on our own. This means we currently have no trade deals with key allies such as Australia, New Zealand or the USA – or important growing economies like India, China or Brazil. Instead of making a deal which is best for the UK, we have to wait for 27 other countries to agree it.

- The EU costs us £350 million a week. That's enough to build a new NHS hospital every week of the year. We get less than half of this money back, and we have no control over the way it's spent – that's decided by politicians and officials in Brussels, rather than the people we elect here.

- You don't have to be a member of the EU to trade with it. Switzerland is not in the EU and it exports more per person to the EU than we do. The big banks and multinationals might be lobbying to keep us in the EU, but small and medium-sized businesses feel differently. Only 6 per cent of UK firms export to the EU, yet all have to abide by EU regulations on their business.

- EU law overrules UK law. This stops the British public from being able to vote out the politicians who make our laws. EU judges have already overruled British laws on issues like counter-terrorism powers, immigration, VAT, and prisoner voting. Even the Government's proposed new deal can be overturned after the referendum: it is not legally binding.

- There are risks in voting either way. Experts, politicians, and businesses are divided. People have to weigh up the risks and potential benefits of each course of action for themselves.

Want to know more? Visit **www.eureferendumfacts.org** or text FACTS to **88802** (standard charges apply).*

referendum involved a multidimensional referendum question that allowed the anti-EU side to place any theme they liked on the agenda and redefine the meaning of the vote. Neither was the Brexit case a typical independence referendum, which normally leads to uphill-struggle campaigns. As opposed to the Quebec or Scotland independence referendums (Bélanger et al. 2018), in the Brexit case the public did not have a long-standing opinion on whether their country was better off inside or outside of the EU. As a result, the campaign had considerable scope to reinvent the question and put a new spin on the meaning of the choice on the ballot paper.

Existing work has highlighted the importance of the campaign among other long-term factors in understanding the Brexit result. In this book, instead of presenting the campaign as one variable amongst many, we offer a comprehensive and nuanced understanding of how the Brexit campaign differed from previous referendum campaigns and how these differences likely contributed to its unexpected outcome. We identify the Brexit campaign's key differences, explain how it was planned and executed, and discuss which campaign strategies and arguments contributed most to the vote choice. In doing so, we do not neglect the long-term factors. By closely studying the well-established habit in British politics of scapegoating the EU, and comparing its impact for early versus late deciders, we explain how this long-standing imbalance structured the choice of campaign strategies as well as contributing to their eventual success.

We argue that the campaign made voting against the status quo for an uncertain future outside the EU easier for a critical section of society. As figures 1.3 to 1.5 depict perfectly, campaign arguments redefined whether departure from the EU was high risk or not. The next chapters show that both the Remain and Leave sides attempted to reach the unsure middle-ground voters and control the status quo bias. Yet when compared with previous EU and independence referendums, the Leave campaigners were more strategic in their campaign decisions and had a closer fit between what they were arguing and the daily lives and feelings of British voters.

Our main argument is twofold. First, given the tradition of *scapegoating the EU* in British politics, the Remain side was at a disadvantage from the outset. The Remain campaigners, being part of the British political elite, which has never been enthusiastic toward the EU, did not feel comfortable promoting or portraying the union in a positive light. Conversely, this scapegoating tradition offered the Leave camp an important shortcut – 'the undemocratic and costly Brussels' – which resonated instantly with voters. This tradition set the stage for the whole campaign by structuring the campaign choices available to the two sides. Second, relying on their previous experience from the 2015 general election and the 2014 Scottish referendum, the Remain camp chose to frame the vote solely as an economic one, emphasizing the costs of departure from the EU. (This position is visible in figure 1.3.) But as the campaign unfolded, the Leave side effectively neutralized these economic arguments and *de-risked a departure from the status quo*. They discredited 'the experts' and proposed their own figures on the economic costs of a Remain vote, famously suggesting that the UK was paying £350 million to the EU budget per week. The style of their documents, seen in figure 1.5 in particular, was chosen carefully to raise the credibility of these claims. The Leave side also successfully increased the number of dimensions in the debate (see figure 1.4), arguing that there would be other risks relating to remaining in the EU, such as losing control of immigration policy and the National Health Service (NHS). They vividly urged the public to 'Take Back Control.' These concrete and emotionally compelling arguments struck an immediate chord with voters. Most intriguingly, the Remain side was silent on these issues without an emotional case to present.

This carefully executed de-risking strategy not only contributed to the referendum result but also had an impact on its acceptance by the public. Moderate Remain voters, who echoed the Leave camp's arguments on the potential consequences of Brexit, found the Brexit outcome more acceptable than other Remain voters did. In other words, the campaign strategies also help us understand why only some Remain voters accepted the result.

The Methodology

We adopt a multi-method approach and build our core argument step by step through interview, media, and survey data. Rich interview findings, involving over 150 face-to-face interviews with campaigners in Scotland and England and across Europe, serve two purposes. First, the data paint a comparative picture of campaign strategies all across Europe, allowing us to place the Brexit campaign decisions within this comparative perspective. Only through comparative lenses can we fully understand the importance of these decisions and their implications.

Second, the extensive interview data serve as a starting point in the analysis by revealing the reasoning behind key campaign decisions in the Brexit referendum. The existing literature on referendums tends to ignore such data, because interviewing the campaigners in a systematic fashion is often challenging and time-consuming. But without input from the campaigners on the formulation of their strategies and arguments, we can have only a limited understanding of the campaign.

These interviews were face-to-face and semi-structured, allowing for follow-up questions. The interviewees included campaigners from all political parties and civil society groups active in the mentioned campaigns. The sampling used for the interviews was based on opportunity and snowball sampling. Opportunity sampling was necessary to maximize access to key campaigners, and snowball sampling helped vastly in reaching individuals from all actively campaigning organizations and thereby in reaching a saturation point. The number of interviewees in each case depended on the number of referendums studied in that country and the number of active organizations that participated in the campaigns. Although this number is lower in some cases, the selection still respects the same breakdown, which implies that these interviewees were key decision-makers and often high-profile campaigners. The appendix includes a full list of the individuals interviewed and the interview questionnaire.

In a second step, we look into media content analyses to assess the extent to which these key campaign arguments were captured by the news media and to track any potential bias in the tone and content of reporting. For this part of the analysis, we rely on two sources, the first focusing on newspaper and press coverage and the second one on online sources. The first is the media analysis of Loughborough University, a study of the news coverage of the Brexit referendum produced on the weekdays between 6 May and 22 June 2016 from the following news outlets. Television includes *Channel 4 News*, *Channel 5 News Tonight*, *BBC1 News*, *ITV1 News, and Sky News*. Press includes the *Guardian, Times, Daily Telegraph, Financial Times, Daily Mail, Daily Express, Daily Mirror, Sun, Star*, and *I*. Our second source offers an analysis of online articles based on a combination of qualitative and quantitative content analysis. This study examines all relevant articles published online over the official ten-week campaign (from 15 April to 23 June). For broadcasters, it includes the *BBC, ITV, Channel 4*, and *Sky News*. For newspapers, it includes the *Daily Mail, Daily Express, Daily Mirror, Daily Star, Daily Telegraph, Financial*

Times, Guardian and Observer, Independent, Times, and *Sun.* For news magazines, it includes the *Economist, New Statesman,* and *Spectator.* For digital only, it includes *Buzzfeed UK, Huffington Post UK,* and *Vice UK.*

The last step in our analysis relies on the use of public-opinion survey data. This step allows us to examine the extent to which the public's voting decision was influenced by these key campaign arguments. This post-referendum opinion survey was conducted by the polling firm Survation in the week following the Brexit vote (between 1 July and 5 July 2016) under our scientific supervision. The survey relied on a representative quota-based sampling approach using Survation's online panel. The fact that it was conducted on an online platform allowed us to incorporate wording experiments, campaign posters, and visuals in the survey, enriching its analytical power. The questionnaire, which includes about one hundred items mostly related to the Brexit campaign, was put to 1,514 UK individuals who were targeted according to their age, sex, and region of residence. (The weighting targets used are based on the 2011 Census's mid-year estimates for 2015.) In the final step of our analysis, we use survey data to understand voting behaviour at the individual level, providing answers to core questions such as how various campaign arguments might have contributed to the vote choice, how risk perceptions affected the voting behaviour, and why some voters accepted the referendum's result while others did not. Importantly, we study the impact of long-term and short-term factors comparatively for the key groups of early and late deciders.

None of the existing studies of the Brexit referendum uses a similarly rich, multi-method dataset to explain the result. The three steps are essential to provide a complete analysis of campaign framing. We examine the *strength* of campaign arguments by analysing the degree to which they tapped into the existing, immediate concerns of the society and by studying whether they did so with memorable, vivid, emotionally compelling campaign materials. The assessment of whether or not these campaign arguments were *effective* or *successful*, on the other hand, is based on public opinion data. We discuss the influence of frames by observing the extent to which campaign frames are echoed by the public in explaining the reasons behind their vote choice. Thus, the success and failure of frames are distinct from their strength or weakness. Our appendix presents a detailed discussion of these methodological steps.

The Plan of the Book

Chapter 2 compares the Brexit campaign to other referendums and addresses exactly how the Leave campaigners differed in their approach. Employing data from over 150 interviews with campaigners, it studies the Brexit referendum strategies through a lens comparing and contrasting them with the most frequently used strategies in EU and Scottish independence referendums. The strategies employed in the Brexit referendum were broadly in line with the strategies used in these previous referendums, but the chapter argues that the Leave side's specific framing choices saved them from key mistakes that others have often made. In comparison to the EU referendums, the Leave side benefitted from the advantages of being on the anti-EU side while successfully avoiding the typical challenge of being seen as extremist. In comparison to the Scottish referendum, on the other hand, the Leave side faced a much weaker opponent and also successfully avoided the usual questions on their exit plan's economic viability. As opposed to the Scottish government, the Leave campaign chose not to present a concrete 'exit plan'. The success of this strategy was demonstrated by the level of criticism that Prime Minister May's 'exit deal' received, as well as its historic rejection in the House of Commons in January 2019 during the actual Brexit negotiations.

The next chapters again use a multi-method approach and make this core argument through interview, media content, and survey data. Chapter 3 relies on rich interview and media content data and reveals how the Remain and Leave sides strategically framed the Brexit choice. This chapter presents the data in two stages; it first details how the long-term habit of scapegoating the EU structured the campaign choices, and then it demonstrates how the Leave camp built its strategy to de-risk the Brexit decision. It uncovers the reasoning behind the critical campaign decisions on 'Project Fear' and the slogan 'Take Back Control' and the use of key themes such as immigration and the NHS. The media-content analysis mirrors the interview data. The Leave side was not only louder than the Remain side in the media but was also very active in de-risking the Brexit decision. In addition to running their 'Project Fear' on the controversial issue of immigration, the pro-Leave sources also became highly involved in the discussion on the economy.

The next two chapters take the analysis to the individual level, using survey data to assess the success of these strategies. Chapter 4 explores how the long-term habit of scapegoating the EU set the stage for the campaign, while chapter 5 discusses how campaign strategies and arguments shaped the way in which the public understood the vote choice. Taken together, these two chapters explain how the long-term and short-term factors interacted to bring about the Brexit decision. To understand how the tradition of presenting the EU in a negative light reflected and contributed to the spread of critical attitudes toward Europe in British public opinion, chapter 4 uses long-term trends in British public opinion as well as three attitudinal variables from our survey (which carry comparable figures to the long-term data): level of attachment to the EU, attitudes toward 'Brussels', and attitudes toward the UK's benefits from the EU. The chapter shows how these long-term opinions shaped the dynamics of the campaign by structuring both the campaign choices and their eventual contribution to the result. This tradition and the resulting lukewarm public attitudes to the EU limited the Remain camp to an unenthusiastic and defensive campaign. In contrast, the tradition provided the Leave camp with the already existing powerful idea of 'undemocratic bureaucrats in Brussels', which served as an important shortcut for voters. Wrapping their campaign around this key theme and urging the public to 'Take Back Control', Leave campaigners attracted the pivotal undecided/moderate voters. Moreover, our data demonstrate that long-term attitudes played a significant role in the voting decision of early deciders but much less so in the vote of the critical group of late deciders. Chapter 5, in turn, investigates the degree to which campaign strategies influenced voting behaviour. It relies on specific survey data on global perceptions of the campaign, opinions on the key campaign arguments, the image of the leaders, the role of emotions, and the perceptions of risk. The statistical analyses demonstrate that the Leave side prevailed over the Remain side in all of these dimensions and reframed the choice, shifting the focus of the debate from the economy to sovereignty. The Leave side's messages on immigration and NHS funding provided a counterpoint to the Remain campaign's arguments on the economic costs of Brexit. We show that adding variables on these short-term factors relating to the campaign increases the explanatory power of traditional voting models based on long-term factors. What is more, the results show that these variables on campaign strategies were in fact more important in explaining the vote choice of moderate/hesitant voters, who made their choice later in the campaign, proving once again that these strategies contributed to the Brexit outcome.

Chapter 6, also using survey data, turns to a key question for democratic politics, analysing why only some Remain voters chose to accept the result while others did not, bringing up the notion of losers' consent. Interestingly, the losers who recognized the legitimacy of the Brexit vote included not only sophisticated citizens capable of overcoming their frustration but also some less-informed late deciders whose moderation helped them accept the outcome. This analysis implies that in de-risking the Brexit choice, the Leave camp also facilitated the rallying of some losers.

Chapter 7 concludes the book by reviewing the major empirical findings, discussing the theoretical contribution of this research, and specifying the policy implications for future referendums, elections, and international cooperation.

2

The Brexit Campaign
in Comparative Perspective

It is far easier to scaremonger about an entity that does not exist ... it is always going to be far easier to fill people with a sense of fear ... about the creation of a brand new entity on the international stage, Scotland as a nation-state, than on a vote on the UK, which is an existing nation state.[1]

Kevin Pringle

The book's core argument is that Leave campaigners reframed the choice in the Brexit referendum, de-risked a departure from the EU, and ultimately made it easier for a critical segment of British society to vote for an uncertain future outside of the union. But studying the Brexit referendum as a single case prevents us from understanding whether what happened was a unique phenomenon. How does the Brexit campaign compare to other referendums in terms of the way in which it was run? Where did Leave campaigners depart from campaigners in other referendums? Is it in fact easier to scaremonger and use certain kinds of arguments or strategies in certain kinds of referendums? Although much has been said about the importance of the Brexit campaign, none of the existing work has studied its strategies comparatively or systematically.

Below, based on a unique dataset of over 150 in-depth interviews with campaigners in Scotland and England and across Europe, we categorize the strategies most frequently used by pro- and anti-EU and pro- and anti-independence campaigners.[2] We also discuss findings of recent research on how much these referendum strategies affect referendum outcomes and locate the Brexit campaigners' decisions within this wide palette of strategies available to them. We detail these choices further with in-depth interview data from the Brexit case in the next chapter. Thus, in this chapter we focus on *what the Leave side did differently* when compared to the campaigners in other referendums, and in the next chapters we show *how they did it* by using a multi-method approach.

Placing the Brexit campaign decisions in this broader comparative perspective demonstrates that referendum strategies are not formulated in a vacuum. The broad parameters of campaigners' decisions are based on referendum politics, as discussed in detail in the first chapter. For instance, campaigners typically try to go beyond their usual voter base to reach the required 50 per cent and to activate or mute the status quo bias. While these dynamics apply to most referendums, there are also some that are specific to EU referendums, such as the inherent advantage of being on the anti-EU side. Campaigners respond to these dynamics in different ways, which in turn affect the success of their frames and their agenda control. A close look at the dynamics of EU and independence referendums tells us that the Leave campaign benefitted from being on the anti-EU side while overcoming the typical challenges that anti-EU and pro-independence campaigners face. The Remain camp, on the other hand, exhausted its position as the defender of the status quo but did not adapt its strategy to counter opponents' claims as the campaign unfolded. We conclude this chapter with a summary of these comparative dynamics in table 2.3.

HOW DOES THE BREXIT REFERENDUM COMPARE TO EU REFERENDUMS?

Because of the EU's complex institutional architecture, and its geographical remoteness from its citizens, referendums on the EU often fall into the category of 'opinion formation' referendums, as LeDuc (2002) has proposed. European citizens are not only unfamiliar with the EU's multiple legislative procedures and its technical terminology but also lack direct interaction with EU institutions in their daily lives. As a result, in referendums on EU-related questions, citizens tend to rely heavily on campaign cues to make up their mind on the subject. But which kinds of campaign strategies are influential on EU referendum outcomes? Below we extract the most frequently used strategies in EU referendums and discuss whether they have an impact on referendum results by surveying the recent literature and using interview data.

In fact, research into EU referendums has only recently turned its attention to referendum campaigns. As discussed earlier, this literature has been dominated by traditional explanations linking referendum results to government approval rates (the 'second-order' approach), European-level policy preferences ('issue-voting' approach), and party cues (e.g., Gabel and Palmer 1995; McLaren 2002; Ray 2003; Reif and Schmitt 1980; Siune, Svensson, and Tongaard 1994). However, detailed survey-based analyses find that dissatisfaction with the government, attitudes toward European integration, and party identification *all* influence the vote choice (e.g., Aarts and van der Kolk 2006; de Vreese and Boomgaarden 2007; Hobolt 2009).

Thus, the next question is how campaign information mediates the extent to which different issues become salient in the minds of voters (Hobolt and Brouard 2011, 310). Existing research shows that political parties *frame the choice* and serve as information providers during campaigns, actively defining the meaning of the vote (Atikcan 2015a; Chong and Druckman 2007a; Hobolt 2009; Laycock 2013; Pammett and LeDuc 2001). In a comparative study of EU referendums, Hobolt (2009) finds that the information provided to voters during campaigns matters. When the negative consequences of a No vote are stressed, more people favour the proposal; when the negative consequences of a Yes vote are stressed, more people oppose the proposal. Garry (2013) similarly shows that perceptions of treaty implications matter the most to voters. Importantly, intense campaigns appear to change these perceptions in the short term. The more that voters' perceptions of the contents of the treaty are aligned with the No campaign, the more they vote No, and vice versa for the Yes campaign (Elkink and Sinnott 2015). Emotions are also shown to matter in EU referendum campaigns. Garry (2014) finds that campaign information can in fact lead to fear or anger and that fearful citizens are more likely to vote for the option that is presented as less risky (see Druckman and McDermott 2008).

Going a step further, Atikcan (2015a) demonstrates that certain kinds of arguments matter more in shaping individuals' minds on the referendum question. Negative and particularly emotive anti-EU arguments, such as those that emphasize the country's national interest, loss of sovereignty, declining pensions, and increasing immigration, tend to drive down the early support for EU referendum proposals. Weaker arguments that rely on technical facts or abstract benefits, on the other hand, are less effective in changing people's minds. For example, in 2005, the French far right anti-EU campaign against the European Constitution used images of the Turkish prime minister signing the document, implying (misleadingly) that the treaty would advance Turkey's accession into the Union, while the pro-EU campaign presented the Constitution mainly as an institutional step toward a better Europe. The emotional arguments of the anti-EU camp connected with voters more effectively than the abstract or technical pro-EU ones.

In line with the broader literature on referendums, a common pattern uncovered in these studies is that the No side in an EU treaty ratification campaign – which aims to reject the EU treaty on offer – has more ability to control the agenda and to advance such arguments on risk if it engages the debate (Atikcan 2018). Put differently, such strategies are particularly *beneficial for supporters of the status quo,* and in EU treaty ratification referendums the status quo is often defended by the *anti-EU campaigners.* The anti-treaty campaigns are typically free to argue that the treaty will cause loss of political autonomy in key fields such as social policy, citizenship rules, immigration, and military neutrality, and on moral issues such as abortion, even when those themes are not present in the treaty at hand. This is why Dinan (2012, 95) describes EU referendums as 'a lightning-rod for Eurosceptics and a scourge for EU politicians and officials'. These argumentation strategies have been shown again and again to be correlated to negative referendum outcomes (e.g., Atikcan 2015a; Hobolt 2009; Mendez, Mendez, and Triga 2016).

But this pattern does not mean that anti-EU campaigners never lose their advantage. It becomes limited when the arguments available to the typical anti-treaty campaigners are reduced due to the contents of the EU treaty or a set of guarantees offered by the EU (Atikcan 2018). Given that the No side does not necessarily need a coherent case and can attack a proposal from multiple angles, multidimensional referendum proposals such as long EU treaties provide more of an advantage to the No side by offering more material to campaign on and more risks to highlight. In contrast, when the proposal is limited to a single topic such as the Fiscal Compact (a short and specific EU treaty on economic and monetary governance), this advantage is reduced. Alternatively, in referendums where the public was asked to vote twice on the same subject, such as the Danish and Irish votes on the Maastricht, Nice, and Lisbon treaties, the EU became involved after the first vote on each referendum, offering guarantees and taking certain arguments off the table and limiting the No side's hand in the second referendum. Such circumstances hence reduce the ability of the anti-EU campaigners to appeal to risk aversion, which is otherwise usually in their control.

On the Yes side – the pro-EU campaigners in EU treaty ratification referendums – detailed data demonstrate that they tend to appeal to risk aversion most successfully when they can tap into the economic costs of an anti-EU vote (Atikcan 2018). For instance, in repeated referendums on the Maastricht, Nice, and Lisbon treaties, voters were told that a second rejection would have significant economic consequences and could even lead to departure from the union. Similarly, in the Fiscal Compact referendum, Irish voters were warned about losing access to EU bailout funds in the event of a negative vote. When such arguments were available to pro-EU campaigners, they could also advance arguments on consequences and risk and could benefit from the status quo bias. Once again, these strategies are repeatedly shown to correlate with more positive referendum outcomes (Atikcan 2015b; Garry, Marsh, and Sinnott 2005; Hobolt 2006b). In the Brexit campaign, as the Remain side advanced a myriad of arguments on the drastic economic consequences of an exit from the EU, the expectation from existing studies on EU referendums would be that this emphasis would dissuade the voters from voting for the Leave option.

Apart from the conditional advantage of the anti-EU side in EU treaty ratification debates, two other factors render pro-EU campaigning more challenging. The first is *the public's general lack of information on the EU*. This lack is due to the EU's political complexity and technical terminology. Initially, the problem resulted from the nature of the policies themselves, such as the completion of the single market. Because these policies were quite technical, the commission mainly targeted the governmental and non-governmental policy elites (Meyer 1999). However, although EU decisions affect approximately 75 per cent of national legislation today, the public still does not debate these decisions on a daily basis (Spanier 2012), generating low general readership demand for EU news and decreasing incentives for the national media to cover the EU sufficiently (Statham 2010).[3]

Second, the EU often gets *negative attention in the domestic sphere*. One part of this problem relates to the media. The majority of media coverage that the EU does receive is negative (Gleissner and De Vreese 2005). The other part of this problem is the habit of national politicians of scapegoating the union – in other words, the 'blame game' (Atikcan 2015a). Since there is no single EU government and the division of competences is rather vague, national politicians can and do easily shift the blame for unpopular policies to the EU. This negative attention suggests that pro-EU campaigners start the debate with a certain disadvantage. Their campaign arguments are compared with what they have said before on the topic. The more negative the existing narrative is toward the European integration project, the more campaigners suffer from credibility problems in advancing pro-EU frames. The opposite is the case for anti-EU campaigners. The habit of scapegoating the EU provides them with easy references and beneficial shortcuts that pave the way for effective framing. In other words, what they say already rings true in the ears of the public. Pro-EU campaigners find these two issues, the lack of information and the usual scapegoating of the EU, to be particularly challenging in their campaign. This difficulty, they argue, often adds to the advantage of the anti-EU side, because the public finds the anti-EU arguments easy to believe even when they might not be accurate (Atikcan 2015a).

As table 2.1 summarizes below, the core strategies used in referendums apply to EU referendums. However, we find that campaigners in these referendums are aware of three additional issues: the anti-EU side's advantage in setting the agenda, the public's lack of information on the EU, and the usual tendency of national politicians and media to scapegoat the union for unpopular policies. These issues prove to be particularly challenging for pro-EU campaigners, and their impact on referendum results is shown in ample data.

For the Brexit referendum, these issues mean that the Leave campaign would benefit from the inherent advantages of being on the anti-EU side. That said, Remain campaigners would be expected to gain from having the key argument on potential economic losses on their side. It should be noted that the Brexit referendum was not on an EU treaty, and thus its dynamics were somewhat different. The side advocating a change was not the pro-EU side but the anti-EU side. However, as the detailed discussions below demonstrate, the Leave campaign strategically challenged the notion of the status quo, and its strategies were thereby closely comparable to those of previous anti-EU campaigns.

Below, we use interview data to discuss the typical strategies employed by EU referendum campaigners. The dataset is based on Atikcan's field research on eleven EU treaty ratification referendums: the European Constitution (Spain, France, the Netherlands, and Luxembourg in 2005), the Treaty of Maastricht (Denmark in 1992 and 1993), the Treaty of Nice (Ireland in 2001 and 2002), the Treaty

Table 2.1
Strategies in EU referendums

Going beyond 50%	Campaigners need to appeal to the undecided voters to reach the winning threshold.
The risk factor	Campaigners seek to activate or mute the status quo bias in order to win. Campaigners seek to avoid a backlash, which occurs when risk-based arguments are not perceived to be credible by the public.
Anti-EU agenda advantage	In EU referendums, the anti-EU side has an agenda-setting advantage when the proposal is a multidimensional one. The advantage switches to the pro-EU side when the arguments of the anti-EU side are restricted and when the pro-EU side can bring up the loss of economic benefits from the EU.
Lack of information on the EU	In EU referendums, pro-EU campaigners struggle in countering the anti-EU arguments due to the public's lack of information on the EU.
Scapegoating the EU	In EU referendums, pro-EU campaigners struggle in advancing enthusiastic arguments or in countering the anti-EU arguments due to the tradition of blaming the EU for unpopular measures.

of Lisbon (Ireland in 2008 and 2009), and the Fiscal Compact (Ireland in 2012). The interviewees included campaigners from all political parties and civil society groups active in the mentioned campaigns. The literature often ignores input from campaigners, as conducting such in-depth interviews is costly and time-consuming. However, hearing the reasoning behind the selection of campaign themes and strategies is crucial for a comprehensive understanding of the campaign process.

Because the target interviewees were often high-profile campaigners, the sampling was based on opportunity and snowball sampling. The interviews were conducted face to face and were semi-structured to allow for follow-up questions. The first chapter presents a detailed methodological discussion, and the appendix provides a full list of the individuals interviewed and the interview questionnaire. The questionnaires used for Brexit and EU treaty referendums were the same because, as discussed, although the Brexit referendum was not on an EU treaty, its dynamics were highly comparable to these previous referendums. The semi-structured nature of the interviews provided the necessary flexibility for the follow-up questions to probe into

Table 2.2
Keywords in interview data

Strategy	Related keywords
Going beyond 50%	reaching/persuading/appealing to undecided/ambivalent/middle/soft voters
The risk factor	use of fear/threats/blackmail backlash/backfiring
Anti-EU agenda advantage	use of multiple/numerous/unrelated/irrelevant themes whether they or the rival campaign had an advantage/ easier job in setting the agenda
Lack of information on the EU	lack of public information/knowledge/understanding technical/difficult/complex language/jargon of the EU
Scapegoating the EU	blaming/scapegoating the EU not selling/explaining the EU sufficiently negative media attention to the EU lack of enthusiasm for the EU

details and to arrive at a comprehensive understanding of these different campaigns.

Table 2.2 presents the keywords used in assessing campaign strategies. In *all* of the EU referendums under study, these strategies were mentioned by a *majority* of the campaigners interviewed. We provide some key quotes in the following sections, each dealing with a specific strategy, to provide examples of how these strategies were visible in the interview data.

Going beyond 50 Per Cent and Trying to Reach the Undecided 'Middle-Ground' Voters

In EU referendums, as in most referendums, both pro-EU and anti-EU campaigners try to find the key issues that undecided voters worry about and to craft messages around those themes. These issues often centre on the economic benefits/costs of EU membership and loss of sovereignty. On the pro-EU side, this task is mostly implicit, because the political mainstream usually campaigns for the EU. The government and all the mainstream political parties almost always campaign on the pro-EU side, as Euroscepticism is confined to the extremes of the political spectrum (De Vries 2009; Taggart 1998; Taggart and Szczerbiak 2013; Usherwood and Startin 2013). These parties therefore may feel less urgency to appeal to the 'middle ground', assuming that the broad and cross-party pro-EU campaign would attract most voters. The task is trickier for the anti-EU side, often portrayed by the pro-EU side as political extremists, as being 'against the peace project'. That image is particularly problematic for appealing to the middle ground.[4] In France, as Claude Debons of the General Workers' Confederation (CGT) put it, 'The Yes campaigners were very defensive ... When the No vote increased in the polls, they started accusing us of xenophobia.'[5] UMP MP Nicolas Dupont-Aignan, a prominent No campaigner, similarly noted, 'As soon as we avoided the trap of being extremists, we won.'[6] In Spain, Initiative for Catalonia Greens (ICV) campaigner Marc Giménez Villahoz also explained that the Yes side frequently portrayed the No side as against Europe, and he identified this as an 'easy counterargument' to their arguments.[7] In Luxembourg too, Trade Unionist Nico Clement (OGBL) criticized certain Yes campaigners for following the logic that 'if you are not for the European Constitution then you are against Europe, then you are in fact for World War in Europe'.[8] This was an issue in Ireland too. Mary Lou McDonald, Sinn Féin MP, mentioned that the Yes side portrayed the No side as extremists.[9] In fact, former Taoiseach Bertie Ahern dismissed the No campaigners as 'loolahs' (lunatics) (Holmes 2008).

Well-planned anti-EU campaigns design specific strategies to counter this image. In Ireland in the first Lisbon Treaty referendum, Libertas, an anti-Lisbon lobby group led by businessman Declan Ganley, took this aspect very seriously. Libertas based its entire campaign strategy on giving the No campaign a non-extreme outlook. The communications director of Libertas, John McGuirk, explained that after conducting research on the public's view of the EU, the lobby group identified two key factors that held them back from voting negatively:[10]

> Number one was the stigma of being seen to agree with people who were outside of the mainstream ... There were lots of people who were in the political centre, who disagreed with the treaty ... They needed to know that there was actually a mainstream group that had support from the business community and the job-creating industries. Secondly, they needed to be ensured of the economic benefits in their minds ... With Lisbon, we felt that we can make the argument that this treaty was economically dangerous. The strategy was to appeal to 20 per cent of the soft Yes voters in the middle.

Libertas's executive director, Naoise Nunn, similarly highlighted the point that Libertas aimed to change the usual complexion of the No side in EU referendums, which is the far left and the far right: 'What we had to do was to make this mainstream, appealing to the middle-class, educated, urban groups. We were seeking to be the acceptable face of the No side ... Our campaign was centre ground, we did not use any inflammatory language, we tried to keep it all straight down in the middle, practical and logical.' He explained that Libertas therefore used arguments on the corporate tax rate, which has been 'a real hot button issue for the business community, for the middle-class, and for the self-employed.'[11]

Irish campaigners agreed that Declan Ganley was able to appeal to the middle ground in the campaign. Déirdre de Búrca of the Green Party emphasized that Ganley did not match the stereotype of the anti-EU treaty campaigners: 'He was not extreme, he was a businessperson, and normally business is pro-EU.'[12] Anthony Coughlan of the National Platform also mentioned that Ganley was a new and unusual voice in the No campaign, never heard before, and different from the previous No campaigners.[13] Pat Cox, campaign director of Ireland for Europe, explained similarly that Libertas animated something that had previously been only marginal, coming from the far left or from a rather fundamentalist Catholic right.[14] In terms of Libertas's economic arguments, Blair Horan of the Civil and Public Service Union (CPSU) emphasized that the Irish electorate had indeed associated the EU with economic benefits in past referendums.[15] According to him, Libertas's corporate tax argument struck a chord with the public by bringing up potential economic damages.

In the Dutch referendum on the European Constitution, the far-left Socialist Party (SP) had a similar strategy. SP Secretary-General Hans van Heijningen openly mentioned that referendums required a different type of strategy than regular elections, referring to their realization that radical leftist messages would not carry them to 51 per cent in the Netherlands. They brought the 'super-state' argument in strategically, as the other arguments had clear left-wing political content. This particular argument suggested that the European Constitution would establish a European federal state with a single constitution in which the Netherlands would be relegated to a powerless province. Responding to their opponents, who blamed the SP for being populist, van Heijningen suggested that they combined socialist messages with people's concerns. He added, 'If populism means communicating with the masses, you can call us populist.'[16] The pro-EU campaigners acknowledged that the 'super-state' argument was a hit. GreenLeft campaigner Bas Eickhout stressed that as a result of the s P campaign, the loss of sovereignty became the fundamental issue.[17] D66 member Gerben Jan Gerbrandy agreed that the s P 'had a very good campaign', particularly because their 'super-state' argument matched the negative mood of the country in the post–Pim Fortuyn era.[18] These specific strategies used by Libertas in Ireland and s P in the Netherlands were shown to be critical in the rejection of the Lisbon and Constitutional Treaties (Aarts and van der Kolk 2006; Atikcan 2015a; Elkink and Sinnott 2015).

In the interview data from the Brexit campaign, as the next chapter details, both Remain and the Leave campaigners openly refer to their strategy of convincing the undecided middle-ground citizens. The Remain side specified the economy as the main issue that would appeal to such voters. This decision was very much based on previous experience in the 2014 Scottish referendum and the 2015 general elections, which had brought them success. On the other side, the official Leave campaign, which was the Vote Leave campaign, chose not to associate itself with Nigel Farage or the Leave.EU campaigns, instead deciding to run a moderate campaign centred on the idea of sovereignty, as Declan Ganley did in Ireland. This move was essential in portraying a non-extreme profile and appealing to the middle ground.

Playing the Risk Card and the Status Quo Bias

In EU referendums, as shown above, pro- and anti-EU campaigners actively seek to define the risks associated with the vote choice. Looking at the strategies used in EU referendums on treaty ratification, the anti-treaty campaigns, being the defenders of the status quo, have a wider palette of arguments available to them. They typically argue that the new EU treaty will cause loss of political autonomy in key fields such as social policy, citizenship rules, immigration, military neutrality, and moral issues such as abortion, even when those themes are not present in the treaty at hand. The pro-treaty campaigners often have difficulty in finding and advancing such risk-based arguments, but they do so mostly in relation to the loss of economic benefits from the EU.

All EU member states witness such arguments in their campaigns, often wrapped around locally sensitive issues. The French referendum on the European Constitution saw a very memorable example of this pattern. The anti-treaty campaigners brought the Bolkestein Directive to the agenda, even though this was not officially part of the Constitution. The directive was a draft EU policy on the liberalization of services, which became highly controversial in France. Employers in one EU country could hire workers from another EU country where the cost of labour was lower, thus increasing their profit and reducing the social welfare of domestic workers. The symbol of this policy was the feared 'Polish plumber' who would come to take jobs away from Western Europeans. The French anti-treaty campaign used the Bolkestein Directive as an example of the European Commission's market-friendly agenda, arguing that the European Constitution would consolidate these 'anti-social' rules in a constitutional document, thereby 'carving it in marble'. In other words, there would be no coming back from a market-friendly Europe. The situation was similar in Ireland. In the first referendum on the Lisbon Treaty, the pro-life Catholic group Cóir argued that a pro-treaty vote would throw away the Irish Proclamation of Independence and make the Charter of Fundamental Rights binding and therefore interfere in Irish laws on abortion. Among their slogans were 'We Will Lose under Lisbon', 'People Died for Your Freedom, Don't Throw It Away', and 'Lisbon, It'll Cost You, More Tax, Less Power'.

The pro-EU side can advance similar arguments. In the second Lisbon referendum in Ireland, the pro-treaty campaigners argued that a second rejection would mean the end of Irish membership in the EU. This idea was presented to the public within the context of the unfolding economic crisis. Combining these two issues, the pro-treaty side claimed that a pro-Lisbon vote would mean more jobs for the Irish, whereas an anti-Lisbon vote would bring economic ruin. Ciarán Toland, a key civil society Yes campaigner in the Nice Treaty referendums, compared the 'jobs' argument of the Yes campaign to the 'abortion' argument of the No campaign, in that both had nothing to do with the treaty in question.[19] What these arguments achieved instead was to instil these themes in the public mind as the risks of the vote ahead. Many studies showed these key themes – the Bolkestein Directive, loss of sovereignty, intervention into abortion laws, and job creation – to be influential in the vote choice (Atikcan 2015a; Brouard and Sauger 2005; Elkink and Sinnott 2015).

In the Brexit referendum, the roles were more nuanced than in the treaty ratification referendums. This time it was the anti-EU side, not the pro-EU side, advocating a change. Therefore, it would be primarily the Remain campaign that would be expected to have the status quo advantage. The detailed interview data show that the Remain side was quite aware of this advantage and chose to pitch its campaign on economic risk. The Leave side, on the other hand, did not passively accept that the Remain side would control the 'risk card'. In the book that inspired the Vote Leave campaign, *Why Vote Leave*, Conservative MEP Daniel Hannan (2016) argued explicitly that, due to the Euro and migration crises, staying in the EU would be a greater risk than leaving. He argued that there was 'no status quo' in this referendum and that a vote to remain would be to vote to be part of the continuing political, fiscal, and military integration of the EU. In his words, 'voting leave would be the safer option'. Following this reasoning, the Vote Leave campaign chose to actively de-risk the economic argument and put different kinds of risk on the table, arguing that there would be risks related to immigration, the NHS, and sovereignty if the UK stayed in the EU. They called this strategy the 'Two Futures' idea, as the next chapter presents in detail.

A related finding is that in EU referendums, often the pro-EU side is blamed for exaggerating the risks of leaving the EU. The Dutch referendum in 2005 witnessed some extreme examples of this. Seeing the anti-treaty campaign's success, some key pro-treaty campaigners resorted to drastic statements warning the public of a potential disaster if they voted against the European Constitution. The Christian Democratic Appeal (CDA) justice minister Piet-Hein Donner warned of the possibility of war and possible Balkanization of Europe if the No campaign won the referendum. MEP Jules Maaten of the People's Party for Freedom and Democracy (VVD) cancelled a TV spot showing images of Auschwitz, the genocide in Srebrenica, and the terrorist bombings in Madrid, which aimed to persuade voters to vote in favour. The video was released and withdrawn within a matter of hours. The D66 (Democrats 66) economic affairs minister Laurens-Jan Brinkhorst remarked that if the Dutch people were to reject the constitution, the 'lights would go off in the Netherlands', 'our country would be locked up', and 'the Netherlands would become the Switzerland of Europe'.

These speeches were criticized severely for backfiring (Anker 2006); most Dutch pro-Treaty campaigners described the statements as 'counterproductive'. Wim van de Donk, the chairman of the WRR (the Scientific Council for Government Policy think tank), characterized the Yes campaign's strategy as clumsy and arrogant.[20] As the minister of EU affairs, Atzo Nicolaï, put it, 'Even though these were only a few statements, it was enough to give people the impression that actually this government was not interested in the voice of the people and the

The Brexit Campaign in Comparative Perspective

outcome of the referendum.'[21] In the Brexit case, as is seen in the next chapter, it was mostly the Remain side that got the blame for exaggerating the costs of a Leave vote, even though the Leave side was criticized fiercely on their £350 million figure.

The Advantage of the Anti-EU Side in Setting the Agenda in Multidimensional Proposals

Moving on to the specific dynamics of EU referendums, the anti-EU side is often more advantageous in setting the referendum campaign agenda. As discussed, the more multidimensional the topic is, the more campaign material the 'No' side has, extending the topic to various controversial themes. The result of this dynamic is often a campaign in which the subject becomes much broader than the Yes campaigners expect.

Once again, this trend is visible in every EU referendum campaign. Anti-EU campaigners typically build their arguments on the existing locally contentious issues. In the Netherlands, the international secretary of the Labour Party (PvdA), Marije Laffeber, pointed to the advantage held by the No side as a significant problem: 'There is something for everybody to dislike. In the Yes camp you are in a defensive position, and you have to explain everything.'[22] In Luxembourg, François Biltgen, the chair of the Christian Social People's Party (CSV) and the minister of labour and employment, echoed the same point, emphasizing that it was easier to be on the No side.[23] Charles Goerens, Democratic Party (DP) MP, agreed, noting that 'destruction is easier than the building process'.[24] Dutch Socialist Party (SP) MP Harry van Bommel acknowledged that this was advantageous to the No side: 'There was a basket of arguments. People sometimes have the wrong reasons to come to the right conclusions. I never mentioned Turkey's membership, but if that was somebody's trigger to vote No, that was fine by me.'[25]

Similarly, pro-EU campaigners complained about the unrelated themes that the No side put on the agenda. Enrique Baron Crespo, member of European Parliament (MEP) with the Spanish Socialist Workers' Party (PSOE), emphasized that some of the No campaign arguments were not accurate.[26] In Luxembourg, CSV MP Laurent Mosar referred to the same phenomenon: 'If somebody says that with the European Constitution we would lose our independence, people immediately believe [it].'[27] In France, Pierre Kanuty from the French

Socialist Party (PS) agreed, claiming that 'the No camp tried to use everything to convince people'.[28] Olivier Ubéda of the Union for a Popular Movement (UMP) explained that unrelated issues became a major obstacle for the Yes side:[29] '[There were arguments such as] Turkey would come into the EU with the European Constitution. Or that you would have eighty millions of Muslims coming into Europe … We had an argument about the Polish plumber, because in the treaty we said that everybody could work everywhere. As if a wave of Polish plumbers would have arrived in France. This is just fears. This is human, you fear things you do not understand, you do not know about … All this from the No camp was just nonsense.'

To open up one example, in the first Irish referendum on the Lisbon Treaty, Brendan Kiely, chief executive of Irish Alliance for Europe, noted that the No side was successful in launching a number of themes in the public's mind: that the Irish Constitution would die, that Ireland would fail to attract foreign direct investment, and that the EU would interfere in Irish corporate tax laws.[30] Dick Roche, minister of state for European affairs, stated his frustration similarly: 'They always come up: Ireland will lose neutrality – no we have not; Ireland will lose its character – no we have not; we will be subsumed in Europe – no we have not; we will lose our culture – no we have not.'[31] Referring to the same phenomenon, Brigid Laffan, chairperson of Ireland for Europe, characterized No campaign themes such as abortion and military neutrality as Ireland's 'neuralgic issues'.[32] Lucinda Creighton, Fine Gael MP, commented, 'People only need one good reason to vote against. It is a major difficulty.'[33] Karen White, member of Irish Alliance for Europe, similarly stated, 'If you are on the No side, you can appeal to different groups with different messages. We had to counter all these different arguments.'[34]

On the anti-EU side, the campaigners accepted this aspect. Naoise Nunn, executive director of Libertas, compared the No campaign to guerrilla warfare in this regard: 'You picked one little issue on which there was some doubt and contention, and then you sold and created enough doubt in the minds of the audience, and the Yes campaigners were struggling, backpedalling, trying to explain, and when they were explaining, they were losing.'[35] These controversial themes were shown indeed to have had an impact on the Lisbon vote (Atikcan 2015a, 2015b; Elkink and Sinnott 2015; Sinnott and Elkink 2010; Sinnott et al. 2009). The pro-EU campaigns often gain a similar advantage when there are fewer arguments available to the anti-EU campaign, either in a repeat referendum or in a referendum on a very specific EU treaty,

The Brexit Campaign in Comparative Perspective 49

such as the Fiscal Compact. As discussed earlier, in all the repeat referendums to date, on the Maastricht, Nice, and Lisbon treaties in Denmark and Ireland, campaigners argued that the pro-EU side controlled the campaign agenda (Atikcan 2018).

In the Brexit referendum, because the referendum topic covered everything relating to EU membership, the anti-EU side could set the agenda around diverse themes. In fact, the deal that David Cameron sought to strike with the EU before the Brexit campaign began could have served as the 'EU guarantees' in repeat referendums and changed these dynamics. Had this deal been substantive and presented to the public as a real change, it could have limited the range of arguments available to the anti-EU side. This was not the case, however. As the next chapter details, campaigners accepted that the Leave side could attack from different angles without needing to be consistent. They did not need to pick one theme; they could run with many. The Remain camp chose to build only on one issue – the economy – whereas the Leave side attacked them on many different fronts – sovereignty, immigration, the NHS. Campaigners also agreed that the Leave side's strategic decision not to specify 'the kind of an exit they would like from the EU' was very beneficial for them. This tactic prevented criticism of the Leave campaign on the specifics of that exit plan. The way in which the Brexit negotiations subsequently unfolded – in particular, the January 2019 rejection of Prime Minister May's exit deal in the House of Commons – demonstrates the importance of that strategy.

The Challenge of the Lack of Information for the Pro-EU Side

EU referendum campaigns usually fall into the particular category of opinion formation campaigns, as discussed earlier. Because the public lacks substantial information on how the EU actually works, they need the campaign information to make up their minds. The pro-EU campaigners often mentioned this lack of information as a major challenge, especially in responding to the diverse attack lines advanced by the anti-EU side.

In the interviews for this study, pro-EU campaigners often complained that in order to counter the various anti-EU arguments, they needed to educate the public quickly on the technicalities of EU decision-making. Anthony Brown, director of research for Ireland for Europe, explained that in order to reply to arguments on neutrality or abortion, the answer had to be related to the EU's 'competences', which he referred to as a 'dread-word' in political debate.[36] In the words of Luxembourg Socialist Workers' Party (LSAP) MP Ben Fayot, 'Citizens have not yet understood the institutional framework and are misinformed about the actual competences of the Union.'[37] Pat Cox, campaign director of Ireland for Europe, noted that many pro-EU campaigners themselves found it difficult to campaign on the content of the Lisbon Treaty: 'Because of the complexity of Article 48A Paragraph 3 ... it is not the easiest terrain.'[38]

A striking example of how the lack of awareness on EU issues can cause problems during intense campaign discussions comes from the Dutch referendum on the European Constitution. One week before the vote, the Dutch government sent every household a short leaflet explaining the content of the Constitutional Treaty. This text was approved by the Referendum Commission, but it became controversial due to a factual error. This leaflet maintained that by saying Yes, the Netherlands would accept the superiority of EU laws over national laws. This legal doctrine, known as the supremacy of EU law, was actually not introduced by the European Constitution and had been long established, as early as 1964. Atzo Nicolaï, Dutch minister of EU affairs, specified the statement as one of the mistakes – an unfortunate one, as people did not understand that the EU laws were already superior to national laws.[39] According also to Jan Jacob van Dijk, Christian Democratic Appeal (CDA) MP, the statement in the leaflet reinforced the feeling among Dutch citizens that they would lose control over their own legislation.[40]

In the Brexit referendum, this lack of understanding of the issues was problematic for the Remain side. As examples in the next chapter demonstrate, Remain campaigners not only had to face a variety of Leave arguments but also struggled in providing quick and easy answers to them due to the complexity of the EU. The entire campaign debate on the economic costs of a potential Brexit decision remained clouded by lack of knowledge. For instance, the figure on how much money could be saved from the EU budget in the case of a departure from the EU caused confusion among the public as well as experts and campaigners.

Scapegoating the EU

Finally, the habit of scapegoating the EU has caused a particular difficulty for pro-EU campaigners. This habit is more pronounced in some countries than in others. Where such scapegoating is a tradition in national politics, it easily creates a credibility issue for the pro-EU side in referendum campaigns.

In both French and Dutch national political arenas, this type of scapegoating is common. In the French referendum campaign in 2005, Gaëtane Ricard-Nihoul, secretary general of the think tank Notre Europe, explained that the long-term use of the EU as a scapegoat had made it difficult for Yes campaigners to suddenly turn around and ask the public to love it.[41] Similarly, in the Dutch campaign, Atzo Nicolaï, minister of EU affairs, said that the main problem was starting the campaign twenty years too late: 'What we did for twenty years was actually negative, to blame Brussels, as a general line, if something did not work out nicely ... This is the negative side, and the positive side is a general feeling after the war, that Europe is good. In between there was not so much.'[42]

In the Brexit referendum, campaigners often referred to the entrenched trend of Euroscepticism and the well-organized and funded Eurosceptic movement in the UK, which, as the above remarks point out, was difficult to change or challenge overnight. The next chapter discusses how this aspect caused a major problem for the Remain side from the outset.

Framing the Choice in EU Referendums

When these dynamics come together in EU referendums, the anti-EU arguments tend to be the stronger ones. The anti-EU side typically broadens the referendum topic to familiar and controversial themes, linking the public's existing and thereby available and accessible concerns to the referendum proposal. These anti-EU arguments are often negative, concrete, and vivid, building an immediate connection to how the vote choice would benefit or harm the public's life. This anti-EU tone is typically emotional, whereas the pro-EU side remains more technical in its language. The availability of the argument on loss of sovereignty touches an emotional chord that offers an advantage to the anti-EU side. On the pro-EU side, the typical emotional argument is that the EU is the peace project that reunited Europe in the wake of the Second World War, and that it needs protection.

In the Brexit referendum, as the next chapter details, the Remain side started the campaign with a major obstacle. As the political elite and the media have scapegoated the EU extensively in previous decades, the pro-EU campaign could not credibly be enthusiastic about EU membership. Figure 1.3 depicts the issue perfectly. Pro-EU campaigners chose to run a purely cost-benefit campaign, leaving the passion to the Leave side. The anti-EU side, benefitting from the lack of information on the EU, de-risked the Brexit decision and created doubts on the economic argument of the Remain camp. As seen in figures 1.4 to 1.6, the anti-EU side broadened the campaign to controversial themes such as sovereignty, immigration, and the NHS. Calling on voters to 'Take Back Control', they struck an emotional and sensitive chord with the public.

HOW DOES THE BREXIT REFERENDUM COMPARE TO INDEPENDENCE REFERENDUMS?

LeDuc (2002) categorizes independence referendums as 'uphill struggles' because the voting public often has an already formed opinion on the question at hand. Although independence referendums are very different from EU referendums in that sense, the Brexit referendum bears an important similarity to them. The Brexit referendum asked the public whether the UK should gain its independence from the EU, which brought to the forefront questions on whether a future in the EU or a future as an independent entity would be better. As in independence referendums, the core question was about leaving the host entity, and an assessment of the risks attached to this change. Would Quebec/Scotland be better or worse off as an independent country? Would the UK be better or worse off outside of the EU's single market? In this section, we specify the kinds of campaign strategies that are influential in independence referendum outcomes by surveying the recent literature and using interview data.

In independence referendums, despite the technicalities of the process, the widespread issue is about the ability of a nation to mount its own economic and social development project (Keating 2009). It is in fact very difficult to calculate whether a county such as Scotland or Quebec would be better or worse off as independent, since estimates are inevitably contested. In the Scottish case, Keating (2009) demonstrates the two sides of the economic argument in great detail, considering public expenditure and transfers as well as North Sea oil, showing that neither the unionist nor the secessionist claims are conclusive because of discrepancies in the calculations of the fiscal imbalance. Nonetheless, the potential economic consequences of independence dominated the 2014 Scottish referendum debate. 'Academics, expert commentators, think tanks, business groups, and representatives of civil society across the United Kingdom offered a range of predictions (positive and negative) of the likely future states of health for the Scottish economy in the event of a Yes vote' (Scott 2016, 154).

In line with the core referendum strategies discussed earlier, the core tasks for the pro-independence movements are thus to persuade the 'soft' or uncertain voters in the middle, to mobilize popular support for substantial changes to the status quo and thereby de-risk the pro-independence vote, and to appeal to the emotions of the electorate with identity-based arguments. By offering a cost-benefit analysis, Meadwell (1993) argues that while a strong sense of identity is an enabling condition, the costs associated with transition to independence are a constraining one. Taking into account the effect of risk aversion is therefore the only way for a nationalist organization to increase its support in the cultural group. This recognition was visible in the wording of the questions used in the Quebec independence referendums. In 1980, the public was asked:

> The Government of Quebec has made public its proposal to negotiate a new agreement with the rest of Canada, based on the equality of nations; this agreement would enable Quebec to acquire the exclusive power to make its laws, levy its taxes and establish relations abroad – in other words, sovereignty – and at the same time to maintain with Canada an economic association including a common currency; any change in political status resulting from these negotiations will only be implemented with popular approval through another referendum; on these terms, do you give the Government of Quebec the mandate to negotiate the proposed agreement between Quebec and Canada?

In 1995, the question was considerably shorter but along the same lines: 'Do you agree that Quebec should become sovereign after having made a formal offer to Canada for a new economic and political partnership within the scope of the bill respecting the future of Quebec and of the agreement signed on June 12, 1995?' The strategy in both referendums was to include a potential economic partnership with Canada in the question itself, thus presumably controlling the status quo bias and assuring the public that a Yes vote would not have drastic economic consequences. A similar dynamic can be observed in the

2014 Scottish referendum. In the Scottish National Party (SNP)'s independence package, the queen would remain as head of state, and Scotland's currency would continue to be the British pound. Therefore, the SNP's approach was to emphasize continuity as well as change. As Mullen (2016) puts it, 'It would not be a leap in the dark.'

The anti-independence side, on the other hand, also seeks to reach undecided voters in the middle, advancing arguments on the risks of a departure from the status quo and invoking fear in the electorate. They typically emphasize that such an economic partnership is not to be taken for granted and reaffirm the risks associated with a Yes vote. In the Scottish referendum, the UK government insisted that sharing a currency with the rest of the UK would not be possible (Mitchell 2016). Similarly, in the 1995 referendum in Quebec, the leader of No campaign often suggested that a Quebec dollar would be very weak and that an independent Quebec would not be able to control the Canadian dollar (Young 1998). The central governments also strategically offer more autonomy for the sub-state unit to render the status quo more desirable. In the Scottish case, when the polls showed a narrow majority for independence in the last two weeks before the vote, the former UK prime minister Gordon Brown, with the apparent approval of the UK government, immediately made a speech in Dundee and set out a timetable for rapid progress toward extensive further devolution (Mullen 2016, 7). Brown's move was followed quickly by the leaders of the Conservative, Labour, and Liberal Democrat Parties making a solemn 'vow', published on the front page of the *Daily Record*, promising 'extensive new powers' for the Scottish Parliament if Scotland voted to remain in the UK. In Quebec as well, in a huge federalist rally, the Canadian prime minister embraced the distinctness of Quebec society and promised a constitutional veto to Quebec (Young 1998).

Ample data link the campaign arguments on economic consequences of independence to a decrease in the Yes vote (Young 1998). For the 1995 Quebec referendum, Nadeau, Martin, and Blais (1999) find proof for status quo bias in voting, as individuals who usually accepted risk more readily tended to choose entirely on the basis of anticipated costs and benefits, but individuals who were more reluctant to take risks gave almost as much weight to the perceived possibility of a 'worst outcome'. Their findings suggest that attitudes toward risk-taking had a modest but significant impact on individual choice, and thus were a contributing factor in the outcome of the Quebec referendum.[43] In the Scottish case, data show that voters did not vote solely on the basis of identity (Mullen 2014, 633). A substantial proportion of those identifying themselves as 'more Scottish than British' voted against independence, implying that the vote was not only conditioned by national identity and that the anticipated consequences of independence were likely influential. Other polling data also suggest that voting intentions strongly correlated with perceptions of the strength or weakness of the Scottish economy after independence (633). Similarly, based on a multi-wave panel survey repeatedly asking respondents their views, Henderson et al. (2015) find that although identity provided core support for both camps, economic risk decided the outcome. The campaign had a significant impact on the public's perception of the consequences of the vote choice. In other words, although independence referendums fall into the 'uphill struggle' category as opposed to the 'opinion formation' one (LeDuc 2002), 'the No campaign did not change what Scots want; just scared them out of going for it' (Johns 2014).

To date, no sub-state movement in the West has succeeded in separating from its host entity via referendum politics, and the studies above suggest that economic costs often trump the emotions surrounding identity. In the Brexit case, as the Remain campaign was indeed centred on the dire economic consequences of a Leave vote, the expectation of these studies on independence referendums would be that the Remain side's focus on economic risks would convince the public not to leave the EU.

We detail below through interview data the strategies employed in independence referendums and how they compare to the Brexit campaign. The data come from Atikcan's fieldwork in Scotland in 2017 with campaigners involved in the Scottish independence referendum campaign. The Scottish case is important for two reasons. First, it is the latest independence referendum to have taken place in an EU member state. Second, and more importantly, given that the referendum took place in the UK, the strategies used in this case and the extent to which they were successful have a direct bearing on the choice of campaign strategies in the Brexit referendum.

The methodological discussion above and the keywords in table 2.2 apply to the Scottish case as well. Keywords, such as 'reaching/persuading/appealing' to 'undecided/ambivalent/middle/soft' voters, and the 'use of fear/threats/blackmail' and any 'backlash/backfiring' to such arguments, were used to identify strategies of going beyond 50 per cent and controlling the risk factor, respectively. Once again, these strategies were mentioned by a *majority* of the campaigners interviewed. We provide some key quotes in the sections below, taking each strategy in turn, to illustrate how these strategies came up in the interview data.

Actors and Arguments in the Scottish Independence Referendum

The Scottish government announced on 21 March 2013 that it would hold a referendum, setting the date as 18 September 2014, which allowed for a very long campaign. In fact, the unofficial campaign had started as early as May 2012. There were two main campaigns: the pro-independence Yes Scotland campaign and the anti-independence Better Together campaign. The Yes Scotland campaign was supported by the Scottish National Party, the Scottish Green Party, and the Scottish Socialist Party. The Better Together campaign was led collectively by the Conservative Party, the Labour Party, and the Liberal Democrats.

The Yes Scotland campaign had three core themes: democracy, prosperity, and fairness. It argued that an independent Scotland would be more democratic and economically better off and would have its own welfare state and thereby better social policies. These arguments pitched an independent Scotland against the policies of the UK that have primarily benefitted the southeast of England. The core slogan was 'Scotland's Future in Scotland's Hands'. On the anti-independence side, the Better Together campaign's main argument focused on the economic loss that would result from Scottish independence, highlighting the uncertainty on key issues such as the currency. This particular aspect is what attached the label 'Project Fear' to the Better Together campaign. An additional argument was brought up around the issue of devolution, with the slogan 'Best of Both Worlds' suggesting that devolution of powers to the Scottish parliament would bring safer and quicker change than independence. Figures 2.1 and 2.2 portray a selection of campaign posters.

Going beyond 50 Per Cent and Trying to Reach the Undecided 'Middle-Ground' Voters

In independence referendums, the typical themes that worry middle-ground voters are the potential costs of departure from the host state and the economic viability of the new independent state. In the

Figure 2.1 Selection of posters for Yes Scotland campaign

Scottish case, both the Yes Scotland and Better Together campaigns said that they tried to convince soft voters in the middle of the political spectrum.

Blair Jenkins, the chief executive of the Yes Scotland campaign, explained that roughly 25 per cent of people told them they would vote for independence, and another 25 per cent said they would definitely vote for staying in the UK; thus their main strategy was to get the remaining 50 per cent to join the conversation and to encourage them to think about it: 'But as we got into debate with people, it became clear that the main obstacle to getting people to vote Yes was economic.'[44] This is why the SNP campaign discussed the issues of currency, monarchy, and ties to the NATO, as a balancing act. The strategic communications director of the SNP, Kevin Pringle, agreed that the economic message was meant mostly for middle-ground voters: 'Essentially the strategy was to win the economic argument about Scotland's economic viability as an independent country, because many people would not go any further in the jungle with you unless they

Figure 2.2 Selection of posters for Better Together campaign

were persuaded that Scotland was economically viable as a country ... I think the reason that we did not manage to get it higher up to the winning threshold was because people had enough doubt in their minds about the economic and financial case.'[45]

On the Better Together side, the picture was similar. Reaching soft voters was the main logic behind the choice of the strategy. Better Together's Rob Shorthouse explained, not unlike Blair Jenkins, that they knew that regardless of attempts to persuade them, 30 per cent of people were always going to vote Yes, 40 per cent of the people were going to vote No, and 30 per cent were in the middle.[46] Then they decided to take a 'brave' decision, in his words:

> We then looked at who the 30 per cent in the middle were ... basically what we learnt was that the people in the middle were

split in a number of ways, but mainly they did not strongly identify themselves as being British. They were not going to make that decision based on what it meant, it was not really a question of national identity ... ultimately the decision they were going to take was based on a cold-heart economic reality. And what we were assured about was that if the debate was about anything other than the cold-heart reality of what this means they would be gettable for the Yes campaign ... So that is why we made the very odd decision of making it about risk and uncertainty. That was a brave decision because the 40 per cent who were going to vote for us became increasingly annoyed with us for ignoring them ... because they wanted union flags.

Shorthouse also explained that while this was Better Together's core message, they noticed that it would only stop the soft voters from becoming Yes voters – it would not necessarily make them No voters. This is why they also developed a message on devolution. Their posters made this point very clear too, as seen in figure 2.2. As he put it, 'The idea was "The Best of Both Worlds." So, if you want to stay in the UK, you can have both the strength and security of the Scottish parliament without the risk and uncertainty of leaving the UK. It was saying, "Here is something to vote for and here is something to vote against."' A board member of the campaign, Phil Anderton, confirmed that the research identified economic consequences as the main issue for the undecided group in the middle, but in his view, the 'Best of Both Worlds' idea was pitched to the voters later in the campaign rather than from the beginning.[47]

Anderton's view was backed by both Jenkins and Pringle from the Yes Scotland campaign, who argued that their polling showed a trend toward an acceptance of independence, and that is what brought in the idea of change and the Better Together's renewed angle on 'Best of Both Worlds' and 'Devolution Max', to offer a change that would be 'faster, safer and better' than the change brought about by independence.[48]

The Brexit campaign was thus very similar to the Scottish campaign in terms of the strategies used to reach the undecided middle-ground voters. In both campaigns, the economic costs of departure from the host entity (the EU or the UK) were identified as the main factor that would sway the voters in the middle. Both campaigns that sought to stay in, Remain and Better Together, chose to abandon the different themes they could have advanced and turned to the economic one in order to convince the critical undecided voters. The other side, the Leave and the Yes Scotland campaigns, ran their campaigns mainly on a message of change, democracy, hope, and taking control of their own future.

Nonetheless, there were two key differences. First, the Better Together campaign, as opposed to the Remain campaign, used a second argument to attack the core argument of the Yes Scotland campaign. Rob Shorthouse explained that the Better Together campaign coupled its arguments on risk with a second argument on bringing change, 'Best of Both Worlds'.[49] The idea of further devolution was put forward in recognition of people's willingness to change the existing situation, and Shorthouse emphasized that this argument responded to the Yes Scotland slogan 'Scotland's Future in Scotland's Hands' in a way that the Remain campaign did not respond to 'Take Back Control'. Given the existing tradition of scapegoating the EU and the considerable level of long-term Euroscepticism, he argued, the Remain side would have gained considerably from a change-based argument.

The second difference was the use of immigration as a campaign theme. Although neither the official Vote Leave campaign nor the Yes Scotland campaign chose immigration as a campaign theme, Vote Leave brought it up later in the campaign. The other Leave campaign groups such as Leave.EU mobilized the immigration theme from the beginning. Given the highly charged nature of the immigration issue, its presence or absence is important in understanding the mobilization potential of the Leave and Yes Scotland campaigns. Rob Shorthouse said, 'The immigration argument gave people an easy answer to their problems ... and the Remain camp just ignored that.'[50] Campaigners from the Remain side echoed this statement, as is discussed in the next chapter.

Playing the Risk Card and the Status Quo Bias

Another key logic in independence referendums is controlling the fear factor and motivating voters on the basis of the status quo bias, which, as shown above, evolves around the economic risks in separating from the host state. In the Scottish independence referendum, as the Better Together campaign chose to pitch its core message around the economic risks of independence, the Yes Scotland campaign had to fight this message from the beginning. Blair Jenkins, the chief executive of the Yes Scotland campaign, explained that the Better Together campaign controlled the fear factor by posing questions about the currency union, Scotland's admission into the EU, the economy's dependence on oil, and more: 'It was all about the negatives, what you would lose if you left the UK.'[51] In order to de-risk the economic argument, he explained, Yes Scotland tried two strategies. First, the SNP tried to emphasize 'continuity' and tell voters that there would be *necessary changes only* and no unnecessary disruptions or ruptures. The social union with the UK would continue, as would the ties to the currency and the monarchy. Second, they pointed to the successful examples of small western European countries about the same size as Scotland, which had the 'best economies and societies'.

Similarly, the SNP's strategic communications director, Kevin Pringle, explained that in their poster (figure 2.1), crossing out the negation in the word 'can't' was designed to de-risk, 'to get people over the hurdle, to create a sense of no barrier'.[52] To move beyond de-risking and to pitch their own risk-based argument, the SNP used the 'Two Futures' idea, much as the Leave campaign would do later on. The idea was to counter the status quo bias and show voters that if Scotland stayed in the UK, there would also be consequences. The poster on the NHS (figure 2.1) was designed to invite voters to think about the harm that future Tory policies – privatization in particular – would do to the NHS.

Nonetheless, Jenkins admitted that 'on balance, people were more concerned about the risks than they were attracted by the potentials.'[53] For the same reason, on their three core campaign themes – democracy, prosperity, and fairness – Jenkins argued that the Yes Scotland campaign had to focus mostly on prosperity, because the Better Together side was completely focused on the economy: 'Therefore we were partly pushing our own arguments on the economic issue, but obviously often defending against the attack from the other side.' Jenkins believed that they won the argument on the other two issues but lost on the economy. Pringle agreed that the arguments on democracy and fairness worked very well but that they had difficulty with the economic viability aspect, particularly in relation to the future currency of Scotland.[54]

The Better Together campaign team were in full agreement that they controlled the fear factor. For Rob Shorthouse, the main factor in that sense was the currency (see figure 2.2). This factor was very tangible in daily life; they argued that keeping the British pound after independence was not guaranteed and blamed the Yes Scotland campaign for not having a 'Plan B'.[55] Shorthouse added, '"Project Fear" was about delegitimizing everything they said – they signed the White Paper, they will keep the BBC, and keep that, and do that ... When we were prepping ourselves for the debates ... we just needed to put in people's minds that whatever Alex Salmond was telling them might not be right. All we had to do was to say, "What if you are wrong?" And that was enough.' As for the risk-based arguments of Yes Scotland, one of which focused on the potential cuts to the NHS under a future Conservative government, Shorthouse accepted that it was difficult for the Better Together campaign to counter it: 'All of a sudden we saw their version of "Project Fear" ... And the reason it was so effective was because a lot of people in the 30 per cent middle group did not like the Tories.' Phil Anderton of the Better Together campaign agreed that the Yes Scotland's emphasis on 'Westminster', 'Tory', and 'the bad guys down there' instead of the word 'English' was cleverly put across.[56] Nonetheless, like everyone else, Anderton added that Yes Scotland's weakness was the economic side of the argument:

> They made it sound like it was going to be a land of milk and honey. So the White Paper, for example, had literally one page on the economics or the future of Scotland. The other fundamental weakness for them was the currency. Most people do not understand what currencies are all about. But they kind of do get a simple thing like 'I kind of know the pound and I want to use the pound and then they are telling us that we may not have the pound and what does that mean? That we will have the Euro?' And they do not fully understand the whole implication of the Euro but they see Greece, they see Portugal, they see all of that, and they think, that is not good for us.

Comparing these strategies to the Brexit case, the Better Together and Remain campaigns share strikingly common ground in their 'Project Fear' approach. The term originates with the Better Together campaign, which tapped into the public's worries regarding the economic risks of Scotland leaving the UK. After seeing this strategy's success, the Remain side deliberately used it in the Brexit campaign. On the other side, both the Yes Scotland and Vote Leave campaigns had to de-risk these economic arguments. In addition, both campaigns tried to put forward the idea of 'Two Futures', in which they sought to specify the risks of staying in. In the words of Blair Jenkins, 'In the EU referendum both sides were running "Project Fear". On the Remain side, they were running "Project Fear" on the economy, and on the Leave side they were running "Project Fear" on immigration.'[57] But such strategies did not work as effectively as in the Scottish case. Campaigners pointed to two major differences.

First, in the Brexit campaign, most campaigners argued that the concerns relating to the economic viability of the separating unit were not as severe as they were in Scotland. The chief executive of Vote Leave, Matthew Elliott, said, 'It was difficult to make the case that Britain was not big enough on its own to survive economically.'[58] Labour MP Gisela Stuart, chair of the Vote Leave Campaign Committee, agreed, emphasizing the size and confidence of the UK compared to Scotland.[59] Pointing to similar issues, the co-founder of Leave.EU, Richard Tice, argued that 'the Scottish "Project Fear" was more credible.'[60] As Kevin Pringle put it, 'It is far easier to scaremonger about an entity that does not exist ... it is always going to be far easier to fill people with a sense of fear ... about the creation of a brand new entity on the international stage, Scotland as a nation-state, than on a vote on the UK, which is an existing nation state.'[61]

Second, another borrowed term was 'Plan B'. The Better Together campaign criticized the Yes Scotland campaign for not having a 'Plan B' and attacked their White Paper strongly on the lack of plans for an alternative currency and all else. Matthew Elliott explained that Vote Leave deliberately avoided being in this position in the Brexit campaign:

We chose to not campaign on the basis of a plan; otherwise the debate would have been precisely over the basis of the plan. If you look at the referendum in Scotland, Alex Salmond had his White Paper. The trouble was, the whole debate was about the White Paper – for example, using the pound and being in the EU after the referendum. I have no doubt that had Scotland become independent, both of those things would have been true. But of course those two points became points of big contention.[62]

The Brexit negotiations that followed the referendum result, the major disagreements over the specific exit deal that the UK should have, prove the importance of Elliott's comment. SNP's Kevin Pringle similarly said that the Leave campaign in the Brexit referendum did not receive much scrutiny on their specific exit plans, 'ironically, because they did not have the equivalent of the independence White Paper.'[63] He added that White Paper was put under a significant amount of scrutiny, tying it back to the issue of differing levels of economic confidence in the two entities. For Pringle, these were the key factors that explained why the status quo bias worked differently in the two cases. Much like the Vote Leave campaign, Pringle noted, 'We tried to develop the concept of "Two Futures". We can either go down this road or that road. But in the media, all of the scrutiny was on the independence option, the change option, and none of the scrutiny was on the no-change option. Ironically of course, in the EU referendum it seemed to be the case that almost all of the scrutiny was on the no-change option, none of the scrutiny was on the change option, which was the opposite of the independence referendum.'[64]

Moreover, just as in EU referendums, campaigners in independence referendums may witness a backlash if their risk-based arguments are not deemed credible. In the Scottish referendum campaign, in March 2014, Chancellor George Osborne denied that there could be a currency union between the UK and an independent Scotland: 'There will not be a currency union in the event of independence. The only way to keep the UK pound is to stay in the UK. Walking out of the UK means walking out of the UK pound. The Scottish government is proposing to divorce the rest of the UK but want to keep the joint bank account and credit card.'[65] This statement, while quite influential and decisive in the end, initially backfired and led to an increase for independence in the polls.

'It was all very well choreographed, because the Labour Party and the Liberal Democrats said the same thing on the same day,' Blair Jenkins observed. 'But it was interesting because it didn't have all that much impact. It annoyed a lot of people ... and backfired a bit ... But there is no doubt that it did also add to the notion of risk.'[66] Pringle argued similarly that Osborne's statement was important but seen as problematic in its immediate aftermath:[67]

> In the initial period it actually gave a boost to the Yes campaign, because it looked like it was really quite unfair. We used arguments like 'the pound is Scotland's currency every bit as much as it is the currency of the rest of the UK, so by what right does George Osborne say we cannot use the pound? It is our pound as well.' So, in the initial period, if anything, it gave the Yes

campaign a bit of a lift, because it looked very heavy-handed, very unfair. But, in the longer term, because there was no agreement that we could use the pound and the UK government and the other parties insisted that we just could not use the pound ... that created enough uncertainty for enough people. They did not feel confident enough to be able to vote Yes.

As opposed to the limited problem that Osborne's statement had, the Remain camp in the Brexit referendum received much more criticism about its figures and timeline regarding the costs of a Leave vote, as the next chapter explains in detail.

Framing the Choice in Independence Referendums

In independence referendums, the winning campaign is the one that can mobilize the 'unsure middle', either by emphasizing the economic risks of independence or by inspiring undecided voters that the best future would be the one 'in their own hands'. The historical record shows that the first prevails over the latter.

The Scottish case paralleled this pattern. The Better Together campaign relied on a cost-benefit approach, while the Yes Scotland campaign chose to use strong emotional arguments. With their slogan 'Scotland's Future in Scotland's Hands', chief executive Blair Jenkins explained, they sought to make a positive emotional case of why Scotland would be better as an independent country.[68] He added that the Better Together campaign, in contrast, was built around a negative case. (Figures 2.1–2.2 demonstrate this contradiction clearly.) Phil Anderton of Better Together also argued that the campaign needed more emotional appeal, discussing the importance of connecting with people's underlying emotional goals, based on neuroscience research: 'There were a few of us on the board who argued strongly that one of the key emotions that people want to satisfy is the sense of security and belonging. And the union, for all its faults, has been a real sense of belonging for the people across the island. And that was something that just was not used at all. And that was a big mistake, because it enabled the SNP to completely own that ground of belonging.'[69] For Rob Shorthouse, however, their campaign's need to persuade the undecided voters led to the 'brave' choice of focusing on the economy and leaving aside the Union flags that their safe vote base was very keen to see in the campaign.[70]

This leads to another point of similarity between the Brexit and Scottish campaigns. The two 'Project Fear' campaigns, Remain and Better Together, have been criticized for approaching the issue purely from a cost-benefit perspective. The Leave and Yes Scotland campaigns, on the other hand, get much credit from campaigners for their emotional appeal, with similar slogans such as 'Take Back Control' (Brexit) and 'Scotland's Future in Scotland's Hands' (Scotland). However, as the empirical research on the Scottish referendum discussed above has shown, the Better Together campaign's focus on economic costs connected quite strongly with the voters. These survey-based studies found again and again that although identity provided core support for both camps, economic risk decided the outcome in the Scottish vote. Why, then, did the emotional arguments of the Yes Scotland campaign not carry it as far as the Leave campaign? Here the campaigners point to two problems for the Yes Scotland campaign.

First, they argue that 'Take Back Control' refers to a successful nostalgic past as opposed to the economically uncertain, untested, forward-looking 'Scotland's Future in Scotland's Hands'. Blair Jenkins, chief executive of the Yes Scotland campaign, explained:[71]

> 'Scotland's Future in Scotland's Hands' is looking forward. 'Take Back Control' is a nostalgic message, it is looking backwards, let's go back to the way we were ... There was a time, there was a rosy period in the past, where we were all happy and prosperous and it was wonderful ... The appeal was a nostalgic appeal to 'Let's Make Britain Great Again'... It was a powerful slogan, because there is no doubt that across the western world many people have a sense that the world is spinning faster than they understand and that they do not have control over their lives, they do not have a job, security, prosperity for their children ... so it was tapping into something quite deep... Our pitch was not a backward-looking one. It was about what kind of country we could be. It has always been outward looking, it has always been about wanting to be part of the world.

Phil Anderton of the Better Together campaign similarly noted that the Leave camp 'nailed it because they came up with the key emotion of "we are out of control"'.[72] SNP's Kevin Pringle also saw a parallel between the two slogans, but he added, 'The difference would be in the motivation for wanting control, and I think we would like to argue that for "Yes Scotland" the motivations were benign, outward-looking, internationalist, to do with social justice, whereas the motivation for "Take Back Control" was quite negative, backward-looking, anti-immigrant.'[73] However, all the campaigners noted, given the economic uncertainty surrounding the idea of an independent Scotland and the lack of such uncertainty in the UK's strong economic past, the nostalgic touch of the Leave campaign was emotionally potent.

A second problem for the Yes Scotland side, as discussed earlier, was that the Better Together side responded with its 'Best of Both Worlds' slogan, the idea of offering a safe and fast change – devolution. Pringle admitted that 'Best of Both Worlds' was effective, offering some control without the uncertainty.[74] In contrast, the Remain campaign did not advance a similar line, therefore choosing not to respond to the emotional argument of the Leave camp. Blair Jenkins (Yes Scotland) noted that in the face of the Leave side's 'Take Back Control', the only response the Remain side had was 'to say you are right, we do not like them either, but we have to be in this club because it is the only way of getting the economy going ... so they conceded so much of their territory to the other side.'[75]

CONCLUSION: BREXIT CAMPAIGN STRATEGIES THROUGH A COMPARATIVE LENS

Looking at the referendums on EU questions and independence, the two most similar categories of referendums to the Brexit referendum, the global expectation would be an advantage for the Remain side. This is primarily because of its capacity to raise the argument on the drastic economic costs of a departure from the EU and its status as the defender of the status quo bias. Nonetheless, the answer lies in the specifics of the campaign. Detailed interview data with campaigners in these referendums highlight the importance of *framing the choice*, the argumentation strategies, in understanding the final choice.

As table 2.3 demonstrates, the strategies employed in the Brexit referendum were broadly in line with the strategies used in EU and independence referendums. But the Leave side's specific *framing choices* saved them from making key mistakes that others often made. Both the Remain and Leave campaigns tried to reach unsure soft voters and to appeal to voters' feelings about the risks of the choice. In comparison with the EU referendum strategies, the Remain side ran its campaign on the economic costs of Brexit, which is the usual strength of pro-EU campaigns. But the Leave side responded to those arguments and placed diverse and potent risks of remaining in the EU on the agenda while maintaining a non-extremist profile, which is a typical difficulty for anti-EU campaigners.

What is more, in EU referendums, the usual advantage of the No campaigners when combined with the lack of information of the public on the complexities of the union can turn into a strong advantage for the anti-EU campaigners. The interview data demonstrate that the Leave side benefitted from these factors. Given the Leave side's lines of attack from a large number of angles without the need for coherence, the Remain campaigners struggled to explain how the EU institutions worked and contributed to the well-being of British citizens. As an added benefit, the Leave camp made highly efficient use of the typical anti-EU argument – the emotional case of losing democratic control over their country – with a brilliant slogan. The Remain camp once again left the stage to them and did not adopt such emotional language.

When compared to the Scottish referendum, on the other hand, the key question is how the Leave side avoided the quintessential problem in independence referendums, which is economic fears trumping national identity in the campaign. The Scottish referendum was especially comparable to the Brexit case, because the Remain side pitched its campaign entirely on economic fears and was labelled as running 'Project Fear' just as the Better Together campaign was. A few differences stand out in the interview data, however. While the Better Together campaign responded to the Yes Scotland campaign with a 'change' argument that proposed increased devolution ('Devolution Max'), the Remain side did not achieve this in the face of the arguments of the Leave campaign. Similarly, although the economic viability of Scotland remained a constant question mark in the minds of the Scottish voters, the Leave campaigners were not bothered by the same concerns, since the UK has already been an independent, economically self-sufficient entity. The Leave side thus had an easier time in de-risking the Remain campaign's economic arguments than the Yes Scotland campaign did. In addition, whereas the Leave side could bring up risks related to the highly controversial theme of immigration, this issue was not part of the Scottish debate. A final difference related to their exit plans. The White Paper that the SNP government decided to draft, detailing their concrete plans for after independence, was

Table 2.3
Brexit referendum strategies in a comparative perspective

	EU referendums	Scottish referendum	Brexit referendum
Going beyond 50%	Pro-EU: – Implicit task for the pro-EU political mainstream Anti-EU: – Avoiding an extremist look – Use of the economy and sovereignty themes	Anti-independence: – Use of the economy theme – Use of the idea of further devolution Pro-independence: – Use of the economy theme – Use of the idea of currency/trade agreement	Remain: – Use of the economy theme Leave: – Avoiding an extremist look – Core campaign on sovereignty and economy, coupled with a separate campaign on immigration
The status quo bias	Pro-EU: – Bringing up the risks of losing the economic benefits of the EU Anti-EU: – Wider palette of arguments	Anti-independence: – Bringing up the economic risks of independence Pro-independence: – Emphasizing continuity and pointing to the success of small states – Proposing the 'two futures' idea – Specific exit plan	Remain: – Defender of the status quo – Bringing up the risks of losing the economic benefits of the EU Leave: – Proposing the 'two futures' idea – Other risks on economy, sovereignty, immigration, NHS – No specific exit plan
Anti-EU agenda advantage Lack of information on the EU Scapegoating the EU	Pro-EU: – Limited availability of arguments – Benefits of a focused treaty or EU guarantees – Difficulty of explaining the EU – Countering existing Euroscepticism Anti-EU: – Wide range of arguments in multidimensional referendums – Advantage for raising doubts from multiple angles – Building on existing Euroscepticism		Remain: – Relying only on economic arguments – No substantive deal with the EU – Difficulty of explaining the EU – Challenge of existing British Euroscepticism Leave: – Wide-range of arguments on economy, sovereignty, immigration, NHS – No specific exit plan – Advantage for raising doubts from multiple angles – Building on existing British Euroscepticism

widely criticized, only adding to the difficulties they faced throughout the campaign. In contrast, the Leave campaign strategically remained vague on their plan in order to avoid such criticism; the importance of this particular decision was demonstrated multiple times in 2019, when the exit plans of both Prime Minister May and Prime Minister Johnson were severely criticised and rejected in the House of Commons. Taken together, these factors contributed to breaking the unbreakable mould in independence referendums.

It is clear what the Leave side did differently from the campaigners in other referendums. Next, we turn to the question of how they did it by employing a multi-method approach. In the next chapter we detail the way in which the Brexit campaign was planned and executed, using in-depth interview data from Brexit campaigners and strategists. We also explore how the news media presented the campaign and its core arguments to the public. The chapters that follow then use survey data to explore how these arguments contributed to the vote choice.

3

Preparing and Executing
the Brexit Campaign

> In the EU referendum, both sides were running 'Project Fear'. On the
> Remain side they were running 'Project Fear' on the economy, and on
> the Leave side they were running 'Project Fear' on immigration.[1]
>
> Blair Jenkins

The Leave campaign was strategic in its framing choices, avoiding
the challenges frequently faced by anti-EU and pro-independence
campaigners. How did they achieve this? A comprehensive, systematic analysis of the Brexit campaign must begin with interviews with
the campaigners and strategists. Only through their eyes can we
grasp the grounding of the campaign, the reasoning behind the choice
of campaign arguments. How did campaigners actively frame the
vote choice? How was the Remain campaign's famous 'Project Fear'
designed? And was it only the Remain side that presented the public
with a 'Project Fear'? It is equally important to understand how these
campaign strategies were reflected in the news media. If the media
transmitted campaign arguments to the public in a different light,
this would constitute an important factor in explaining the outcome.
How did the media portray these messages to the voting public?

Table 3.1 builds directly on previous chapters and exhibits once
again the 'kit' of strategies most frequently used in referendums. Using
these categories, we detail the strategic decisions that Brexit campaigners took, relying on in-depth interview and media content data (see
appendix). The methodology used for the Brexit interviews follows
the same steps used for the EU and Scottish independence referendums.
These interviews were similarly face-to-face and semi-structured to
provide the necessary flexibility for probing questions. Opportunity
and snowball sampling were prioritized in order to target and reach

Table 3.1
Strategies in the Brexit referendum campaign

Scapegoating the EU		Remain: – Challenge of existing British Euroscepticism and lack of credibility Leave: – Building on existing Euroscepticism
De-risking the Brexit decision	Going beyond 50%	Remain: – Use of the economy theme Leave: – Avoiding an extremist look – Core campaign on sovereignty and economy, coupled with a separate campaign on immigration
	The status quo bias	Remain: – Defender of the status quo – Bringing up the risks of losing the economic benefits of the EU Leave: – Proposing the 'two futures' idea – Other risks on economy, sovereignty, immigration, NHS – No specific exit plan
	Anti-EU agenda advantage Lack of information on the EU	Remain: – Relying only on economic arguments – No substantive deal with the EU – Difficulty of explaining the EU Leave: – Wide-range of arguments on economy, sovereignty, immigration, NHS – No specific exit plan – Advantage for raising doubts from multiple angles

interviewees who were key decision-makers on the campaign strategies. (For a detailed methodological discussion, see chapter 1; for a full list of the individuals interviewed and the interview questionnaire, see the appendix.)

In analysing the interview data, we focused on the keywords listed in table 2.2 to identify the strategies used in the Brexit campaign. *All* of these strategies were mentioned by a majority of the campaigners interviewed. In that sense, the Brexit case closely parallels the other referendums. But taking a step further, we assess the ways in which these strategies resembled or differed from those used in previous referendums. In this chapter, we devote each section to a specific strategy and through detailed quotes from the campaigners discuss in detail how the Brexit campaigners prepared for the campaign battle and how they reassessed their strategies as the campaign unfolded.

We present the interview data in two stages. First, there was a structural aspect that defined the campaigns. The Remain side was at a disadvantage from the outset: given the long tradition of *scapegoating the EU* in British politics, the Remain campaign had to promote an unpopular institution. Second, as the campaign unfolded, the Leave camp actively *de-risked a departure from the status quo* by reaching middle-ground voters, challenging the status quo bias, and benefitting from the advantages of being on the anti-EU side. In other words, while the usual habit of scapegoating the EU posed a challenge for the Remain side from the beginning, the other campaign decisions shaped how the two sides portrayed the voting decision and the extent to which the Leave side could de-risk leaving the EU. Table 3.1 summarizes these strategies, and we discuss each aspect in turn. In the chapter's final section, we turn to the media coverage of the campaign to understand whether the media conveyed the campaigners' messages to the public in the way that campaigners intended.

SCAPEGOATING THE EU

Campaigners enter referendum debates with a history. If the referendum question is not entirely new, they may need to take into account in formulating their campaign arguments what they have already said on the topic. In that sense, the pro- and anti-EU sides did not start the Brexit campaign on an equal footing. On LeDuc's (2002) spectrum, the Brexit referendum falls into the middle, where the voters already had a clear sense of what the EU meant to them but lacked information on the specifics of their membership in the EU and what a future outside of the EU would mean. The Brexit campaigners thus needed to both engage with the existing narrative on European integration and invent new arguments on the specifics of the referendum question.

In the interviews, campaigners often referred to the long-established trend of scapegoating the EU and to the well-organized and well-funded Eurosceptic movement in the UK, which we take up in the next chapter (see Evans and Norris 1999; Evans and Butt 2007; Forster 2002; Gifford 2014; Startin 2015; Vasilopoulou 2016). This tradition was difficult to challenge or change overnight. The chief executive of the Yes Scotland campaign, Blair Jenkins, summarized the issue succinctly: 'It was highly unusual that both the Remain and Leave campaigns started from the premise that the EU was not an institution to be admired. I do not think anyone has thought enough about how to make a positive emotional case that would connect to people about Europe.'[2] From the outset, this tradition structured the choices of the Remain and Leave campaigns, conditioning their campaign positions and arguments.

The Remain campaigners, part of the British political elite who often blamed the EU for unpopular measures, found it difficult to switch to a highly enthusiastic mode advancing inspirational arguments on European integration. Condemned to defend a partnership long been presented and perceived as unpopular, the Remain advocates chose to focus their argument not on the benefits of the EU for their country but instead on the negative economic consequences of no longer being a part of it. The posters in figure 1.3 present this emphasis clearly. The history of blaming the EU has thus favoured a strong focus on the economy, and the Remain campaign turned this focus to a core campaign strategy, aiming to appeal to middle-ground voters and relying also on their previous experience in the Scottish referendum and the 2015 general elections.

For the Leave side, such scapegoating paved the way for a strong framing from the beginning. They could immediately rely on voters' existing resentment toward the EU and easily resort to the use of heuristics, because shortcuts such as 'costly and inefficient European bureaucracy' were already available in the public mind. As such, the tradition of scapegoating the EU was highly instrumental in advancing their arguments. It also provided a strong campaign infrastructure for the Leave side. As Matthew Elliott, chief executive of Vote Leave, put it, 'What mattered was the campaign over twenty-five years.'[3] Vote Leave drew upon the past quarter-century of previously constructed infrastructure, with pressure groups, think tanks, and grassroots organizations, he explained: 'Some of these were quite significant bodies and what that meant was that, first of all, people have been putting out leaflets for many years, and secondly when it came to the campaign we already had a grassroots structure.'

Throughout the campaign, the Remain side was strongly criticized for not breaking the existing unpopular outlook of the EU with energetic and enthusiastic arguments. Labour MP Alan Johnson explained the long-term reasons behind this:[4]

Britain has never been in love with the EU. We were not there at the start ... In the end when we came in it had been going on for almost twenty years, and we were the new kids on the block. We did lead the single market, and that was very important, but there has always been this anti-European feeling in this country, in a way that it has not been in most other European countries. Part of that is, of course, we did not have the same experience in the war. We were not invaded, we did not have our soil running red with blood. For Germany, for Italy, for France, there was a very emotional argument about having seen two world wars in the first half of the twentieth century. Peace on their continent. Never really caught on over here ...

We were trying to find inspirational arguments for remaining in the European Union. Ours was the status quo, it was what people were used to for forty, fifty years. It did not generate much excitement, and it did not have the same immediate impact as the kind of slogans of Leave.

Campaigners also pointed to the impact of the Eurosceptic tabloid press in reinforcing the negative view of the EU. The chief campaign spokesperson of the Remain side, James McGrory, said that the tabloid press had been running a two-decade campaign against EU membership and they continued with it.[5] Similarly emphasizing the amount of Eurosceptic newspaper coverage during the campaign and in the previous decades, Labour MP Alan Johnson said that it was 'a wonder that the result was so close, actually'.[6] The existing Euroscepticism and the habit of scapegoating the union thus gave the two campaigns a different footing in their initial positions.

DE-RISKING THE BREXIT DECISION

We now turn to the typical referendum strategies and how they were used in the Brexit case as the campaign unfolded. What were the specific choices made by the Remain and Leave campaigns in each of these categories? How were these strategies used to shape the risk perceptions of the public? How was the Remain campaign's famous 'Project Fear' designed? How exactly did the Leave camp argue that remaining in the EU would in fact be riskier than leaving it? What was the reasoning behind the key slogan 'Take Back Control'?

Going beyond 50 Per Cent and Trying to Reach
the Undecided 'Middle-Ground' Voters

In the interviews, both the Remain and the Leave campaigners mentioned the core referendum strategy of trying to reach undecided, middle-ground voters. The Remain side prioritized the economy as the main issue that would appeal to the middle-ground voters. The Vote Leave campaign, on the other hand, chose not to associate themselves with Nigel Farage or the Leave.EU campaigns and decided to run a middle-ground, moderate campaign centred on the idea of sovereignty.

The director of strategy of the Remain campaign, Ryan Coetzee, explained that they studied the campaign 'territory' in great detail, compartmentalizing the voters into different groups based on regular polling data. The secure groups were given names such as 'ardent internationalists' or 'EU hostiles', and the middle-ground groups had names such as 'disengaged middle' or 'hearts versus heads'. As Coetzee put it, 'Essentially this referendum boils down to a question of framing. Will a voter think the economic issues are the most important issues, or will they think of sovereignty and immigration? The middle segments are persuadable ... So, our strategy is, first of all, frame the referendum as a choice on the economy.'[7] Lord Rose, the chair of the Remain campaign, similarly said that the pollsters they used constantly warned the campaign team that the most important issue on which to convince the middle voters was the economy:[8]

> We were repeatedly told by the pollsters who were working for us that, yes, immigration matters, yes, the National Health Service matters, yes, all of these other things matter, but all of them pale into insignificance when it comes to the economy. And they brought in historical comparison – 'Look at what happened in the first-past-the-post referendum, look at what happened in the Scottish referendum, look at what happened in the 2015 general election.'

On the Leave side, Matthew Elliott raised similar concerns:[9]

> The easy thing for us would have been to base our campaign around UKIP ... But we realized two things: firstly, their limit was 30 per cent, and secondly, if you wanted to get above 50 per cent, those swing voters you needed to attract basically did not

like UKIP or Nigel Farage. They did not want to feel like they are voting for UKIP by voting Leave. So it was essential to have a non-UKIP, cross-party, business-led mainstream campaign, which would appeal to those swing voters. Because we knew that basically all the UKIP followers would vote leave in any case ... what we needed to do was to have all that [middle segment] to actually get us to 50 per cent. The vast majority of voters were in the centre. How do you appeal to the vast majority? You go for the median voter. How do you go for the median voter? You have messages and messengers that appeal to the median voter. Hence the platform that Michael Gove, Boris Johnson, Gisela Stuart all felt comfortable joining.

To maintain a non-extremist look, Elliott said, they chose the core issue of sovereignty because all voters who were attracted by anti-migrant feelings were mostly also UKIP supporters. The approach mirrors that successfully used by Declan Ganley in the Lisbon referendum. Elliott added, 'Now, if you talked in those terms [sovereignty] with voters, it doesn't mean anything to them. The association is with monarchy and the Queen. Hence our slogan "Take Back Control". That did resonate with people, because they could understand what we were going to do. We were going to "take back control" – "Take Back Control" of our borders, our money, our law-making.' This was why, with Dominic Cummings, they specified the three core points of the campaign as 'our money our priorities, take control, safer choice'. Elliott explained their reasoning: 'What's the most popular thing in the UK? The NHS ... The first leaflet was "How to save the NHS."' (See figure 1.4.)

Going beyond the segments of already-decided voters and appealing to the unsure middle was thus the first step that defined the campaign ground. The Remain side chose to prioritize the economy card above all other messages, whereas the main campaign on the Leave side pitched its campaign around these carefully selected themes to avoid an extremist outlook. Importantly, this move also laid the groundwork for agenda setting and moving the discussion away from the economic field to key controversial themes that were very important in the public eye.

Playing the Risk Card and the Status Quo Bias

By asking the public to vote for leaving the EU, the anti-EU side advocated a change in the Brexit referendum as opposed to the usual case in the treaty ratification referendums. The Remain campaign was thus widely expected to have the status quo advantage. However, the Leave side pitched its campaign around the 'Two Futures' theme, arguing that there would be risks if the UK stayed in the EU (on sovereignty, exemplified by immigration and the NHS).

On the Remain side, Ryan Coetzee said in March 2016 in the early days of the campaign that the main goal was to present a personal, concrete, and credible economic risk to voters.[10] His objective was to be 'crunchy' about the details and to make them local and regional: 'So how many jobs in the northeast? How many jobs in the car industry? What is the impact on farming communities?' Discussing the challenges the Remain side potentially faced, Coetzee admitted that the risk for them was the immigration argument of the Leave side gaining traction. He argued that the challenge of the Leave campaign was, in turn, choosing between the themes of economy or immigration. He added, 'If I were them, I would actually try to de-risk the economy, to de-risk leaving on the economy.'

In fact the Leave side did not need to choose between the economy and immigration, as the interview data show below. The co-founder of Leave.EU, Richard Tice, indeed said, 'The status quo bias was our biggest fear, people not voting for change, for the unknown.'[11] Vote Leave's Matthew Elliott also noted that they needed to 'overcome the status quo bias':[12]

> We tried to de-risk the whole thing. We did that by basically saying that there was no status quo. We said that Leave was the safer option. We set it up as two futures for the UK, with a future where we stayed in the EU and we had all the risks of Remain, as we called it. More power and money going to Brussels, more migration, threats of the Eurozone crisis. So they were the risks of Remain. When you contrast the risks of Remain with the benefits of leaving, Leave was the safer option. Faced with the two different futures for the UK, where the status quo was not an option, Leave was the safer choice.

Echoing Coetzee's assessment, Elliott also thought that the weak point for the Remain campaign was immigration, just as the economic argument was the weak point for the Leave side. Although the Leave camp did not have the big multinational corporations on their side, Elliott explained that they still had major entrepreneurs and local business people. Labour MP Gisela Stuart, chair of the Vote Leave Campaign

Committee, emphasized that the de-risking of the Remain side's economic argument went hand in hand with the UK's size and confidence, as it was not a small country to feel threatened.[13] On that point, the chief campaign spokesperson of the Remain side, James McGrory, noted, 'They did not nullify our economic argument ... but they managed to suggest that the economic opinion was divided, that business opinion was divided, when it was nothing of the sort.'[14] MP Alan Johnson, who led the Labour Party Remain campaign, added, 'They [de-risked the economic argument] and their great coup was getting Boris Johnson on their side. It could have gone either way. Michael Gove, as he was a significant cabinet member, for him to be on their side as well, that was a big surprise. They did not expect Gove to be against it [EU membership]. And they did not expect Boris Johnson to be against it.'[15]

The Remain side was therefore under significant attack from the Leave campaign regarding its economic arguments. Instead of attacking the Leave side with a full set of arguments, they chose to stay on the economic message throughout the campaign and thereby locked themselves into a defensive mode. McGrory, on the Remain side, discussed how the Remain campaign started out with three messages – the risks to the UK's economy, its place in the world, and security – but focused more and more on the economy as the campaign took off.[16] According to McGrory, as for Lord Rose, this tactic was closely related to the success of the Conservative campaign in the 2015 general elections, which relied strongly on an economic message. However, in the Brexit referendum, McGrory argued, the Leave side put forward other arguments that sounded risky to people:

> For example, the way of living. They made that a risk issue because that affected public services and local neighbourhoods. The economic risk arguments only work for people who feel they have a definitive stake in the nation's economy. And the Leave campaign piled up votes in communities, which have completely legitimate grievances about being left behind and ignored for years. In many communities, particularly in the Midlands, in the north of England and parts of Wales, the effects of de-industrialization and globalization were present, as well as the feeling that London and politicians do not care about them ...
> A great achievement for the Leave campaign is that they turned the NHS and public services into such arguments.

80 Framing Risky Choices

Lord Rose agreed that on the Remain side there was 'a fundamental misreading of what was bothering people':[17]

> People increasingly think that they are no longer in control … that their voices are not being listened to, that politicians do not care about real people, real jobs, and real concerns. The faulty promises made by [the Leave campaign] about all the wonderful things that will happen if we can get the £350 million a week that will go to the NHS, that we will control immigration, that we will actually get wage increases, that we will have more control over our lives and our destinies, became a powerful weapon … they were very clever at reading the zeitgeist.

Matthew Ellery of Get Britain Out explained that once the status quo bias was taken away, the sovereignty argument became all the more powerful: 'Once you have stripped away the perception of the status quo, people were free to say, "This is about these people creating our laws or somebody else creating our laws." If you strip it back to that, and remove all the other arguments about the economic impacts, you are left with a stark choice about who should create laws for this country. That is a very easy and persuasive argument to win.'[18]

The Remain side therefore agreed that the Leave campaign successfully put different arguments on the agenda and carried the discussion into different realms of 'risk'. As the interview data demonstrate, campaigners agreed that the main weakness of the Leave side was the economy, and the main weakness of the Remain side was immigration. But the Leave campaign acted to launch an attack on the economic argument, while the Remain campaign simply did not discuss the other risks brought up by the other side. Vote Leave's Elliott criticized the Remain campaign for not building a case for why freedom of movement was good in contrast with the Leave side's ground work on the economy: 'They were left high and dry on migration … They did not rule the pitch.'[19] MP Alan Johnson, who led the Labour Party's Remain campaign, also emphasized the importance of immigration in the campaign:[20]

> The defining moment for me was when the Office for National Statistics produced the latest net migration statistics. And this was on something like 25 May, just about a month before the poll. The figure was 333,000, the highest it had ever been, a

record, higher even than when Britain allowed the accession countries to come in in 2004 ... You could feel the argument slipping toward the Leave side ... But the umbrella Remain campaign decided very early on that the economy was our strongest argument and immigration was our weakest argument; we should not talk about immigration, we should just talk about the economy. We fired all of our best bullets very early on in the campaign, including Obama coming over saying 'You are left to be at the back of the queue, if you want a trade deal'. They were all fired quite early. That would be well fired by the time this net immigration figure came out. And there was no attempt to engage with this argument about immigration. So, when the argument did start going against us, the umbrella Remain campaign continued with this whole line of just not talking about it. And that was not the way to tackle it ... It was not a lost debate. I think there was an answer to it. I think we could have made an argument that actually leaving the EU would mean we lose control, we lose the Dublin regulation.

But the Remain camp chose not to respond. As Remain's McGrory explained, 'We did not tackle immigration as an issue. We said we are going to run on economic risk. The logic to it was that we were always going to lose on it, so why would you spend time talking about your opponent's strength when we can talk about our strengths, which is the economy? Every minute spent talking about immigration was a wasted minute, and every minute spent talking on the economy was a positive minute.'[21] This particular campaign decision left the stage fully open for the Leave side to make its case.

Furthermore, in the Brexit case, it was mostly the Remain side that got the blame for exaggerating the costs of a Leave vote, even though the Leave side was also fiercely criticized on their £350 million figure. In the early days of the campaign, in March 2016, Remain's Ryan Coetzee explained that their strategy was to advance a risk argument on the economy that was proportionate, detailed, and from a credible source.[22] Nonetheless, toward the end of the campaign, the Remain arguments were criticized quite harshly for not being realistic. Lord Rose, the chair of the Remain campaign, argued that the Leave campaigners could easily de-risk the Remain side's economic argument because they themselves actually made the Leave side's job easy by exaggerating:[23]

They could easily debunk it ... We overemphasized the financial consequences, which was nearly as bad as lying – which the other side did. All the comments that came out, whether they were from George Osborne, or the prime minister, said there was going to be an immediate economic recession, there was going to be a collapse in property prices, pensions were going to suffer, etc. And it was so obviously exaggerated that people saw straight through it. So, ironically, it was easier to believe a lie about the £350 million a week ... There is of course going to be very difficult times ahead but it was not going to happen immediately.

He added that he was under pressure from Number 10 not to say anything about the Leave vote having no immediate consequences. Labour MP Alan Johnson fully agreed: 'The government, George Osborne in particular, went over the top with the stuff they were saying. The Treasury papers suggested that banks were going to crash straight away, we were going to be into a period of recession. And, of course, none of that was going to happen immediately, because we were not going to leave the EU for at least two years. So that was really overdone.'[24] He contrasted this stance with the credibility that Boris Johnson added to the Leave side's arguments.

The Leave campaigners had the same impression. Matthew Ellery of Get Britain Out explained that the Remain side's economic argument was very strong but that it was pushed too far; he pointed to Cameron's statement that Brexit had the potential to trigger World War III.[25] That remark was very similar to the ones used in the Dutch referendum, which had also backfired. Labour MP Gisela Stuart agreed: 'Osborne in particular misjudged how to project "Project Fear". So, when Osborne comes out saying in five years' time you are going to be £4,322 worse off than you would normally be, people thought that was ridiculous. He overplayed his hand. Or Obama saying we need to go to the back of the queue ... And it was when that punishment budget showed no impact anywhere that we knew their capacity to threaten had run out.'[26] Vote Leave's Matthew Elliott added, 'Our figures had more credibility, even the £350 million one, because people know that we actually do send money to the EU. That cannot be challenged. You can challenge the government's forecasts.'[27] Echoing Alan Johnson, he emphasized that the Leave side's figures gained more credibility when Boris Johnson decided to back them up.

Preparing and Executing the Brexit Campaign

On the Leave side, the £350 million figure was widely criticized for exaggerating the real figure. Nonetheless, the more it was repeated, and the more the Remain side tried to debunk it, the more it stuck in the public's mind, whether or not it was judged to be accurate.

The Advantage of the Anti-EU Side in Setting the Agenda in Multidimensional Proposals

The Brexit referendum covered everything about the EU. When such broad proposals are on the ballot paper, the anti-EU side has been shown to be more effective in extending the topic and placing a wide range of controversial themes on the agenda. This is exactly what the Leave side achieved in the Brexit case. What is more, David Cameron could have had a chance to limit the campaign debate to a subset of issues, had he secured a substantial deal from the EU before the campaign began. In the past, EU member state governments have used such strategies and obtained a set of guarantees from the EU right before campaigns, to knock such arguments off the table. Lacking a deal as such, the Remain side found itself fighting the full palette of Eurosceptic arguments.

Remain's Ryan Coetzee maintained in his early statement in March 2016 that the Leave side had to choose between the themes of economy and immigration for their campaign.[28] Indeed, the Vote Leave campaign stayed away from immigration at the beginning of the campaign; however, campaigners from both sides agreed that Vote Leave brought the issue in during the second part of the campaign. Thus, in the end, the Leave side did not need to choose a single angle and could use as many different arguments as it liked.

On the Remain side, James McGrory noted that it was very helpful for the official Vote Leave campaign to have on the fringes groups and politicians such as Nigel Farage, despite all the squabbling and infighting.[29] Leave campaigners agreed that this was the case. The co-founder of Leave.EU, Richard Tice, noted that having two campaigns, Leave .EU and Vote Leave, ended up helping, although it was more by accident than good judgment.[30] Adding that Leave.EU spent almost the same amount of money as Vote Leave, despite not having the official designation, he explained that the two groups used different images and language. Leave.EU focused on local communities, using tougher messages to highlight the changes these communities were facing in relation to uncontrolled low-skilled immigration, while Vote Leave's focus was on control and sovereignty, which worked mostly for Leave voters in the southeast. Vote Leave's Matthew Elliot similarly underlined the point that despite the differences between the two campaign groups, the activists worked together at the grassroots level.[31] Matthew Ellery of Get Britain Out added that they also tried to complement the Vote Leave campaign by focusing on the democratic control of policies and being active on social media.[32]

As the campaign advanced, it became clear that the Leave side would not need to choose between the economy and immigration. Labour MP Alan Johnson stressed that the Leave side was free to choose any theme they wanted:[33]

It is only the rhetoric, but the rhetoric can be quite effective. So, the rhetoric of saying, 'Look, there are all these countries that we could be making deals with, we could be making deals with India, China, all these growing economies.' The enemies of the EU said it was like being shackled to a corpse. Of course, it was rubbish. Once you get into the details, you know, we export more to Ireland than we do to all fifty-two commonwealth countries put together. There was even an argument about immigration that people like Farage were using, that if we didn't have free movement from the EU, we could let more Pakistanis in, which of course was the last thing they were going to do.

Remain's James McGrory explained that they initially did not think the Leave side would make the immigration issue a big one:[34]

But they just hammered us on money, laws, borders. So immigration, sovereignty and EU budget. And I think actually the way they won is that we did not really come up with an effective answer on any of those three questions, which matter for people. Particularly on immigration. It was quite a seductive argument, so you pay these people too much money, they tell us what to do and they let all these immigrants in … In both focus groups, people who were voting Leave, or inclined to vote Leave, could reel off what they do not like about the EU. 'We have to pay them billions of pounds. And [they] make all our laws. And all the immigrants, I do not like the immigrants.'

Vote Leave chair Gisela Stuart echoed the same point: 'Simple and empowering messages. These are your borders, your taxes and your laws ... A perfect example was the EU's tampon tax, when speaking to a group of women.'[35] The campaign used every debate, every opportunity, to talk about taking back control, she added.

For the Remain side, the multiplicity of arguments launched by the Leave camp was difficult to counter. James McGrory stressed that the Leave side peddled easy answers to extremely complicated questions – much like Trump's promise to build a wall – without specifying what leaving the EU would look like: '"Take Back Control. I want my country back". From where? From whom? To do what?'[36] Lord Rose agreed: 'They did it deliberately. They did not propose a plan. They had a different argument every day, they were selling dreams ... They were telling you that the land across was full of milk and honey.'[37]

On the Leave side, Vote Leave's Matthew Elliott stressed that not having a concrete plan was a strategic choice:[38]

So let's say we had a very long plan and said things like, 'Once we leave the EU, we would have no tariff barriers on trading goods'. Anybody with half a brain knows we will get to a situation with no barriers on trading goods because there is a huge trade deficit, so it will be illogical for the EU to impose tariffs on trading goods. You can argue on financial services, where we have a huge surplus, but trading goods, nobody would argue that we would have that. Had we had a manifesto with that in, all the member states of the EU would say, 'there would be tariff barriers'. Even though it would be completely illogical for them to say that, they would say it for political reasons. So we wanted to neutralize that threat by not having a plan.

Gisela Stuart agreed: 'The more you get specific, the more you get the specifics torn to shreds, and you lose the general principles, which is the bit you want to get across. Details become just like snares which just trap you.'[39] Richard Tice of Leave.EU said that his group in fact wanted to present a vision of what Brexit would look like, as opposed to Vote Leave, which got the official designation, but he agreed that it 'might have given more ammunition to the enemy to tear us apart'.[40] The power of this specific strategy became highly visible during Prime

Minister May's Brexit negotiations, as her deal was very quickly 'torn to shreds'.

The Leave campaign was thus able extend the topic to different risks, successfully bringing up a combination of themes, sovereignty, immigration, the NHS, and budget spending, in addition to the economic benefits of leaving the EU. They deliberately kept vague their vision of the UK outside of the EU, which further helped them in the debate. The Remain side, in return, did not have answers to these non-economic Leave arguments.

The Challenge of the Lack of Information for the Pro-EU Side

The Brexit referendum was no exception when it came to the low level of public knowledge on the EU. As in other EU referendums, the pro-EU side struggled to clarify the misperceptions that surrounded the EU system. Remain's James McGrory explained that because the world was extremely complicated, their arguments had to be quite 'high-minded', but that the complexity of their arguments was a difficulty in the campaign:[41]

> If you were to ask a voter what was good about the EU, they would just talk vague concepts about how it was good for the economy, but without any specific knowledge about why that was. Single market, regulation, these never permeated through to people ... I think [the Leave side] ran very effectively on the simplistic argument that we should control everything. Now myself and others consistently said that 'we have got to make the argument that it is not that simple in the modern world.' If you follow the idea that you are sovereign as a nation because you choose to do things entirely on your own, then the most sovereign nation is North Korea. But Britain has been an enthusiastic signer-up to international treaties. Does the signing up to the international defence against torture make us less sovereign? No. But we did not use this. Does signing up to NATO? That is pooling of sovereignty ... The misinformation that is spread about the EU ... What was our message? 'We are better off in Europe and if you come out of the EU, the country will be worse off and you will be worse off personally.' That was it. That was easy to understand. We won 48 per cent of the vote.

More complex arguments like the nature of pooled sovereignty and the globalized world are more difficult to get across to the regular voter.

Labour M P Alan Johnson echoed the point:[42]

When they said we had lost our sovereignty, you had to sit down for half an hour to explain, 'Look, every country loses some sovereignty for the greater good', blah blah. Take them through the whole course of history from the Second World War, whereas all they had to say was "Take Back Control" ... They talked about unelected people running Brussels. And then you would say, 'Look, every decision made by the EU is made by ministers of elected governments.' And you have to explain that if you elected the commissioners, then it would be like another country. The whole point of the system is that it is not another country, it is an umbrella group to bring countries together. And so, all of that was quite complex ... And, of course, they would say that we are spending 18 to 20 billion a year. The net figure was something like 8 to 10 billion a year, but they were making an argument using the gross figure. Let someone else say 'but the net amount it is much lower'. So, the figures they were using were not inaccurate, they were not wrong, they were just skewed.

Lord Rose, chair of the Remain campaign, similarly said, 'It was very hard for us. It is like you try to get a bar of soap and it keeps slipping through your fingers. Very hard to grip to the facts.'[43]

The Leave side agreed with these remarks. Matthew Ellery of Get Britain Out argued that the £350 million figure had a major impact for the same reason.[44] He explained that the more the Remain side mentioned and debated this figure, the more it stuck in the public consciousness. Lord Rose concurred: 'The actual net number that we paid was not 350 million ... But the number stuck because it was stuck on the bus, it was said so many times that even if you tried to say it is not true, nobody believed you.'[45] Labour M P Gisela Stuart also noted that a lot of people and a lot of M Ps had no idea what the 'single market' was.[46] Leave.EU's Richard Tice underlined that there was a lack of understanding and information on the topic, and that his group initially designed their core slogan to build on that: 'When You Are in the Know, You Vote No.'[47] He added that they decided to abandon this slogan when the referendum question was taken out of the Yes/No format and the Remain/Leave format no longer rhymed with 'know'.

Facing these various attack lines from the Leave camp, strategically presented to the public in a document imitating a government leaflet (figure 1.5), Remain campaigners struggled to provide the background information to important concepts such as the pooling of sovereignty. This difficulty once again paved the way for anti-EU arguments and helped the Leave side to de-risk the Brexit decision.

WHICH SIDE'S ARGUMENTS DID THE CAMPAIGNERS PERCEIVE AS STRONGER?

Campaigners on both sides perceived the pro-Leave arguments to be much stronger. The Leave campaign matched the existing worries of the public closely with key themes such as immigration, loss of control in a globalizing world, and the deterioration of the NHS. The Remain side allowed the Leave side to take the stage on these contentious issues. Although the Remain side also had a powerful argument on the economic risks of a departure from the EU, the Leave side brought their own figures to the debate and actively contested the economic risks. Not only were the Leave side's arguments very available, accessible, and applicable for the public, but they were also presented in an image-provoking, emotive, and inspirational light around the slogan 'Take Back Control' or the famous £350 million figure (figure 1.4).

Campaigners criticized the Remain side for running a purely cost-benefit campaign. They added that the passionate argumentation was on the Leave side. Labour MP Alan Johnson argued that the Remain side lacked inspirational arguments:[48]

'Take Back Control' was three words, very important … whereas the strategy for the umbrella Remain campaign was just the economy, the economy, the economy. For many people, they do not understand, they have better things to do at the time. I mean, nobody loves some market: that does not inspire. So, to start about the single market and customs union and about trade and complexities of trade deals, it was over people's heads.

Preparing and Executing the Brexit Campaign

All campaigners interviewed agreed that the slogan 'Take Back Control' was very potent and that the Remain side did not provide an emotional response to it. Labour MP Gisela Stuart explained:[49]

> I remember having a conversation with someone on the Remain side who said, 'Take Back Control' is a slogan to which there was no answer. And that is why it was genius. And the genius of it was twofold; when I first came in, I said 'Take Control,' and Dominic [Cummings] said it was 'Take Back Control'. As opposed to 'Take Control', 'Take Back Control' encompasses both the future and the past. It's a forward-looking nostalgia.

Remain's Lord Rose agreed: '"Take Back Control". What did we have to say? We could not find an alternative; it was almost impossible for us to find an alternative ... So they had a very powerful weapon that was very emotional.'[50]

HOW DID THE MEDIA PORTRAY THE CAMPAIGN MESSAGES?

Although campaigners initiate the framing process, it is the news media that transmits these frames to the public. Before delving into how the media covered the Brexit issue, it is important to state that all the campaigners stressed in their interviews the significance of the existing Euroscepticism in the British media. This point once again links to the long-term scapegoating of the EU, and the disadvantage it created for the Remain side from the outset. As Labour MP Alan Johnson put it,[51]

> You have to remember this drip of European rubbish from our media, particularly from the newspapers for years and years and years. If you looked at the media, and you looked at the fact that *Daily Mail...* opted for Leave, *Daily Telegraph* was for Leave, the *Sun* was for leave, the *Star* was for leave, the *Daily Express* was for leave, it was only the *Financial Times*, the *Guardian*, who were for Remain. The *Times* were just about for Remain. And you looked at the amount of really emotional stuff that was coming out, like the Turkish border, like the NHS, this money could go to the NHS, these billions of pounds could save the

NHS, Leave the EU and save the NHS ... it is a wonder that the result was so close, actually.

Campaigners made comparisons to the 2015 election campaign, in which the Conservative Party also ran on the economy issue, yet they also pointed to a stark difference. This time, in the Brexit campaign, the tabloid press was completely against the government and its pro-EU case. Campaigners argued that this stance made a difference. In this case, campaigners stressed, the tabloid press did not find the 'Project Fear' credible, openly arguing against the figures proposed by the Remain side and George Osborne. Put simply, Leave.EU's Tice said, the media, because of this long-term scapegoating, helped the Leave side.[52]

Turning to the empirical side of the topic, just how partial was the British news media in its coverage during the referendum campaign? The University of Loughborough has carried out the most detailed study of the referendum news coverage, including outlets from both television and the press.[53] Their report demonstrates that the media coverage was very much in line with the elite campaign framing presented in the interview data. To begin with, the study presents findings on the directional balance in the campaign. The study finds the *Mirror*, the *Guardian*, the *Financial Times*, the *I*, and the *Times* to be pro-Remain, and the *Star*, the *Daily Telegraph*, the *Daily Express*, the *Sun*, and the *Daily Mail* to be pro-Leave. The non-weighted results illustrate that the relative volume of news items was split between the two sides at 43 per cent pro-Remain versus 57 per cent pro-Leave. But when weighted by circulation, the figures show a striking difference between the two sides – 19.5 per cent pro-Remain versus 80.5 per cent pro-Leave – due to the higher circulation of pro-Leave papers. This result confirms campaigners' remarks on how the existing scapegoating tradition in the media created a structural challenge for the Remain side.

The media content analysis goes on to show that three themes – the drama and dynamics of the campaign, the economic implications of leaving the EU, and immigration and border controls – dominated the media agenda. Importantly, the study finds this narrow issue agenda to be consistent across television news, pro-Remain newspapers, and pro-Leave newspapers, as can be seen in table 3.2.

In the interview data, the Remain campaigners discussed their initial idea of pitching the campaign on three themes (economy, security, the

Table 3.2
Issue balance in the media coverage of the referendum in percentages

	All media	Pro-Remain newspapers	Pro-Leave newspapers	Television news
Referendum conduct	30.9	33.5	29.6	28.9
Economy/business	18.9	18.9	18.9	18.8
Immigration	13.2	9.9	14.8	15.6
Public opinion	8	8.8	5	11.3
Constitutional/legal issues	6.1	5.8	6.7	5.5
Employment	3.6	3.9	3.4	3.4
Security/defence	3.4	2.9	4.4	2.7
Political standards/corruption	2.4	2.1	4.2	0.3
Health	2.3	2.7	2.2	1.7
EU activities	1.7	1.4	1.6	2.4
Housing	0.9	0.7	1.1	0.8
Crime	0.9	1.1	1.2	0
Social security	0.8	0.6	1.2	0.7
Devolution in UK	0.8	0.8	0.3	1.5
Other foreign policy	0.7	0.8	0.7	0.5
Taxation	0.6	0.6	0.7	0.5
Public services	0.6	0.1	1	0.6
Agriculture	0.6	0.6	0.3	0.9
Environment	0.5	0.7	0.6	0
Education	0.5	0.4	0.7	0.2
Other issues	2.7	3.5	1.5	3.4

Source: Centre for Research in Communication and Culture 2016

UK's place in the world), admitting that they had abandoned the latter two in favour of the first. The media content data in table 3.2 confirm this focus, as the other two issues were not visible on the agenda. Similarly, as expected, the pro-Remain newspapers gave little coverage to the issue of immigration relative to the pro-Leave papers, once again very much in parallel with the interview data from Remain campaigners, who felt 'every minute spent talking about immigration was a wasted minute'.[54]

The pro-Leave newspapers, on the other hand, paid as much attention to the economy as the pro-Remain newspapers did. This pattern once again follows the interview data closely. The Leave side chose to actively contest the Remain campaign's figures on the economic costs of leaving the EU. With regard to Vote Leave's campaign message on taking back control of the UK's borders, money, and law-making, and their catchy slogans on the NHS, at first glance these themes do not seem to have been dominant in the campaign, according to the individual attention given to them in table 3.2. Nonetheless, in attempts to de-risk the Brexit decision, the Leave campaign linked some of these themes, especially money and the NHS, with the core argument on the economic costs of staying in the EU and claimed that leaving the EU would allow a better economic management of the UK's budget and the NHS. In that sense, the high level of attention given to the economy could be seen as covering the money as well as NHS aspects. Similarly, the Leave side's border argument is captured as an important aspect in the high degree of attention given to immigration.

Overall, the issue balance in table 3.2 confirms the core message coming from the interview data. Both sides were running 'Project Fear' in the Brexit referendum. As Blair Jenkins put it, 'On the Remain side they were running "Project Fear" on the economy, and on the Leave side they were running "Project Fear" on immigration.'[55] To further illustrate this point, figure 3.1 below compares the media coverage on the economy and immigration.

Although economic news exceeded the coverage of immigration for all weeks except for one, figure 3.1 shows that the gap between them narrowed considerably toward the end of the campaign. The report underlines the fact that the issue of immigration received more than twice as much media attention as the issue of sovereignty, which contradicts the post-referendum claims from Vote Leave that immigration was not central in the referendum campaign. This weight is confirmed in our interview data. While the Vote Leave campaign argued that initially they deliberately stayed away from the issue of immigration, campaigners from both sides agreed that they put the issue on the agenda in the second half of the campaign.

Another detailed study of British media coverage of the same period, based on a combination of qualitative and quantitative content analysis of online articles, closely parallels these findings (Moore and Ramsay, 2017).[56] In terms of issue coverage, this study shows that on online platforms as well, the economy was the most covered campaign issue (7,028 articles), followed by immigration (4,383 articles). Very much in line with our core argument, economic claims, despite falling into the most covered domain, were highly contested, and 'warnings about the repercussions of Brexit were routinely dismissed as deliberate Remain "scaremongering" – a term used 737 times' (ibid., 8).

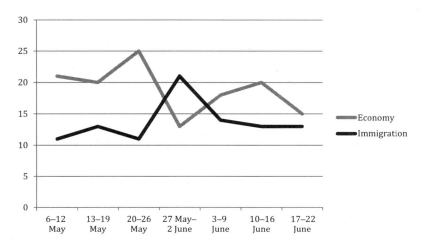

Figure 3.1 Media coverage on economy versus immigration in percentages

Source: Centre for Research in Communication and Culture 2016

Although immigration was second in line, coverage of it tripled during the campaign, as our interview data suggest. This coverage was predominantly negative, blaming migrants for many of Britain's economic and social problems. What is more, 'sovereignty' as a term appeared in almost 2,000 articles, and almost half of these articles associated sovereignty with 'taking back control'. This finding reaffirms how successful the Leave side was in priming this key idea. Perhaps the most interesting finding of this study is that 'every week of the campaign saw both sides engage in mutual accusations of lying (552 articles), of misleading (464 articles) and of dishonesty (234 articles)' (10). This finding highlights the contradictory evidence used by the Remain and Leave camps to back up their alternative arguments and, in turn, the vast opportunities for post-truth politics.[57]

CONCLUSION: CAMPAIGN STRATEGIES AND MEDIA REPORTING IN THE BREXIT REFERENDUM

The interview data confirm the core argument of this book: the Remain side started the campaign with a considerable disadvantage. For decades, the political elite had been warning the British public about the shortcomings of the EU. Given this structural limitation, and relying on their previous experience in the 2015 general elections and the 2014 Scottish referendum, the Remain campaigners chose to frame the vote solely as an economic issue, emphasizing the economic costs of a departure from the EU. The Leave camp actively sought to de-risk the Brexit decision and thereby clouded the sole defence line of the Remain camp. The Leave camp was more strategic in its choices, choosing to couple a core campaign on sovereignty and economy with a separate campaign on immigration, to avoid an extremist look. Pitching a 'Two Futures' idea, but one without a specific exit plan, the Leave campaign also avoided questions on what exactly Brexit would look like, while at the same time successfully arguing that there would be risks relating to remaining in the EU. These strategies increased the number of dimensions in the debate, adding losing control of the immigration policy and the NHS, to which the Remain side chose not respond. What is more, campaigners perceived pro-Leave arguments to be much stronger than the pro-Remain ones, connecting with voters by raising already contentious issues and doing so with highly emotional language. Campaigners agreed that 'Take Back Control' and the famous £350 million figure were entrenched in the public consciousness.

The power of the Leave side is visible in the media analysis as well. Two points deserve special attention. First, in line with the habit of scapegoating the EU, the Leave side was louder in the media than the Remain side. Second, the Leave side was also very active in de-risking the Brexit decision in the media. The two 'Project Fears', one on immigration, the other on the economy, were visible in the news media. However, the data show that the pro-Leave sources not only ran their 'Project Fear' on the controversial issue of immigration but also became actively involved in the discussion on the economy, pitching their own 'Project Fear' on the topic. The pro-Remain sources were much less vocal in questioning the contentious issue of immigration.

Based on this foundation of how the campaigners chose to present the Brexit choice to voters, and how the media transmitted these messages, we now turn to the final step of our multi-method analysis. Using survey data, we explore how these campaign arguments might have shaped public opinion and the degree to which the scapegoating of the EU and the de-risking strategy contributed to the vote choice.

4

How Did the Scapegoating of the European Union Affect the Vote Choice?

What mattered was the campaign over twenty-five years.[1]

Matthew Elliott

The interview and media data analysed in the previous chapters suggest that in its campaign choices the Leave side was more strategic than the Remain side. We now turn our attention to survey data to shed additional light on these strategic decisions and to try to understand their contribution to the vote choice. In this chapter, we pay particular attention to the consequences of the long-term tradition of scapegoating the EU in UK politics. We argue that the long-entrenched critical attitude of British political elites toward the EU reflected and clearly helped cement such views in the eyes of the public and consequently *set the stage for the campaign*. In chapter 5, we study the extent to which the specific campaign strategies and arguments may have *affected public opinion*. Together these two chapters aim at explaining how these long-term and short-term factors interacted in bringing about the Brexit decision. We thus provide a better understanding of how successful the Leave and Remain sides were at both reinforcing Britons' pre-existing attitudes toward the EU and developing campaign arguments to sway the vote.

We begin this chapter by examining how the habit of scapegoating the EU incarnated a particular view of European integration in the UK. We review how the predominantly negative tone of the media and political elites over several decades reflected and contributed to the spread of critical attitudes toward Europe in British public opinion and depleted a crucial reservoir of support for the European project at the time of the Brexit referendum. As previous chapters have made clear, this situation constrained the Remain camp's hand

and led them toward a campaign based on economic calculations rather than enthusiasm for Europe. For the Leave campaigners, the scapegoating tradition was only a benefit, facilitating their campaign planning and organization. It also had a key impact on the resonance of their core message.

In the second part of this chapter, we turn our attention to the role that long-term attitudes to the EU played in the final vote decision. Three indicators are used to seize the impact of scapegoating the EU on the vote: level of attachment to the EU, attitudes toward Brussels, and global assessments of British membership of the EU. While the measurement of these long-term attitudes is limited to our post-referendum survey, the values they carry are highly comparable to the trends in regular surveys, as we detail below. First, we study the impact on the Brexit vote of long-term EU attitudes, along with other long-term factors such as socioeconomic variables.[2] Next, we compare the impact of these attitudes among the groups of early and late deciders. Our results suggest that the tradition of scapegoating the EU contributed to reinforcing Britons' Eurosceptical attitudes, which the Leave camp successfully mobilized in their campaign.

SETTING THE STAGE: THE LONG-TERM TRADITION OF SCAPEGOATING THE EU IN BRITISH POLITICS

The notion that Euroscepticism has represented a central feature of British politics and public opinion over the past decades is largely shared among scholars. Forster (2002) compellingly shows that the tendency among the British party elites to be critical of the European integration project goes back more than half a century. Gifford (2014) suggests that Euroscepticism has been a systematic feature of British politics since the reorganization of Britain from imperial state to European Union member state in 1973. Startin's (2015) study of the British tabloid press coverage of the EU illustrates how the media too have contributed to making Euroscepticism mainstream in the UK. These works often echo many episodes in the tumultuous relationship between the UK and the EU, such as the battle of Prime Minister Margaret Thatcher against the EU's bureaucratic centralization or the Exchange Rate Mechanism crisis in the early 1990s (Rasmussen 1997; Evans 2003). In brief, there is a considerable body of work demonstrating the British tradition of Euroscepticism and presenting the EU in a negative light in domestic politics (e.g., Geddes 2013).

In parallel to this widespread critical stance in the elite's discourse regarding European integration, we find similarly sceptical views of the EU in British public opinion (Clarke, Goodwin, and Whiteley 2017; Evans and Norris 1999; Evans and Butt 2007; Bølstad 2015). Britons' mixed feelings toward the EU were already widespread in the 1950s. Anderson and Hecht (2018, 630) show with a unique dataset starting in 1952 that public support for European integration has been systematically lower in the UK than in France, Germany, and Italy.[3] More precisely, the authors conclude that 'the dynamics of UK opinion stand apart from the other major European states: it has displayed consistently lower levels of support since the 1950s ... [and] comes closest to exhibiting a level of support that acts like an anchor to which opinion inevitably returns after moving up or down over time' (631–2). Confirming these trends, a compilation of eighty-eight Eurobarometer surveys from 1973 to 2015 similarly shows that the proportion of respondents viewing their country's membership to the EU as a good thing has been consistently and significantly lower in the UK than in the rest of Europe (DR's Investigative Research Team 2016).[4]

A rich source of information on Britons' views of the EU over time can be found in the British Social Attitudes Survey (BSA), an annual survey conducted in Great Britain since 1983 by the National Centre for Social Research. The BSA involves detailed interviews over a large variety of topics with more than three thousand respondents selected using random probability sampling. One item included in the questionnaires is particularly interesting. Since 1996, respondents to BSA surveys have been presented with a list of national identities associated with the UK and/or Ireland and asked which ones best describe the way they think of themselves. Crucially, among those included on the list is 'European'. Figure 4.1 shows the percentage of those who think of themselves as 'European', either exclusively or in combination with other identities.[5] The extremely low proportion of respondents expressing a European identification is striking, with an average of 12 per cent, and the high and low at 17 per cent and 10 per cent, respectively. This weak sentiment of identification with the European Union is not without consequences. According to Curtice and Evans (2015, 7), 'The persistently low level of identification with Europe certainly creates conditions in which it is more likely that Euroscepticism will prosper.'

Another important item in the questionnaires directly measures citizens' attitudes toward the UK's membership of the EU. Since the

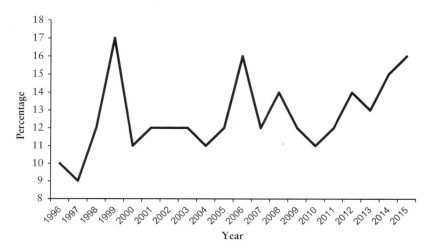

Figure 4.1 Trends in 'free choice' European identity, 1996–2015

Source: Curtice 2015

beginning of the 1990s, respondents were asked, 'Do you think that Britain's long-term policy should be to leave the EU, to stay in the EU and try to reduce EU's powers, to leave things as they are, to stay in the EU and try to increase EU's powers, or to work for the formation of a single European government?'[6] Figure 4.2 illustrates the level of support for these options over time, revealing interesting patterns. First, even in the early 1990s when opinion was more favourable toward Europe, Britons showed no real appetite for strengthening the EU at the expense of their national sovereignty. Second, the domination of 'autonomist' options (fewer powers for the EU, or leaving it) over 'integrationist' ones (more powers for the EU, or a single European government) grew significantly after 1995. The combined level of support for the autonomist options hovered around 50 per cent between 1995 and 2008 before jumping to approximately 65 per cent in the years leading to the Brexit vote. Meanwhile, the proportion of respondents backing a stronger EU dropped to approximately 10–15 per cent of the electorate. Various episodes of scapegoating the EU occurred during this period in reaction to events such as the Maastricht Treaty, the Schengen agreement, the EU's ban on British beef exports, the introduction of the Euro, and the enlargement of the EU to twenty-eight countries. The recurrent use of an anti-EU narrative

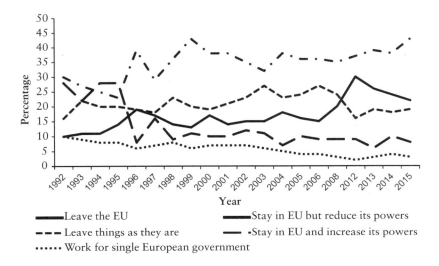

Figure 4.2 Attitudes toward the UK's relationship with the EU, 1992–2015

Source: Curtice 2015

in reaction to these events certainly reaffirmed Eurosceptic sentiments among the British public and possibly helped strengthen them.

Overall, these public opinion findings suggest that Eurosceptic sentiments represent stable, long-lasting, and deeply entrenched attitudes for a significant number of Britons.[7] These attitudes, developed long before the 2016 referendum campaign, can be characterized as anchor variables that played a central role in many voters' final decision. (See also Clarke, Goodwin, and Whiteley 2017.) The attitudes can also be characterized as lukewarm and sceptical at best, if not outright negative, vis-à-vis the European integration project. They have developed in parallel with a recurrent scapegoating discourse on the part of the UK political elite. Whether this elite discourse shaped these long-term public attitudes or simply reflected them is an issue beyond the scope of the current analysis.[8] At the very least, we can conclude that the two have reinforced each other. From the perspective of the Brexit referendum campaign, what matters is that the public opinion climate in the UK had long been unenthusiastic about the EU and the UK's membership in it. These long-held Eurosceptical attitudes provided fertile ground for the Leave campaign's anti-EU arguments and prevented the Remain campaign from using certain pro-EU arguments.

Below, we begin our examination of the determinants of voting with another set of long-term factors, the socioeconomic variables, which are generally considered to be the most remote from the vote decision (e.g., Campbell et al. 1960; Lewis-Beck et al. 2008), before moving on to estimating the impact of the EU attitudes.

SOCIOECONOMIC STATUS AND THE VOTE CHOICE IN THE BREXIT REFERENDUM

The relationship between socioeconomic status and the Brexit vote has been extensively studied at the aggregate level (Goodwin and Heath 2016; Becker, Fetzer, and Novy 2017; Clarke, Goodwin, and Whiteley 2017; Matti and Zhou 2017; Colantone and Stanig 2018). These studies have shown that support for the Leave option was systematically higher in areas with greater proportions of older, male, less well-educated, less affluent voters. As Goodwin and Heath (2016, 331) summarize, these relationships, especially those involving age and education (or qualifications), strongly suggest that 'the vote for Brexit was delivered by the "left behind" – social groups that are united by a general sense of insecurity, pessimism and marginalisation, who do not feel as though elites … share their values, represent their interests and genuinely empathise with their intense angst about rapid social, economic and cultural change'.

Evidence at the individual level has been scarcer, with Hobolt (2016), Swales (2016), and Clarke, Goodwin, and Whiteley (2017) providing the key reference points. These studies confirm the existence of a strong association between support for Leave and the variables of age and education with survey data. These two objective characteristics thus appear as the most important socioeconomic factors explaining the Brexit vote choice. Regarding gender, Hobolt (2016) and Swales (2016) report that men were slightly more supportive of the Leave option than women, but Clarke and colleagues (2017, 155) present a null relationship between an individual's gender and the decision to vote in favour of Brexit. As for the impact of an individual's affluence on the vote choice, extant studies have focused on two indicators: household income (Hobolt 2016; Swales 2016) and assessment of change in one's personal financial situation (Hobolt 2016; Clarke, Goodwin, and Whiteley 2017). Both indicators are shown to affect an individual's inclination to vote Leave, although their respective relationship to the vote choice is not nearly as strong as that of age and education.

Below we study the individual-level association between these four core socioeconomic variables and the vote choice using our own survey data, coming from an online post-referendum public opinion survey conducted during the first week of July 2016 by the British polling firm Survation. In our analyses below, the dependent variable is the choice to vote Leave over Remain. The weighted data from our survey produce an accurate estimation of the Leave support (51.9 per cent).[9] The details of data collection and coding are presented in our appendix.

Table 4.1 shows the bivariate relationship between age group and vote choice in the Brexit referendum, which broadly confirms the findings from the literature. There is a positive and strong association between an individual's age and the tendency to vote Leave. Support for Brexit reaches only 34 per cent among the youngest group of voters (18–34 years old) but rises above the 50 per cent threshold among the other two age groups: 53 per cent of the 35–54 year olds and as many as 63 per cent of those over 55 years old. Clearly, the oldest and youngest generations are found at the opposite ends of the Brexit debate, and this generational divide constitutes one of the defining features of the outcome. During the weeks that followed the Leave victory, this divide also manifested itself in the calls for a new referendum although, as seen in chapter 6, young voters were not significantly more likely to be 'sore losers'.

Do men and women differ in their level of support for the Brexit? The bivariate relationship displayed in table 4.2 suggests that they do. In line with some (although not all) of the results in the extant literature, the majority of men (55 per cent) voted to Leave, whereas the majority of women (52 per cent) voted to Remain. That said, the statistical test results at the bottom of the table indicate that this gender gap is not particularly strong and that it may not survive in a multivariate model, as we see below.

Previous studies have specified education as one of the largest socioeconomic divides reflected in the Brexit referendum outcome. Citizens with low qualifications are among the most affected by the economic and social changes brought about by free trade and immigration. They were thereby among the most likely to hold grievances against EU policies and the UK's relative loss of control over its sovereignty (Goodwin and Heath 2016; Hobolt 2016; Becker, Fetzer, and Novy 2017; Clarke, Goodwin, and Whiteley 2017; Matti and Zhou 2017; Colantone and Stanig 2018). The data in table 4.3 lend significant support to these claims. As can be seen, 63 per cent of those individuals

Table 4.1
Relationship between age
and the referendum vote

	Remain	Leave	N
18–34	66	34	(346)
35–54	47	53	(460)
55 or more	37	63	(512)
Pearson χ^2	66.62***		
Gamma	.35***		

Note: Entries are row percentages. *** p < .001.

Table 4.2
Relationship between gender
and the referendum vote

	Remain	Leave	N
Female	52	48	(652)
Male	45	55	(665)
Pearson χ^2	5.96*		
Gamma	.13*		

Note: Entries are row percentages. * p < .05.

with the lowest level of qualifications voted in favour of Brexit. Support for that option decreases to 48 per cent among the middle category and to 46 per cent among individuals within the highest category of qualifications.

The more affluent are usually more supportive of European integration, because trade liberalization tends to favour individuals with higher levels of income (Gabel 1998). Income is certainly an important indicator of socioeconomic status that frequently determines electoral behaviour (e.g., Lipset 1960). However, recent work has suggested that labour income alone is not necessarily the best measure of an individual's affluence, since it ignores other sources of revenue – usually referred to as capital income – that also determine political preferences. (For the British case, see Lewis-Beck, Nadeau, and Foucault 2013.) Our opinion survey measures both sources of revenue, household income as well as the number of assets owned,[10] which we combine (average) into a single measure of an individual's wealth. By taking assets into account, we are better able to capture the recent

Table 4.3
Relationship between education and the referendum vote

	Remain	Leave	N
No qualifications/ formal apprenticeship	37	63	(254)
GCSEs/O-levels	52	48	(482)
Diploma/AS-levels/ Professional qualifications/Degree/postgraduate Degree	54	46	(488)
Pearson χ^2		20.75***	
Gamma		−.18***	

Note: Entries are row percentages. *** p < .001.

Q: Which of these qualifications do you have? (If your UK qualification is not listed, please tick the box that contains its nearest equivalent. If you have qualifications gained outside the UK please tick appropriate UK equivalent, if none please tick 'Other'.)

- A formal apprenticeship
- NVQs/GNVQs/RSA diploma
- GCSEs/O-levels
- Diploma (general)
- AS-levels
- A-levels
- Professional qualifications (i.e., Teaching, Nursing, Accountancy)
- Degree/postgraduate degree (i.e., BA, BSC, MA, MSC, MRes, MBA, PGCE)
- Other (incl. Vocational training, i.e., forklift licence, construction skills certification scheme (CSCS), food hygiene certificate, and foreign qualifications)
- No qualifications

increase in economic inequalities in advanced industrial democracies such as the UK (e.g., Piketty and Saez 2003). Indeed, table 4.4 displays a negative relationship between an individual's wealth and support for the Leave option. A clear majority (58 per cent) of individuals in the top tier of our wealth variable voted in favour of remaining in the EU. This relationship is strong, and appears to be stronger than the one found in the extant literature between an individual's household income alone and vote choice in the Brexit referendum (Hobolt 2016; Swales 2016).

In a nutshell, the individual-level socioeconomic profile of Leave supporters could not be clearer. Voters in favour of Brexit tend to be older, male, less well-qualified, and less affluent. These findings lend support to the idea that the referendum outcome reflected deep frustration among parts of the population vis-à-vis globalization and loss of control in the face of EU policies on free trade and free movement of workers. However, as Goodwin and Heath (2016, 331) conclude as well, 'the left-behind thesis cannot explain the entire Brexit vote'.

Table 4.4
Relationship between wealth and the referendum vote

Wealth	Remain	Leave	N
Low	41	59	(353)
Medium	44	56	(424)
High	58	42	(459)
Pearson χ^2	29.64***		
Gamma	−.24***		

Note: Entries are row percentages. *** p < .001.
Q: What best describes your household income, including all benefits, but before tax is deducted?

- Less than £10,000
- £10,000–£14,999
- £15,000–£19,999
- £20,000–£29,999
- £30,000–£39,999
- £40,000–£49,999
- £50,000–£59,999
- £60,000–£69,999
- £70,000–£79,999
- £80,000–£89,999
- £90,000–£99,000
- £100,000–£149,999
- £150,000–£199,999
- £200,000 or more
- Don't know / prefer not to say

Do you, or someone in your household hold the following assets: home or apartment; a country house, a savings account; a business; rental properties; stocks?

We agree that these socioeconomic variables do not tell us much about citizens' specific views of the EU or their agreement with campaign statements, especially those that triggered long-held negative perceptions of the EU. We next turn to this aspect.

WHAT DID BRITONS THINK ABOUT THE EU?

While part of the Brexit vote is certainly anchored in long-term socioeconomic variables, clearly other factors also played an important role. Continuing with the long-term factors, we find that attitudes toward the EU certainly informed the vote choice. We examine these perceptions closely to better understand the campaign ground and the structural advantages and challenges experienced by both campaigns.

Once again, we rely on our post-referendum survey to measure these long-term variables, which is a limitation. Nonetheless, the values that these variables carry closely parallel the long-term trends measured by the regular surveys discussed above.

To begin, do British voters feel attached to the EU at all? Is there evidence that they have an emotional bond with the EU? Feelings of national identity have been shown to represent a serious impediment to the European integration project (Carey 2002; Hooghe and Marks 2004; McLaren 2006; Curtice and Evans 2015).

The results in table 4.5 indicate that the level of attachment to the EU varies among our survey respondents. Whereas 31 per cent indicate being very much or somewhat attached to the EU, 47 per cent feel the opposite way (not attached or not attached at all). In addition, only 7 per cent mention feeling 'very much attached' to the EU. It is interesting to compare these figures to those on attachment to the UK. Table 4.5 also reports that 39 per cent of respondents indicate being very strongly attached to the UK, and another 39 per cent report feeling somewhat attached. Only 6 per cent and 3 per cent indicate feeling not attached or not attached at all to the UK, respectively. British citizens do not display a particularly strong level of attachment to the EU, especially in comparison to their feelings toward their own country. This means that the referendum question was asking them to decide whether the UK should remain part of a larger entity toward which they held lukewarm feelings at best. This factor illustrates quite well the challenge that the Remain campaign faced when it came to selling the EU to the voters.

In turn, the data in table 4.6 highlight British citizens' most widespread grievance against the EU, which is its excessive centralization. No less than 62 per cent of the respondents in our survey believe that the EU intervenes too much in the affairs of their country, while just 17 per cent think the opposite (18 per cent of the respondents hold a split opinion on this issue). Importantly, in our experiment, this figure increases to 66 per cent when the question explicitly refers to 'bureaucrats in Brussels' instead of 'the EU'. With this formulation, only 11 per cent of the respondents mention disagreement with the question.[11] The results are clear: the perception that the EU exerts too much influence on British decisions was quite widespread at the time of the Brexit referendum, once again constituting a handicap for the Remain camp.

The next task, then, is to identify the specific areas in which this intrusion was perceived as being excessive and if, despite everything, this

Table 4.5
Feelings of attachment toward the UK and the EU

	(1) UK	(2) EU
Very weak	3	29
Weak	6	18
Neither weak, nor strong	13	22
Strong	39	24
Very strong	39	7
Number of respondents	1514	

Note: Entries are percentages.

Table 4.6
Opinion on the degree of EU intervention

	A	B
Strongly agree	36	41
Agree	26	25
Neither agree nor disagree	18	17
Disagree	13	9
Strongly disagree	4	2
Don't know	4	6
Number of respondents	780	733

Note: Entries are percentages.
Q: A Would you say that the *European Union* intervenes too much in the affairs of the UK?
Q: B Would you say that *the bureaucrats in Brussels* intervene too much in the affairs of the UK?

negative aspect could be seen as the exception in a globally advantageous partnership. The next three tables help us answer this question.

Table 4.7 indicates that, on balance, British citizens see their country's membership in the EU as generally beneficial. Close to half (46 per cent) of our survey respondents think that EU membership of the UK has been beneficial or very beneficial, while a quarter of them believe that the benefits for the UK have been 'average'. Only 29 per cent hold a negative opinion about the benefits of EU membership. These results indicate that, despite views about the EU being too centralized, a significant number of voters perceived British membership in the EU as beneficial to their country. This positive overall assessment constituted

Table 4.7
Evaluation of the benefits of British membership in the EU

Not beneficial at all	12
Not beneficial	17
Average	25
Beneficial	30
Very beneficial	16
Number of respondents	1514

Note: Entries are percentages.

an important reservoir of support for the Remain camp, but the numbers were not sufficient to win the referendum. That is why both campaigns sought to target the voters who held middle-ground views about EU membership.

In this respect, the data in table 4.8 make it clear that British citizens distinguish the economic and political dimensions of the European project. In the case of the economy, Britons generally approve of an increase in trade through the establishment of a free trade area between their country and the European continent. To the question 'Do you think that the European integration project has gone too far or not far enough in the field of free trade among member states?', no less than 62 per cent of respondents express a sense of satisfaction or openness: 50 per cent feel that this integration has reached an appropriate level, and 12 per cent believe that this integration could even be pushed further. The evaluation is very different in the field of immigration. In this case, 50 per cent of respondents believe that integration has gone too far, whereas 22 per cent think the level is appropriate and only 12 per cent think it should be pushed further. The economic and political dimensions, which the Remain and Leave campaigns converted into the fault lines of the referendum debate, clearly emerge here, and the results highlight the relative satisfaction of the British voters in the first case and their dissatisfaction in the second.

These questions lead us directly to the issue of assessing the performance of the EU in a number of important areas. This issue constitutes the ultimate test, since, for example, an individual could judge that the union is too centralized but nevertheless effective. The data in table 4.9 complement and enrich the figures in the previous tables. These figures relate to assessing the performance of the EU in

108 Framing Risky Choices

Table 4.8
Opinion about the European integration project on free trade and immigration

	A Immigration	B Free trade
Gone too far	50	18
About right	22	50
Pushed further	12	12
Don't know	16	20
Number of respondents	1,514	1,514

Note: Entries are percentages.
Q: Do you think that the European integration project has gone too far or not far enough in each of these fields?
A   Immigration
B   Free trade among member states

five areas: the economy, immigration, social benefits, tackling crime, and the environment. A first observation concerns the relatively small number of respondents who do not have an opinion on the performance of the EU in these areas. This percentage is barely 4 per cent for immigration and reaches 10 per cent for social benefits, a result that seems to signal once again the importance of the immigration issue in the debate.

These assessments of different EU policies are interesting for several reasons. First, the area where evaluations are the most positive, that is, the environment (+20 for the balance of favourable opinions, 42 per cent, and unfavourable ones, 22 per cent), corresponds to an issue that was almost completely absent from the referendum campaign. The issue of crime, where evaluations are also quite favourable (+6), is similar. However, the issues of social benefits (through the NHS debate), the economy, and immigration were all the focus of campaign debate. While in the first two cases the EU's performance evaluations are slightly negative (−10 for social benefits and −7 for the economy), they are extremely negative in the case of immigration. On this key issue, no less than 40 per cent of respondents consider the performance of the EU very bad, and 23 per cent consider it bad. This means that at the time of the Brexit vote, almost two out of three respondents thought that the EU's record was negative for this key issue.

The overall picture that emerges from these figures is that the EU's track record at the time of the Brexit referendum was rather negative in the eyes of British voters. This dissatisfaction is particularly clear

Table 4.9
Performance of the EU in dealing with various issues

	A Economy	B Immigration	C Social benefits	D Fight against crime	E Environment
Very badly	16	40	15	11	9
Fairly badly	22	23	22	17	13
Neither well nor badly	24	18	26	30	27
Fairly well	23	11	21	27	30
Very well	8	4	6	7	12
Don't know	7	4	10	8	9
Number of respondents	1,514	1,514	1,514	1,514	1,514

Note: Entries are percentages.
Q: How well do you think the European Union handles: A, The economy; B, Immigration;
C, Social benefits; D, The fight against crime; E, The environment?

in the case of the union's political dimension. The European institutions are perceived as being too centralized, too burdensome, and too insensitive to the concerns of the British citizens, especially on the issue of immigration. In addition, British voters do not feel particularly attached to the EU. The balance sheet is not entirely negative, however. Respondents rate the EU's record on the economy (essentially free trade), the environment, and the fight against crime more positively. These elements reflect the support of many British citizens for a project facilitating trade with the European continent and collaboration between EU governments on issues of common interest, such as environmental protection and the fight against terrorism. Yet these same figures also seem to reflect some dissatisfaction with the perceived unresponsiveness of the European institutions and their encroachment on British sovereignty – a dissatisfaction that the Leave campaign successfully mobilized through its core arguments on immigration and the NHS. The next section takes a closer look at the relationship between these general attitudes toward the EU and the vote choice in the referendum.

SCAPEGOATING OF THE EU AND THE BREXIT VOTE

How did these (mostly negative) views about the EU relate to the vote choice? What did these relationships imply for the two campaigns?

What kinds of opportunities and challenges did they present? Below, we provide a preliminary answer to these questions by examining the bivariate relationship between these EU-related variables and the referendum vote. In the next chapter, we address these questions further with direct variables on campaign arguments.

We first look at this relationship as it pertains to the two attachment variables. Table 4.10 focuses on attachment toward the UK. Recall from table 4.5 that as many as 78 per cent of the survey's respondents expressed a 'strong' or 'very strong' level of attachment toward their country. We see that a significant reservoir of support for Brexit (64 per cent) is found among those who say that they are very strongly attached to the UK and who represent an important section of the electorate – 42 per cent of the respondents. Those who feel 'strongly' attached to the UK are rather split; 52 per cent report having voted to Remain in the EU, but this proportion is not high enough to compensate for the strong pro-Leave tendency found among the 'very strongly' attached group. Support among those individuals feeling much less attached to the UK (the other three answer categories) is clearly in favour of Remain, but again they do not constitute a large enough group of voters to give the Remain campaign a comfortable victory.

Feelings of attachment toward the EU are even more strongly associated with the referendum vote decision than the levels of attachment toward the UK. As can be seen in table 4.11, 72 per cent of the respondents feeling 'weakly' attached to the EU and as many as 95 per cent of those feeling 'very weakly' attached voted Leave. Recall from table 4.5 again that these respondents make up about half of our survey sample (with as many as 31 per cent expressing a 'very weak' level of attachment toward the EU), thus tipping the balance significantly in favour of the Leave option. While 92 per cent of the respondents who reported being 'very strongly' attached to the EU decided to vote Remain, their overall number is extremely low (7 per cent of the sample), and they were not able to reverse the trend toward Brexit. Taken together, the findings of tables 4.10 and 4.11 suggest that the widespread (and, for the most part, long-held) negative feelings vis-à-vis the EU – especially in comparison with the much more positive feelings of attachment to the UK – constituted a significant liability for the Remain campaign.

This impression of an uphill battle for the Remain camp is only reinforced by the data in table 4.12. On the question of whether the

Table 4.10
Support for Leave and feelings of attachment toward the UK

	Very weak	Weak	Neither weak nor strong	Strong	Very strong
Leave	23	35	38	48	64
Remain	77	65	62	52	36
N	35	80	151	501	550
	(3)	(6)	(11)	(38)	(42)
Pearson χ^2			66.82***		
Gamma			.36***		

Note: Entries are percentages in columns and entries in parentheses are row percentages (n=1317). ***p< .001.

Table 4.11
Support for Leave and feelings of attachment toward the EU

	Very weak	Weak	Neither weak nor strong	Strong	Very strong
Leave	95	72	31	12	8
Remain	5	28	69	88	92
N	408	228	278	314	89
	(31)	(17)	(21)	(24)	(7)
Pearson χ^2			662.12***		
Gamma			−.87***		

Note: Entries are percentages in columns, and entries in parentheses are row percentages (n=1317). ***p< .001.

EU (or the 'bureaucrats in Brussels') intervene too much into the affairs of the UK, recall from table 4.6 that the typical response was 'strongly agree'. Table 4.12 shows that among this group of respondents, no less than 88 per cent voted Leave. Those who voted Remain hold more positive views regarding the EU's degree of intervention into British affairs, but this group only makes up about a third of the survey sample – a figure that includes the voters neither agreeing nor disagreeing with the statement.[12] In short, the widely held perception that decision-making in the EU is too centralized, which we have shown was one of the core arguments of the Leave campaign, was a difficult one to counter for those advocating remaining in the EU. These perceptions (along with other factors such as the previous campaign experience) therefore provided a powerful shortcut to the Leave campaign and led the Remain campaign to a focus on the economy.

112   Framing Risky Choices

Table 4.12
Support for Leave and opinion on the degree of EU intervention

	Strongly	Agree	Neither agree nor disagree	Disagree	Strongly disagree	Don't know
Leave	88	42	18	4	5	36
Remain	12	58	82	96	95	64
N	551	331	211	144	42	39
	(42)	(25)	(16)	(11)	(3)	(3)
Pearson χ^2			569.9***			
Gamma			−.83***			

Note: Entries are percentages in columns, and entries in parentheses are row percentages (n=1317). ***p< .001.

Q: Intervention: Would you say that *the European Union* intervenes too much in the affairs of the UK? OR, Would you say that *the bureaucrats in Brussels* intervene too much in the affairs of the UK?

The interview data presented in the previous chapters showed that one of the key strategies of the Leave campaign was to target and persuade citizens holding moderate views on the EU. At first glance, citizens' positive evaluations of the benefits that the UK receives from the EU had the potential of bringing victory to the Remain side. Indeed, recall from table 4.7 that 46 per cent of British voters believed that EU membership was globally beneficial for their country, compared to only 29 per cent holding the opposite view. Table 4.13 shows, unsurprisingly, that support for the Remain option was huge among the first group (84 per cent), the opposite being true among the second group (8 per cent). The real surprise comes from the significant group of voters (24 per cent of the sample) holding mixed views about the contribution of the EU to their country. Among this pivotal group, no less than 70 per cent of voters chose to support the Leave option. This result strongly suggests that the Leave campaign was successful in mobilizing this middle group, in line with their campaign strategy to reach the middle-ground voters, which was evident in our interview data. A very similar figure emerges in the responses of British voters on the potential economic consequences of Brexit, confirming once again the Leave side's success in reaching the undecided middle ground, which we present in the next chapter (see table 5.10).

Tables 4.14 and 4.15 examine the bivariate relationships between the referendum vote choice and the views on the preferred degree of European integration. As seen in the previous section (table 4.8), a

Table 4.13
Support for Leave and evaluation of the benefits of British membership in the EU

	Not beneficial at all	Not beneficial	Average	Beneficial	Very beneficial
Leave	91	92	70	20	8
Remain	9	8	30	80	92
N	165	241	313	392	207
	(12)	(18)	(24)	(30)	(16)
Pearson χ^2			622.8***		
Gamma			−.85***		

Note: Entries are percentages in columns, and entries in parentheses are row percentages (n=1317). ***p< .001.

slim majority of British citizens think that European integration has been 'about right' in the domain of free trade. Table 4.14 shows that the vote choice among this group of voters was in favour of remaining in the EU but not overwhelmingly so (56 per cent). In fact, we see some degree of polarization on the issue of free trade. The Remain camp has a slight edge among voters who expressed an opinion on this question. Nonetheless, the very strong preference for leaving the EU (83 per cent) among those citizens who think that integration in the area of free trade has 'gone too far', combined with the surprising support for Leave (56 per cent) found among those individuals not having an opinion on this question, somewhat counterbalances the Remain advantage on this economic dimension.

Opinions are clearly more negative on the preferred degree of integration in the domain of immigration. About half of our sample considers that European integration has 'gone too far' in this policy area (table 4.8). This view is closely associated with a Leave vote (74 per cent), as table 4.15 indicates, thus providing the Leave camp with a clear edge on this question. Responses in the other three answer categories tend to favour the Remain option, but we must note two caveats here. First, we find a smaller number of individuals expressing no opinion on this question than for the free trade issue, so their slightly greater support in favour of Remain weighs a bit less than the Leave majority found among those that had no opinion on the economic dimension of European integration (see table 14.4). Second, among those individuals who do express an opinion about the degree of integration on the immigration issue, we do not find the same linear relationship with the vote choice as we do on the free trade

114   Framing Risky Choices

Table 4.14
Support for Leave and opinion about the European integration project
on free trade

	Gone too far	About right	Pushed further	Don't know
Leave	83	44	33	56
Remain	17	56	67	44
N	242	670	168	236
	(18)	(51)	(13)	(18)
Pearson χ^2		138.0***		
Gamma		−.33***		

Note: Entries are percentages in columns, and entries in parentheses are row
percentages (n=1317). ***p< .001.

Q: Free trade among member states: Do you think that the European integration
project has gone too far or not far enough in each of these fields?

Table 4.15
Support for Leave and opinion about the European integration project
on immigration

	Gone too far	About right	Pushed further	Don't know
Leave	74	16	32	43
Remain	26	84	68	57
N	689	281	169	178
	(52)	(21)	(13)	(14)
Pearson χ^2		310.1***		
Gamma		−.68***		

Note: Entries are percentages in columns, and entries in parentheses are row
percentages (n=1317). ***p< .001.

Q: Immigration: Do you think that the European integration project has gone too far
or not far enough in each of these fields?

issue. Indeed, one would expect support for the Remain option to
increase as we go from one extreme (integration on immigration has
gone too far) to a middle-ground view (about right) to the other
extreme (not far enough). This is not exactly what we find in table 4.15,
with the Remain vote standing at 26 per cent among the first group
of respondents, rising to 84 per cent among the second group, and
then dropping to 68 per cent among the third group. Of course, the
number of respondents found in the latter group is rather low (they
form only 13 per cent or so of the sample), but this unexpected pattern
revealed by the table seems indicative of the difficulty of the Remain

Scapegoating of the European Union   115

campaign in mobilizing support based on the political dimension of European integration as encapsulated by the immigration issue.

MULTIVARIATE MODELS

In this section, we propose a multivariate model of the vote decision in the Brexit referendum that considers long-term socioeconomic factors as well as general attitudes toward the European Union. These various factors form the two blocks of variables that are successively added to the estimation. This 'block-recursive' approach allows us to introduce additional blocks of explanatory variables in the next chapter, particularly those directly relating to the campaign. But here we start with the first two blocks, which refer to determinants that are the most distant from the referendum vote in terms of time (e.g., Campbell et al. 1960; Lewis-Beck et al. 2008; Nadeau et al. 2017). The dependent variable is voting Leave (coded 1) as opposed to voting Remain (coded 0). The model is estimated via logistic regression, given the dichotomous nature of the outcome.

Figure 4.3 presents the results from our first regression model, which can be considered as the baseline model since it includes only the block of socioeconomic determinants. These long-term variables include those previously examined in this chapter (age, gender, education, and wealth), to which we add the individual's self-placement on a left-right ideological scale. Ideology is included in this model as a long-term political attitude that can determine (or 'anchor') electoral behaviour, like other variables found at the top of the funnel of causality. Figure 4.3 presents the average marginal effect (with a 95 per cent confidence interval) associated with each of the model's independent variables, based on the logistic regression model found in the appendix table A3.1 (model 1).

To begin with, this baseline model's results confirm some of the previously discussed relationships. Leave voters are significantly older, less qualified, and not as affluent as Remain voters. To this set of socioeconomic determinants, we can add ideology, as the model indicates that those individuals self-locating more on the right of the ideological divide are significantly more likely to vote Leave than those self-locating more on the left. Note, however, that the gender variable does not have a statistically significant effect on the vote choice according to this baseline model. That is to say, the bivariate relationship that we initially observed (in table 4.2) between gender and vote choice

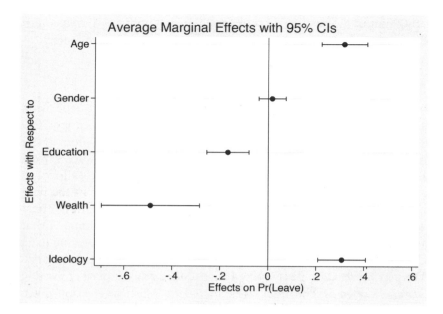

Figure 4.3 Logistic regression model of the Leave vote including socioeconomic variables (baseline model)

is not robust enough to survive in the face of the impact of several other key long-term determinants. Among these more important effects, we can note that wealth, age, and ideology are the most prominent variables. For example, moving from the lowest wealth category to the highest decreases the probability of voting Leave by 42 percentage points on average. The marginal effects associated with the age and ideology variables are very similar in magnitude, with probability changes of 32 and 31 percentage points, respectively. Education has less of a total impact (17 percentage points on average, from the lowest level of qualification to the highest) but is still statistically significant, unlike gender.

Figure 4.4 adds a second block of determinants to the model's estimation. This block includes variables that measure British citizens' views on various aspects of European integration. Three aspects are included. The first involves the attachment that Britons feel toward the EU as compared to the UK, and it is measured by calculating the difference between the attachment score for the UK and the one for

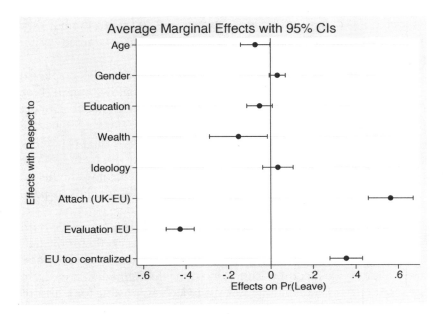

Figure 4.4 Logistic regression model of the Leave vote including socioeconomic variables and attitudes toward the EU

the EU. The greater the difference between these two attachment scores, the greater the probability of voting Leave. The second aspect has to do with the evaluation of the benefits of EU membership. The more an individual thinks that the UK has benefitted from belonging to the EU, the less probability that he or she will vote Leave.

The third and last aspect concerns what emerged in the previous sections as British citizens' most important grievance – namely, the notion that the EU is too centralized and that it intervenes too much into British affairs. To measure this dimension, we use a question from our survey that asks respondents whether they think 'too many issues are decided on by the EU' (coded 1), or 'more issues should be decided on by the EU' (coded 0), or 'the number of issues decided by the EU at present is about right' (coded 0.5, including 'don't know' responses). About 62 per cent say that the first statement (too many issues) comes closest to their view, 34 per cent choose the third statement (number of issues is about right), and 4 per cent think that more issues should be decided by the EU. Not only do these answers accurately reflect the general opinion that the EU is too centralized an institution but they also nicely encapsulate the other related questions examined earlier in this chapter.[13]

Multivariate regression estimates for this second model, displayed in figure 4.2 and appendix table A3.1 (model 2), show that all three of these dimensions are closely associated with the choice to support Brexit. The attachment variable exerts the greatest impact (a positive change of about 56 percentage points on average in the probability of voting Leave from its lowest to highest value) but not by much. The centralization variable leads to an increase of 35 percentage points on average in the probability of supporting the Leave side. For its part, the evaluation of the benefits variable yields an average marginal effect of 43 percentage points (in the negative direction, as one would expect). This evaluation variable thus compensates partly for the pull exerted by the other two EU-related attitudinal variables. It does not, however, provide a comfortable reserve for the Remain campaign in the face of arguments that present the EU as responsible for a host of problems, the key one being the loss of British sovereignty over important policy areas in the current socio-political context.

Finally, at this second stage of the model's estimation, two socio-economic variables from the first block of determinants still exert a statistically significant effect on the vote decision, namely, an individual's age and affluence – although their impact is diminished (average marginal effects of 7 and 15 percentage points, respectively) and even reversed in the case of age. This decrease in the effect of the first block of variables is not entirely unexpected, since the inclusion of the EU-related attitudinal variables into the equation estimation improves the model fit substantially (for instance, the percentage of correctly predicted vote choice increases from 64 to 87 going from the first to the second model; see appendix table A3.1).

EARLY AND LATE DECIDERS

An important question concerns the behaviour of those who made their decision earlier or later during the campaign. We devote more attention to this topic in the next chapter, where we study the extent to which the specific campaign strategies and arguments may have shifted public opinion. But it is important at this point to establish if, as expected, the long-term factors examined in the previous sections played a bigger role for those who made their decision earlier compared to the presumably more hesitant individuals who made their decision closer to the polling day.

To distinguish between early and late deciders, we use the following question: 'If you voted, when did you make up your mind on how you would vote in the referendum on British membership of the EU: at the time the referendum was announced, fairly early in the campaign, in the final week of the campaign or on the referendum day?' The results show that about four voters out of five (78 per cent) can be considered 'early deciders' since their decision was either made at the outset of the referendum campaign or quickly after its launch. This leaves about one voter out of five (22 per cent) who waited until the last week of the campaign or even until the referendum day to make up their mind. Given the discussion in the previous sections about long-standing attitudes toward the EU, this relatively large proportion of early deciders is not unexpected.

The values of the pseudo-R-squared displayed in figures 4.5 to 4.7 show the contribution of the socioeconomic profile and the long-term EU attitudes to the vote choice for all respondents, including both early and late deciders. A few findings stand out for the entire sample of voters. First, the socioeconomic and ideology variables included in our baseline model explain a bit more than one-eighth (0.13) of the variance of our dependent variable. Second, the contribution of the bloc of variables measuring the impact of long-term attitudes toward the EU is, as expected, sizable. The level of explained variance of our dependent variable substantially increases to 0.70 with the inclusion of variables measuring long-term attitudes toward the EU. This result gives strong support to the idea that the 'campaign over 25 years', to borrow Mathew Elliott's words, has mattered in the Brexit referendum.

The results for the early and late deciders displayed in figures 4.6 and 4.7 are perhaps even more interesting. They show that the contribution of long-term attitudes toward the EU in explaining the vote is about twice as important for early deciders as for late deciders (pseudo-R^2 of 0.78 versus 0.40). These findings confirm that long-term attitudes played a major role in the voting decision of the important bloc of early deciders but much less of a role for the smaller but pivotal group of late deciders. These results help us to better understand the campaign choices of the Leave and Remain sides. In brief, the substantial contribution of long-term EU attitudes to the vote choice of the early deciders is a powerful reminder that years of debates on

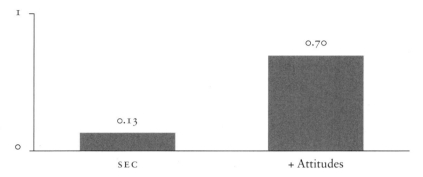

Figure 4.5 Pseudo-R-squared with different models among all respondents

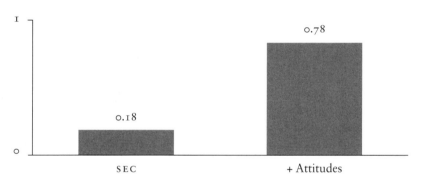

Figure 4.6 Pseudo-R-squared with different models among early deciders

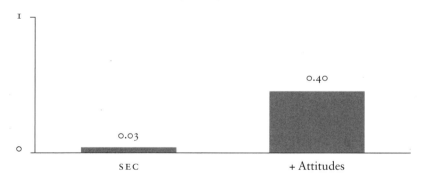

Figure 4.7 Pseudo-R-squared with different models among late deciders

Europe with a clear Eurosceptic bias set the stage for the Brexit campaign and constrained both sides' strategic choices. But the relatively low impact of the same variables on the late deciders' vote shows that the campaign arguments and the performance of leaders from both sides also mattered significantly.

CONCLUSION: SETTING THE STAGE FOR THE CAMPAIGN

Our baseline model explores the impact of a number of long-term variables that 'anchored' the vote choice of British citizens. This initial model delineates the various socioeconomic divides revealed by the Brexit debate: a generational gap (with older Britons being greater supporters of leaving the EU than younger ones), an educational gap (with less-qualified voters supporting Brexit in greater numbers than more-qualified ones), and an affluence gap (with wealthier citizens being more supportive of remaining in the EU than less-affluent ones). The latter finding about the role of wealth in the vote decision is particularly noteworthy due to the originality of the measure we used, which considers both income and assets. Taken together, these initial estimates strongly confirm the 'left-behind' explanation of the Leave victory. Yet they only tell one part of the story, since these socioeconomic determinants relate only indirectly to the various frames employed by the Leave and Remain campaigns.

Our analysis therefore turned to Euroscepticism in British politics. The habit of scapegoating the EU and the resulting scepticism toward certain EU policies among both the public and the elite form the bedrock of political arguments in favour of Brexit. We looked more specifically at three attitudinal variables that relate to Britons' long-established critical stand toward the EU: the degree of attachment to the EU, the attitudes toward the EU and its perceived centralized character, and the opinions on the benefits of EU membership. The results from this part of our empirical analysis could not be clearer. The scapegoating of the EU, exemplified by long-held arguments and opinions about the EU being too centralized and by the relatively weak attachment of Britons toward this supranational political community, constitutes a central dimension of the public debate over Brexit. In addition to the socioeconomic cleavages, existing attitudes toward the EU provide a fundamental element for understanding the vote choice.

These long-term beliefs do not fully explain the referendum outcome either, particularly for the significant bloc of voters who made their decision late in the campaign. Of course, the existing opinions of the public about the EU mattered, but the campaign largely contributed to link these long-held views to the referendum question. As discussed, the Brexit referendum was not an entirely new issue for the public, but it nonetheless produced a technical debate in which voters needed the campaign information to make up their mind. Importantly, campaigners determined which of these long-term views would become relevant for the vote choice and which would remain dormant. As Curtice put it (2015, 17), 'the campaign seems to have exacerbated the social and cultural division about the merits of EU membership that already existed in British society'. The Leave side strategically chose to campaign with the valuable shortcut of 'undemocratic bureaucrats in Brussels' by pitching their campaign around the powerful slogan of 'Take Back Control'. The Remain campaign, on the other hand, let slip some key themes, such as the environment and the fight against terrorism, whose mobilization potential is evident in our survey data.

Our central argument in this chapter is that the two sides did not start the campaign on an equal footing. The tradition in national politics of presenting the EU in a negative light *set the stage* for the campaign. This was a major reason behind the Remain camp's over-reliance on the economy. The Remain campaigners, being part of the British political elite which has never been enthusiastic toward the EU, did not feel comfortable promoting or defending the union in a positive light. Moreover, the appeal of the pro-Remain arguments, even those on the economy, were significantly undermined by the fact that they were advocated by actors such as Prime Minister Cameron himself who, until the very last moment, was very critical of the EU. Conversely, the existing lukewarm public attitudes to the EU offered the Leave camp strong arguments that resonated with voters. The public's slightly positive assessment of the benefits that membership in the EU have brought to the UK – including the benefits of belonging to a free-trade zone – were effectively counterbalanced by the Leave campaign's priming of other more negative dimensions of European integration. Chief among them was the widespread view that British political sovereignty was taken away by the *bureaucrats in Brussels* in key policy areas. Such general attitudes toward the EU, fuelled over the long run by party and media elites, offered simple shortcuts (or cues) to the Leave campaign, which in turn helped many voters, *particularly the late deciders*, to make up their mind about the relatively complex issue of whether the UK should continue to be a member of the EU. Importantly, our data also demonstrate that this tradition was instrumental in paving the way for the Leave campaign to attract the *pivotal group of undecided/moderate voters*, which was crucial for crossing the 50 per cent threshold.

The next chapter explores the degree to which specific campaign strategies and arguments may have *affected public opinion*. In doing so, it builds on this background in this chapter and studies how the Leave side used this key shortcut effectively to de-risk the Brexit decision and reverse the status quo bias.

5

How Did the Perceptions of Risk Affect the Vote Choice?

> In referendums, about two-thirds of the time, the status quo wins. We tried to de-risk the whole thing. We did that by basically saying that there was no status quo ... We set it up as two futures for the UK, with a future where we stayed in the EU and we had all the risks of Remain ... more power and money going to Brussels, more migration, threats of the Eurozone crisis ... Faced with the two different futures for the UK, where the status quo was not an option, Leave was the safer choice.[1]
>
> Matthew Elliott, chief executive of Vote Leave

A campaign analysis is incomplete without specific survey data on the degree to which strategies were effective and how far arguments might have resonated with the public. How successful was the Leave camp's de-risking strategy? How did voters react to the campaign strategies used by the Remain and Leave camps? How did the Brexit supporters perceive the key message 'Take Back Control'? Below, using our survey data, we show that the Leave side's messages on immigration and NHS funding effectively countered the Remain campaign's arguments on the economic and political costs of Brexit.

The Brexit referendum campaign saw both camps trying to frame the issue strategically in order to influence the vote choice. In the previous chapters placing the Brexit case in a comparative perspective and relying on interviews and media content analysis, we argued that the Leave side's strategy was able to de-risk the decision to leave the EU. In this chapter, we examine this argument with individual-level data. We pay attention to the impact of campaign arguments on the vote choice, with an eye to assessing the effectiveness of the various strategies that the Leave camp used in de-risking the economic aspect, such as reaching middle-ground voters, taking advantage of being on the anti-EU side in agenda setting, and avoiding a specific 'exit plan' (unlike the Scottish pro-independence campaigners). We suggest that, toward the end of the campaign, the Leave side successfully used these strategies to persuade a significant number of hesitant voters.

We begin our analysis with voters' global perceptions of the campaign. Next, in line with the Michigan voting model previously introduced, we study the resonance and then the impact of the key campaign arguments on the vote.[2] We continue our examination of the campaign effects by analysing the role of leader images and emotions on the voting decision. Importantly, the impact of these factors is then compared among the groups of early and late deciders. Finally, we present data on risk attitudes that signal once again that the de-risking strategy of the Leave side has been influential.

HOW DID VOTERS PERCEIVE THE CAMPAIGN GLOBALLY?

As chapter 1 discussed in detail, there are different kinds of referendum campaigns. Those on less-familiar issues such as the European Constitution are more likely to see drastic swings in vote intentions, the opposite being true when voters are called upon to decide on less complex and more frequently debated issues, as in the Quebec and Scottish independence referendums. The question of the UK's membership in the European Union is certainly not new. We have seen how campaigners could easily use shortcuts as a result of the widespread practice of scapegoating the EU by the British political elite. Yet while it was familiar, the issue also presented extremely complex terms that voters knew little about and had little control over. Therefore, the stakes in the Brexit referendum were hybrid, presenting both camps with a series of challenges and opportunities. How, then, did the voters react to their strategies of mobilization and persuasion?

One interesting aspect of the campaign is what *it could have been*. The initial goal of the Brexit referendum was to allow citizens to decide on David Cameron's deal with the EU on the country's new terms of EU membership. But this aspect remained invisible during the campaign, both in campaign arguments and in the media. The data in table 5.1 confirm that the deal occupied only a small place in voters' minds. Indeed, about one in four respondents (26 per cent) said that they were unable to comment on the agreement that was supposedly at the centre of the campaign. While only 28 per cent felt that the agreement was beneficial for the UK, as much as 46 per cent believed that it was not beneficial for their country. Moreover, among those with a positive opinion of the agreement, support for remaining in the EU was massive (78 per cent), but among those with a negative opinion of the agreement, it was very weak (26 per cent). Among voters who said they had not heard of the agreement, opinion was quite divided (58 per cent).

These figures suggest that the Cameron government failed to reach an agreement that could potentially have presented the UK's membership of the EU in a more favourable light as well as demonstrating Europe's openness and flexibility to the demands of their country in the future. The failure also had the disadvantage of painting Remain advocates as mild Eurosceptics: they appeared to have been dissatisfied with the UK's EU membership before the deal was reached. This position fuelled Euroscepticism at a time when pro-Remain campaigners should have actively been promoting the European Union. In short, the data in table 5.1 suggest that the last-minute deal reached between the Conservative government and the EU was a false start for the campaign. That said, it could also be argued that the deal's lack of visibility resulted from the sound and reasonable decision of the Remain camp to downplay an unsatisfactory agreement. Whatever the case, the inability of David Cameron to reach a convincing agreement with the EU in the months leading to the Brexit referendum has been portrayed by many analysts as a missed opportunity.

Another noteworthy lens for understanding the Brexit campaign is voters' opinion on how the two campaigns performed. These opinions could involve a projection effect from proponents of each side concluding that their side led the best campaign (Grand and Tiemann 2013; Granberg, Kasmer, and Nanneman 1988; McAllister and Studlar 1991; Nadeau, Niemi, and Amato 1994). Also, voters on the losing side tend to develop a more positive attitude toward the winning side (Cigler and Getter 1977; Joslyn 1998), and they could logically conclude that the Leave campaign had the best campaign, since it won. Nonetheless, this tendency does not entirely discount voters' perceptions of the quality of the Leave and Remain campaigns. In fact, there have been many examples in the past, especially during important referendums, in which voters clearly recognized that the losing side had run a better campaign than the winning side (the reverse being observed frequently as well).[3]

How, then, did British voters view the Leave and Remain campaigns? To measure these attitudes, we asked the following question:

Table 5.1
Opinions about David Cameron's deal and the vote

	Opinion on the Deal	Support for Leave
Beneficial	28	22
Not beneficial	46	74
Never heard, don't know	26	42
N	1,514	1,122

Note: Entries are percentages.
Q: David Cameron struck a deal with the European Union before calling the referendum. Overall, do you think this deal was beneficial for the UK?

'Leaving aside how you voted, how successful would you say that each side was in putting forward a clear vision of the UK it wants?' The answers to this question are presented in table 5.2. While more than one in two respondents (52 per cent) believed that the Leave side put forward a clear message during their campaign, only one in four voters (25 per cent) held that opinion about the Remain side. Conversely, only 22 per cent had a rather negative view of the Leave campaign, against almost double that figure (43 per cent) for the Remain side. Splitting up these responses according to the responder's vote choice is even more revealing. While Remain supporters took a more positive view of the Leave campaign than of the Remain one (45 per cent vs. 37 per cent), the situation is completely different for Brexit supporters. Those supporting Leave were four times more likely to have a favourable opinion of their own side's campaign than that of Remain (64 per cent against 16 per cent).

Despite their potential limitations based on projection effects, the figures in table 5.2 suggest that, in the eyes of the voters, the Leave campaign was better in formulating and spreading a clear and persuasive message during the campaign. Another revealing indicator of this attitude lies in the evaluations of how each side's leader performed during the campaign.[4] This information is presented in tables 5.3 and 5.4. The data in table 5.3 show that Jeremy Corbyn presented a challenge for the Remain camp, as almost one in three respondents (33 per cent) identified him as the leader who performed worst in the campaign. Perceptions of David Cameron are more positive, but it is Boris Johnson who stands out. He has the largest proportion of respondents identifying him as the best leader (21 per cent), and he also has the lowest proportion of respondents identifying him as the worst (8 per cent). Despite Nigel Farage's negative evaluations overall, the

Framing Risky Choices

Table 5.2
Evaluations of campaign success in 'putting
forward a clear vision of the UK it wants'

A All Respondents (n = 1514)

	Leave	*Remain*
Not successful at all	8	14
Not successful	11	29
Average	29	32
Successful	37	20
Very successful	15	5

B Partisans of Leave Only (n =684)

	Leave	*Remain*
Not successful at all	3	20
Not successful	7	34
Average	26	30
Successful	41	14
Very successful	23	2

C Partisans of Remain Only (n = 634)

	Leave	*Remain*
Not successful at all	12	9
Not successful	15	26
Average	28	29
Successful	35	28
Very successful	10	9

Note: Entries in columns are percentages.
Q: Leaving aside how you voted, how successful would say that each side was in putting
forward a clear vision of the UK it wants?

dominance of the Leave camp leaders is clear. One in three voters (33 per cent) responded that Leave leaders performed best during the campaign, whereas only one in five (20 per cent) named the Remain camp leaders. On the flipside, only 26 per cent said the leaders of the Leave side were the least effective, compared to 48 per cent who said the same about the leaders of the Remain camp.

The figures in table 5.4 on each leader's perceived persuasiveness complement and nuance these results. Once again, Boris Johnson prevails. He is clearly perceived as the most convincing leader in the campaign, while Jeremy Corbyn is perceived as the least convincing. Perhaps the most revealing fact from this table is that the level of positive ratings is essentially the same for David Cameron and Nigel Farage (41 per cent in both cases). These results have two important implications. The first is that Boris Johnson appears to have dominated the campaign. The second is that there was a striking imbalance between the two camps: the Leave campaign had two 'convincing' leaders (one highly convincing and one moderately so), whereas the Remain side only had one (only moderately convincing).

The Leave camp thus prevailed in many dimensions of the campaign in the eyes of the voters. A plausible consequence of such dominance would be that the voters who made their decision later on in the campaign were a little more inclined to support the Leave option. The data in table 5.5 confirm that this seems to be the case. Support for Brexit reaches 56 per cent for those who report making their decision during the final week of the campaign or on the day of the vote. The figure goes down to 51 per cent for those who report having made their decision before this period. This gap of 5 percentage points between late and early deciders is significant for two reasons.[5] First, it lends clear support to our core argument. Second, the opposite trend would have led the Remain camp to a comfortable victory.[6]

These global findings suggest that the dominance of the Leave campaign contributed to its final victory. It is important to reiterate, as we have shown in the previous chapter, that long-term factors, such as deeply entrenched attitudes toward the EU, also played a crucial role in explaining the vote choice. We examine more specifically below the arguments put forward by both camps and the extent to which the pro-Leave campaigners succeeded in reframing the debate to de-risk the Brexit decision. These analyses notably show that these campaign factors were particularly important for late deciders in general and for moderate voters in particular.

THE RESONANCE OF CAMPAIGN ARGUMENTS AMONG THE ELECTORATE

In the preceding chapters, we argued that the Remain camp distilled its campaign arguments into a single frame: a departure from the EU would have drastic economic costs. This choice was partly because of the long-established habit of scapegoating the EU and partly because

Table 5.3
Leaders' performance during the Brexit campaign

	Best	Worse	Difference
Cameron	14	15	−1
Corbyn	6	33	−27
Johnson	21	8	+13
Farage	12	18	−6
Leave advantage	+13	+22	

Note: Entries are percentages.

Q: Thinking overall about how politicians performed during the referendum campaign, which politician do you think performed best: David Cameron, Jeremy Corbyn, Boris Johnson, Nigel Farage? And, overall, which politician do you think performed worst during the referendum campaign: David Cameron, Jeremy Corbyn, Boris Johnson, Nigel Farage?

Table 5.4
Leaders' persuasiveness during the Brexit campaign

	Convincing	Unconvincing	Difference
Cameron	41	51	−10
Corbyn	22	65	−43
Johnson	57	35	+22
Farage	41	50	−9

Note: Entries are percentages.

Q: How convincing would you say each of the following campaign actors was: David Cameron, Jeremy Corbyn, Boris Johnson, Nigel Farage?

Table 5.5
Time of decision and the vote in the Brexit referendum

	Early deciders	Late deciders
Leave	51	56
Remain	49	44
N	1032	285

Note: Entries are percentages.

Q: If you voted, when did you make up your mind on how you would vote in the referendum on British membership of the European Union?

Early deciders = At the time the referendum was announced or fairly early during the campaign; Late deciders = In the final week of the campaign or on the referendum day.

of previous campaign experience prioritizing the economy over other issues. Importantly, the Leave campaign successfully exploited the Remain camp's single line of defence. It diluted this proposed economic risk, relied on voters' resentment toward European bureaucracy, and broadened the debate by reframing it around the political cost of the status quo: to remain in the EU would result in the loss of political autonomy. This was the essence of the Leave camp's 'Two Futures' strategy. They put forward two specific issues to demonstrate these disadvantages: immigration and NHS funding. By refocusing the debate on these two themes, the Leave camp managed to redirect voters' attention away from the economic losses of a Brexit decision toward the gains of such a decision – allowing the UK greater control over immigration and gaining better funding for the health service.

In tables 5.6 to 5.9, we study the extent to which voters agreed with these core arguments. The data in table 5.6 look into how citizens perceived the potential consequences of leaving the EU. In terms of the Remain campaign's core message, almost one in two respondents (47 per cent) expressed apprehension about the economic consequences of a Brexit decision, believing that it would lead to a drop in trade with Europe and job losses. In addition to this large group of worried voters, a strong contingent of nearly one in four voters (24 per cent) said they were uncertain about the economic consequences of leaving the EU. However, table 5.6 also demonstrates why this economic argument of the Remain side was not sufficient. First of all, we can see that respondents were divided about the consequences of Brexit on the UK's international influence and ability to ensure security against the rise of terrorism. Moreover, table 5.6 clearly shows that the Leave camp convinced an important section of the electorate that remaining in the EU would increase immigration, result in funding cuts for the NHS, and mean further losses for their country's sovereignty.

These figures confirm the interview data on campaign strategies in many ways. First, they show that the Leave side effectively clouded the key idea that leaving the EU would be an economic disaster. This result is all the more important considering that the Leave campaigners' figures were in striking contrast with those of 'the experts'. A sizable group of voters had doubts as to whether leaving the EU would actually be costly. This is in line with the Leave side's reported campaign strategy of actively contesting the arguments on the economy to undermine the impact of risk aversion. It also highlights an important difference between the referendums on Quebec and Scottish

132   Framing Risky Choices

Table 5.6
Perceptions of the consequences of a Leave vote

	Unlikely	Neither unlikely nor likely	Likely
Loss of trade and jobs	29	24	47
Immigration decrease	31	22	47
NHS better protected	31	25	44
Sovereignty protected	19	25	56
UK less secure	43	19	38
UK weaker on world stage	44	21	35

Note: Entries are percentages. Respondents' level of agreement with these claims was measured on a 5 point scale where 1 means very unlikely, 3 neither likely nor unlikely, and 5 very unlikely. The first two (unlikely) and last two (likely) categories are merged in Table 5.6. Don't know answers (3 per cent on average) are merged with the neither unlikely nor likely category.

Q: A number of claims were made about what leaving the EU would mean to the UK. For a UK outside the European Union, how likely would you say the following would be? There would be loss of jobs, trade and investment? The level of immigration in the UK would decrease? The National Health System (NHS) would be better protected? The British culture and sovereignty would be protected? The UK would be less secure? The UK would be weaker on the world stage?

sovereignty and the Brexit referendum. While in the first two cases a significant number of voters were sensitive to the idea that their region's interests would be best defended by concluding economic association agreements with the host countries and by continuing to be part of the G7 to enjoy a strong political and economic stature (Bélanger et al. 2018), voters in the UK did not seem to share the same feeling that they needed to belong to a larger entity like the EU in order to achieve such goals.[7] This apparent confidence confirms the insistence by campaigners in the interviews that although the economic viability of Scotland remained a constant question mark in the minds of the Scottish voters, the Leave campaigners were not bothered by the same concerns, since the UK had already once been an independent, economically self-sufficient entity. This difference was arguably related to the Leave camp's strategy of not announcing a specific exit plan, avoiding the pitfalls of the contested White Paper of the Yes Scotland campaign.

These figures also suggest that the Leave side's 'Two Futures' strategy was effective in making the public think that there was no safety in the status quo. Table 5.6 illustrates that the Leave camp successfully exploited the Remain side's simplistic economic vision of Europe by

Perceptions of Risk

reframing the debate around the political and financial gains associated with Brexit. In the Scottish referendum, although the Yes Scotland campaign relied on the same 'Two Futures' theme, arguing that remaining in the UK would also have consequences (e.g., for their social policy), detailed studies of the Scottish vote found that it was the economic risk that decided the outcome (Henderson et al. 2015).

Specifically on the issue of immigration, the interview data underlined the importance of the battle between two 'Project Fears', one on the economic costs of Brexit (led by the Remain camp) and the other on the dangers of mass immigration (led by the Leave camp). The pro-Leave arguments on the topic met with no effective answer from the Remain campaigners, who practically gifted their opponents the ownership of this question. The data in table 5.7 confirm just how important this issue became for voters. As many as six out of ten respondents (60 per cent) approve of a drop in immigration, and of this group, almost four in ten (37 per cent) want this reduction to be extensive. Looking at the data in these tables together, the Leave side's arguments on immigration appear to have succeeded in two ways. First, the arguments matched voters' widespread desire to reduce immigration into the UK. Second, the arguments convinced voters that a Leave victory was the best way to obtain the desired result. What is more, these figures once again underline how the absence of this theme in the Scottish debate likely made the job of the Better Together campaigners easier.

THE IMPACT OF CAMPAIGN ARGUMENTS ON THE VOTE CHOICE

So far, we have presented results that demonstrate the extent to which the arguments of the two camps resonated with the electorate. Next, we look into whether these arguments might have influenced the vote choice. To explore this question, we first examine the reasons that respondents gave for their vote choice when presented with a list of possible justifications. Although limited by the tendency of voters to rationalize their choice after the fact (e.g., Blais, Martin, and Nadeau 1998), this information nonetheless offers a first glance at voter motivations.

The main reasons offered by the Leave and Remain voters are shown in tables 5.8 and 5.9, respectively. The results fall in line with the previous observations. For the Leave supporters, the most frequently

134 Framing Risky Choices

Table 5.7
Opinions about the level of migration in the UK

	%
Decreased a lot	37
Decreased a little	23
Left the same as it is now	25
Increased a little	6
Increased a lot	3
Don't know	5
N	1,514

Note: Entries are percentages.
Q: Do you think the number of immigrants from foreign countries who are permitted to come to the United Kingdom to live should be increased, decreased, or left the same as it is now?

mentioned reason is that exiting the EU would allow their country to regain control over major national decisions (65 per cent). This reason is followed by reducing immigration (50 per cent), the perceived excessive contribution of the UK to the EU (40 per cent), dissatisfaction with the EU's functioning (32 per cent), and better funding for the NHS (25 per cent). Leaving aside the answer on dissatisfaction with the EU, which echoes the scapegoating tradition discussed in the previous chapter, Leave supporters were particularly sensitive to the pro-Leave message about the need for Britain to regain its political sovereignty so that it could control immigration and protect the NHS.

Table 5.9 in turn reports the reasons mentioned by the Remain supporters. The data show that both general economic concerns and fear that Brexit would lead to job losses and a decline in trade with Europe played a central role in motivating the Remain voters. These findings seem to vindicate the Remain campaign's strategy of focusing on the economy. However, we also observe two limitations. First, a significant proportion of the Remain supporters justified their vote choice by citing arguments that were not prioritized by the Remain campaign, such as the UK's ability to fight more effectively against terrorism or to play a more important role on the international scene as part of a larger supranational body. As the interview data discussed in chapter 3 showed, these arguments were initially designed to be part of the Remain campaign but were jettisoned later on in favour of the economic argument. That decision appears to have been a

Table 5.8
Arguments mentioned by Leave voters

	% *mentioned*
Control on national decisions	65
Decrease immigration	50
Pay too much to EU	40
Discontent with the EU	32
Protect NHS	25
EU: too many members	21
UK more secure	17
UK: stronger on world stage	13
Economy more secure	12
Discontent: UK government	5
Lack of information	3
N	684

Note: Entries are percentages.
Q: Which of the following describe best your reasons for voting for British membership of the European Union? Please tick THE THREE MOST IMPORTANT reasons.

Table 5.9
Arguments mentioned by Remain voters

	% *mentioned*
Loss of jobs and trade	57
Economy more secure	56
Preventing terrorism	43
UK: stronger on world stage	34
Protect NHS	22
Decrease immigration	7
Avoid Scottish Independence	7
N	634

Note: Entries are percentages.
Q: Which of the following describe best your reasons for voting for British membership of the European Union? Please tick THE THREE MOST IMPORTANT reasons.

mistake, as table 5.9 illustrates the mobilizing potential of these arguments. Second, the Leave supporters mentioned more reasons in support of their choice than did Remain supporters. These two findings suggest that the Remain campaign did not use its full mobilizing potential.

The findings in tables 5.6–5.9 suggest that the interview data closely match the survey data in explaining the campaign dynamics. Next, we turn in a more systematic way to the effect of these arguments on voters' choice, through the use of bivariate and multivariate analyses. Specifically, we examine the impact of the three main arguments put forward during the Brexit campaign on the economy, immigration, and the NHS. Unsurprisingly, and confirming the significance of a frame analysis, the data in table 5.10 present a strong link between supporting each of these arguments and the vote choice. Support for Brexit falls to 16 per cent among voters who believe that the withdrawal of the UK from the EU will lead to economic losses and reaches 77 per cent and 80 per cent among those who believe that this departure would reduce immigration or better fund the NHS, respectively.

To a certain degree, the magnitude of the effects seen in table 5.10 is once again attributable to a projection effect that causes respondents to rationalize their vote choice by imbuing it with positive consequences. That being said, a closer inspection of table 5.10 highlights a key result that explains the Remain campaign's main weakness, which handed the victory over to the Leave side. At first glance, the strongest association is observed between the beliefs about the negative economic consequences of Brexit and the vote choice. In line with the 'kit' of strategies we developed in chapter 2, this result confirms that the Remain campaign built on the traditional strength of the pro-EU campaigners by using the argument on economic costs. Nevertheless, the relationship between these two variables also highlights some limitations. A key group for this analysis is composed of those who are undecided about the economic benefits of Brexit (25 per cent). Within this pivotal group, no less than 72 per cent of the respondents voted to leave the EU. These figures are important for several reasons. First, a shift of a few percentage points within this group could have made the difference and led instead to a Remain victory. Second, these figures, along with the previous similar findings in table 4.13, show that the Leave side was more successful than the Remain side in reaching middle-ground voters, which was linked to their core strategy in going beyond the 50 per cent threshold. The result also points to the

Leave campaign's success in maintaining a non-extremist profile, which is usually the main problem of anti-EU campaigns. Third, these figures also help us understand why we do not observe the well-documented relationship between risk aversion and political choice in the Brexit case; the respondents who were undecided about the economic consequences of Brexit should have opted for the status quo. The Remain camp's economic argument was indeed the only decisive one in favour of remaining in the EU, yet the Leave camp's strategies convinced an important number of moderate voters to support Brexit and helped the campaign reach the winning threshold.

Next, we observe whether these opinions on the three main campaign arguments still have a significant effect once all the other factors that may have influenced the vote choice have been taken into account. Furthermore, we are interested in measuring the impact of this variable (campaign arguments) on the vote choice not only for the entire electorate but also among particular groups, such as moderate voters and late deciders.

Figure 5.1 presents the results of a multivariate regression that includes these variables. As in the previous chapter, regression coefficients and goodness-of-fit measures are presented in appendix table A3.1. The results, reported in figure 5.1, are the average marginal effects of the explanatory variables in a logistic regression model of the Brexit vote. This model includes the anchor variables and the attitudes toward the EU discussed in the previous chapter, to which we add variables on campaign argumentation. These variables measure agreement with the three proposed consequences of a Leave vote: a decrease in trade and an increase in unemployment; a decrease in the level of immigration; and the opportunity to better fund the NHS by not paying into the EU. The average marginal effect represents the average change in the probability of voting Leave when we move from the minimum category of a variable (for instance, being totally in disagreement with pro-Leave or pro-Remain arguments) to its maximum category (to be totally in agreement with these arguments).

Importantly, these regression results, involving the variables on campaign arguments, match the more descriptive observations in the previous sections and together offer a coherent story. First of all, the argument most closely linked to the vote choice is the one related to the negative economic consequences of Brexit. (All things being equal, supporting this argument leads to a decrease of 25 percentage points in one's probability of voting Leave; see figure 5.1.) This result

138   Framing Risky Choices

Table 5.10
Relationship between support for three campaign arguments and the vote

	Unlikely	Neither unlikely nor likely	Likely	Gamma
Loss of jobs and trade	92	72	16	−.86**
Decrease of immigration	20	41	77	.72**
NHS better protected	12	43	80	.77**

Notes: Entries represent percentages of support for the Leave option. The gammas in the last column measure the strength of the relationship between supporting these claims and the vote. ** p < .01.
For the question, see Table 5.6.

confirms once again that the strongest argument for pro-EU campaigners is the economic one and that the Remain side benefitted from this strategy. However, the data also suggest that the combined effect of the Leave camp's arguments on immigration and the NHS (supporting them increases the likelihood of voting Leave by 18 and 20 points respectively) allowed them to partially counter the effect of voters' economic fears by reframing the debate around the political and financial gains associated with Brexit. These figures offer evidence for the widely observed agenda-setting advantage of anti-EU campaigners. The Leave side fully benefitted from this advantage by broadening the agenda via the issues of immigration and the NHS to the political costs of losing sovereignty and countered the economic risks of the vote choice.

An important question is whether the Remain campaign could have been more effective in neutralizing its opponents' arguments. The data presented earlier showing perceptions of the Remain camp as unconvincing suggest that this could have been the case. Two experiments provide further evidence on this possibility. The Leave side's edge as being the best option to protect the NHS dropped from thirteen to three points (see table 5.6) in a subgroup of respondents who answered the same question after seeing a specific pro-Remain poster. This poster highlights a study from the University of Oxford arguing that leaving the EU would result in a £40 billion cut for the NHS (see figure 1.3).[8]

Another experiment shows that the argument 'the UK's financial contribution to the EU is largely offset by what it receives in increased trade' would have been more effective if presented in a concrete and vivid fashion. The proportion of respondents agreeing that the UK's contribution to the EU is fair (36 per cent) is almost at par with those

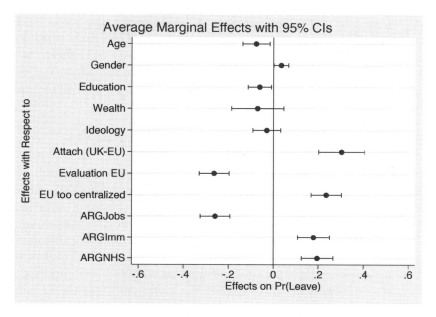

Figure 5.1 Logistic regression model of the Leave vote including socioeconomic variables, attitudes toward the EU, and opinions on campaign arguments

thinking otherwise (41 per cent) for a subgroup that received a strong version of this argument. This strong version was framed as follows: *Some say that the UK sends an important amount of money to the EU. Some others say that for every pound we put into the EU, we get almost 10 pounds back through increased trade.* This result is in clear contrast with a large negative gap (28 per cent versus 43 per cent) for those exposed to a weaker version of the same claim. The weaker version had the following wording: *Some say that the UK sends an important amount of money to the EU. Some others say that what the UK receives in increased trade is way more than it sends to the EU.*[9]

The results from these two experiments suggest that there was potential for pro-EU arguments, yet the Remain campaign kept some of its best arguments partly invisible. The partisans of Europe could have promoted a larger array of arguments to advocate remaining in the EU (particularly on social issues) and could have presented them in a crisper fashion. In other words, the advantage of the Leave side concerning the 'unfairness' of the British contribution to the EU and its presumed consequences for the NHS funding was not inevitable.

At the very least, the data show that the Remain camp could have matched their rivals' arguments on this question. Their inability to do so allowed the Leave camp to add additional dimensions to the debate that were key to partially offsetting the Remain side's advantage on the economic dimension, and to give concrete examples about the need to take back control from Brussels.

LEADER IMAGES AND THE VOTE CHOICE

As we discussed in the first chapter, frame strength mostly depends on the message content. Emotional and vivid arguments, especially those evoking fear, anxiety, and anger, are expected to be more enduring than those that do not elicit an affective response, all else being equal. But speaker credibility may also affect frame strength. For instance, research has shown that voter motivations on a region's political independence can rely on emotions and messenger credibility (e.g., Clarke and Kornberg 1996; Clarke, Goodwin, and Whiteley 2017; Hobolt 2016; Johnston et al. 1996; Liñeira, Henderson, and Delaney 2017; Martin and Nadeau 2001; Nadeau, Martin, and Blais 1999).

As we noted earlier, Boris Johnson was perceived as the most convincing leader during the referendum campaign, followed by David Cameron and Nigel Farage, who were tied, with Jeremy Corbyn following far behind (see table 5.4). The data on leader images in table 5.11 complete this picture. There we see that respondents ranked Boris Johnson most favourably, with an average score of 47 compared with 44, 35, and 34 for Cameron, Corbyn, and Farage, respectively. Yet the most revealing figures are those on how respondents' viewed the leaders of their own camp. Leaders of the Leave campaign enjoyed much greater popularity among the Leave supporters than the Remain leaders did among Remain supporters. Being able to count on leaders who were popular within their support base was a decisive advantage for the Leave camp, given the very close results of the Brexit referendum.

Figure 5.2 presents the results from a regression analysis that includes variables measuring leader popularity.[10] As the data show, adding the leader-popularity variables reduces but does not eliminate the impact of attitudes on the EU and campaign arguments on the vote. The impact of each leader's popularity on the vote choice is revealing. There is a strong negative correlation between David Cameron's popularity and support for the Leave option. Support for

Table 5.11
Leaders' ratings

	All	Remain	Leave
Cameron	44	48	40
Corbyn	35	44	27
Johnson	47	30	62
Farage	34	14	52

Note: Entries are percentages.
Q: On a scale going from 0 to 100, where 0 means you really dislike a leader and 100 means you really like him, how do you feel about: David Cameron, Jeremy Corbyn, Boris Johnson, Nigel Farage?

voting Leave falls by fourteen points among the respondents who have a very favourable opinion of Cameron, compared to those who have a very negative opinion of him. The reverse relationship is also observed between the perceptions of the pro-Brexit leaders and support for voting Leave, the effects being ten and twelve points for Boris Johnson and Nigel Farage, respectively. The lack of relationship for Jeremy Corbyn confirms his underperformance during the campaign and signals once again how the Remain camp was at a disadvantage. Remain was caught in an uneven fight, having only one popular leader rather than the two more popular leaders of the Leave side, who were better able to mobilize their base. It is thus not surprising that the late deciders favoured the Leave option.

EMOTIONS AND THE VOTE CHOICE

We now turn our attention to the link between emotions and the vote choice. There are two reasons for this interest. First, as discussed, emotions are shown to be a significant factor in understanding framing effects. Politicians who use emotional language tend to shape public opinion more than those who do not. Moreover, the interviews conducted with Remain and Leave strategists revealed that emotions occupied an important place in a referendum campaign that some have characterized as the battle between two 'Project Fears', one capitalizing on the economy and the other on immigration.

In spite of its relevance, the study of emotions presents some challenges. The biggest is to establish a clear causal link between the

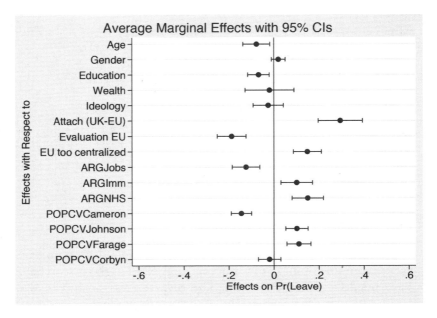

Figure 5.2 Logistic regression model of the Leave vote including socioeconomic variables, attitudes toward the EU, opinions on campaign arguments and leader images

emotions reported by respondents and their behaviour. In our case, the respondents' emotions were measured after the actual referendum. As such, it is entirely possible that the link between these measures and the choice to support Brexit is the product of a projection effect, with the winners expressing their satisfaction and the losers their disappointment. For this reason, the results on the joy or anger expressed by our survey respondents must be interpreted with caution.

The results presented in table 5.12 present the relationship between the respondents' post-Brexit emotions and their reported vote choice. The very strong association between these two variables is not surprising. It goes without saying that an individual who claims to be deeply angry after the Leave victory is very likely to have supported Remain, with the opposite being true as well. That being said, two aspects of these results are of interest. First, the Leave side prevails within an important category of individuals who expressed having mixed feelings about Leave's victory. The other significant fact revealed in table 5.12 is that the percentage of respondents expressing positive feelings after the referendum is higher than that of those expressing

Perceptions of Risk

Table 5.12
Relationship between supportive emotions toward the Leave victory and the vote choice

	Remain	*Leave*	*Total*
1 (very angry)	100	0	20
2	92	8	17
3 (neither angry nor happy)	47	53	20
4	14	86	22
5 (very happy)	5	95	23
Pearson χ^2		798.2**	
Gamma		.93**	

Notes: Entries are row percentages. ** p < .001.
Q: Now we would like to know something about the feelings you have toward the referendum result. How do you feel about the victory of the Leave camp? Please locate yourself on each of this emotion scale: 1 = very angry, 2 = angry, 3 = neither angry, nor happy, 4 = happy, 5 = very happy.

their anger (45 per cent vs. 37 per cent). This result is all the more unexpected since many observers pointed out that the Leave side's victory was a surprise for a good number of people, many of whom might have voted differently or have chosen to vote if they had known the outcome. However, the results in table 5.12, which deal with the reactions of voters as well as non-voters, do not show that kind of remorse following Leave's victory.[11] We take up this issue in detail in the next chapter on losers' consent.

Figure 5.3 presents the regression analysis that includes the emotion variable. The strength of the relationship between the emotions expressed and the vote choice highlights the importance of this variable in understanding the referendum outcome. More specifically, it confirms the interview data that the Remain camp's inability to appeal to emotions indeed contributed to its defeat. As a final point, the results in figure 5.3 demonstrate that even the inclusion of such a powerful explanatory variable does not eliminate the effect on the vote of attitudes toward the EU, campaign arguments, and leader images. This finding is telling, given the Leave side's edge on all these dimensions.

EARLY AND LATE DECIDERS

The findings presented so far underscore the importance of examining campaign effects on early versus late deciders. To distinguish between these two groups, we rely on the same question presented in chapter 4,

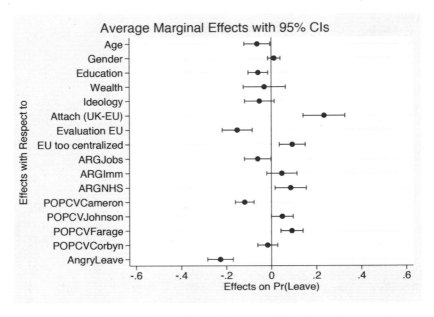

Figure 5.3 Logistic regression model of the Leave vote including socioeconomic variables, attitudes toward the EU, opinions on campaign arguments, leader images, and emotions

which allows us to separate respondents who made their decision at the time the referendum was announced or early after its launch (78 per cent) from those who waited until the last week of the campaign or the referendum day itself to make up their mind (22 per cent).

The values of the pseudo-R-squared displayed in figures 5.4 to 5.6 show the contribution of opinions on campaign arguments, leader images, and emotions to the explanation of the vote for all respondents, as well as for early and late deciders. As the results show, the inclusion of opinions on campaign arguments in the model for all respondents increases the explained variance by 9 percentage points (from 0.70 to 0.79). Tellingly, the impact of these variables is significantly higher for late deciders than for early deciders. The explained variance increases by 12 percentage points in the first case (from 0.40 to 0.52) compared to 8 percentage points in the second case (from 0.78 to 0.86). Put differently, the overall results that emerge from figures 5.4 to 5.6 suggest that the early-decider vote choice was strongly determined by long-term variables that reflected strong

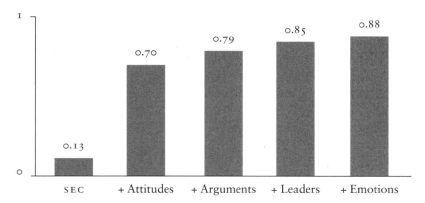

Figure 5.4 Pseudo-R-squared with different models among all respondents

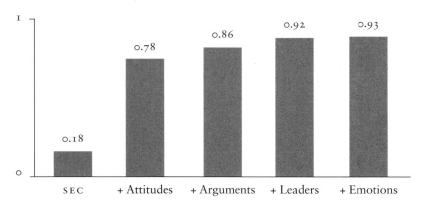

Figure 5.5 Pseudo-R-squared with different models among early deciders

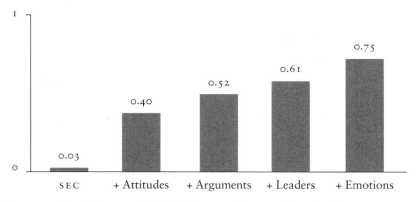

Figure 5.6 Pseudo-R-squared with different models among late deciders

attitudes toward the EU, while the late-decider choice was less structured and largely determined by short-term factors, such as the campaign arguments.

Adding the block of variables concerning leader images also contributes to a significant increase in the explained variance in voting choices, with the model's pseudo-R^2 increasing from 0.79 to 0.85 for all respondents. Once again, the impact of this campaign factor is greater for late deciders (+9) than for early deciders (+6). This result, which is in line with work suggesting that late deciders are more susceptible to being influenced by leader images than early deciders (Chaffee and Rimal 1996; Cattelani and Alberici 2012), once again underlines the importance of the campaign for the pivotal group of undecided voters

Finally, including a measure of emotional reactions to the outcome also contributes to the explanation of the vote, but quite differently among different groups of voters. Figures 5.4 to 5.6 show that the 3 percentage points increase in the explained variance for the whole sample is almost entirely due to the impact of this variable among the late deciders (+0.14 versus + 0.01 for early deciders). Overall, the roles of campaign factors, leader images, and emotions are not only important for the study of framing: they are highly relevant also for understanding campaign dynamics because they seem to be more influential for late deciders whose rallying was crucial for the tight referendum outcome.[12]

RISK ATTITUDES AND THE VOTE CHOICE

We conclude this chapter by looking at the link between risk attitudes and the vote. To do so, we examine the impact of three variables that measure an individual's disposition to *various* forms of risk. The use of these unique indicators requires some explanation. The first measures the general disposition to risk (GENRISK), the second relates to risks of an economic nature (ECNRISK) and the third, very rarely used in opinion polls, measures the political risk (POLRISK).[13] As discussed in chapter 1, the relationship between individuals' appetite for risk and their political choices has been the subject of a significant body of work (e.g., Kam and Simas 2012; Nadeau, Martin, and Blais 1999; Morgenstern and Zechmeister 2001). Several of these studies have used an individual's *general* disposition to risk (Ehrlich and Maestas 2010; Nadeau, Martin, and Blais 1999; Steenbergen and Siczek

2017).[14] Attitudes toward *financial* risks have also been widely studied (Collard and Breuer 2009; Weber and Hsee 1998; Weber, Blais, and Betz 2002). Given the nature of the Remain camp's arguments, it is crucial to examine the impact of financial-risk tolerance on support for Brexit. Taking a step further, we also add a variable on disposition to *political* risk, which has received little attention from researchers. It is necessary to examine the effect of this variable on the vote choice because supporting Brexit was a political decision with a great deal of uncertainty and risk surrounding it (Steenbergen and Siczek 2017). Moreover, the Leave camp actively tried to reorient the debate by focusing on the political gains rather than the economic costs of Brexit.

The results for the regression analysis including the three measures of risk attitudes are presented in figure 5.7. Given that the crux of the campaign strategies of both sides was to frame the risk dimensions associated with the Brexit decision (to activate it or to mute it), we estimate the impact of these variables with a model that includes opinions on campaign arguments. The results demonstrate that the vote choice is linked neither to the respondents' general disposition to risk (GENRISK) nor to their appetite for financial risk (ECNRISK).[15] On the other hand, the willingness to take political risks (POLRISK) appears to be significantly related to one's decision to support Brexit or not. The data in figure 5.7 show that the likelihood of voting Leave is 11 percentage points higher for respondents with a high tolerance for political risk, compared to those with the opposite view. These results, showing the dominance of political risk over financial risk in the vote decision, parallel the interview data and confirm that the Leave campaign's strategy on risk was influential. The conventional indicators measuring an individual's appetite for risk are not related to the vote choice. It seems that the Remain camp failed in its attempt to make the idea of risk more prominent in the vote choice. The result regarding political risk, on the other hand, implies that the Leave camp successfully managed to mitigate the worries of moderate voters, the pivotal group in any referendum.[16] By shifting the debate away from economic losses and toward the political gains of Brexit, the Leave side reached these middle-ground voters.

CONCLUSION: REVERSING THE STATUS QUO BIAS?

We argue that the key to understanding the Brexit referendum's unusual outcome – a critical group of British voters choosing an

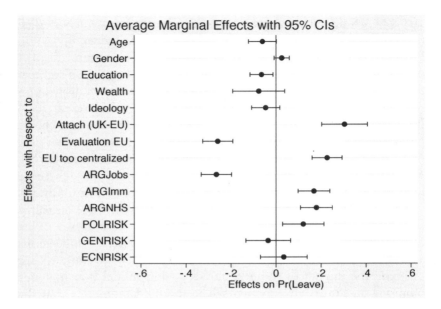

Figure 5.7 Logistic regression model of the Leave vote including socioeconomic variables, attitudes toward the EU, opinions on campaign arguments, and risk attitudes

uncertain economic future as opposed to the safe status quo – relates deeply to the campaign. This chapter has presented this core argument by using survey data. The Leave camp's success in de-risking the choice and reversing the status quo bias manifests itself in three ways. The first is at the message level. As our survey results indicate, many people believed that the Leave camp led a more convincing campaign than that of its opponents. The Remain camp was wise to focus its campaign on the economic costs of Brexit, following the example of successful pro-EU campaigners up until this point; yet this argument proved to be insufficient to improve the image of the EU, tarnished by decades of scapegoating in British politics. Also, as the campaign unfolded, the Remain side failed to actively counter the more varied, more concrete, and more emotionally charged message put forward by the Leave camp. This was the key difference between the unsuccessful 'Project Fear' of the Remain campaign and the successful 'Project Fear' of the Better Together campaign in Scotland, which brought up the idea of 'Devolution Max' to counter the arguments of the Yes Scotland camp. On the flipside, the Leave side benefitted fully from being on the anti-EU side and from the existing unpopularity of the EU. Unlike in the usual pro-independence campaigns, they neither suffered from the questions on the economic viability of the UK nor proposed a specific economic exit plan. It was in this context that the Leave camp pitched its de-risking strategy and directed voters' attention away from the possible economic risks of Brexit toward the political and financial costs of remaining in the EU. They clouded the economic argument of the Remain camp, despite going against 'the experts'. This was because their campaign message was vivid and touched a sensitive chord, urging voters to regain control of their national borders to limit immigration into the UK and to recuperate the money sent to the wasteful Brussels bureaucracy in order to strengthen their health-care system. This message proved to be both reassuring and mobilizing, and it convinced a significant number of moderate and hesitant voters to support the Leave side. In that sense, the Leave side was successful in reaching middle-ground voters and thereby obtaining the winning threshold. The Remain camp's message on the economic costs of Brexit was successfully countered by the pro-Leave arguments on immigration and NHS funding.

Second, the data show that the Leave campaign also had an advantage in terms of campaign leaders. In the eyes of voters, Boris Johnson emerged as the most convincing leader, while Jeremy Corbin's underperformance turned the referendum debate into an uneven struggle. The complementary nature of the two Leave leaders allowed Boris Johnson to give the Brexit decision a non-extremist profile that reassured moderate voters – the key challenge for most anti-EU campaigners. Nigel Farage, on the other hand, freely capitalized on the more emotionally charged issue of immigration. This synergy between one moderate and one extremist leader was thus a benefit for the Leave camp, which did not face a similar two-leader combination (one conservative, one progressive) on the other side. This lack was again a lost opportunity for the Remain side.

A final factor was the battle of emotions. The general unpopularity of the EU and the Remain side's entirely negative arguments to defend it did not generate any enthusiasm among Remain supporters and so limited their mobilization. The Leave side, on the other hand, exploited the resentment felt toward the bureaucrats in Brussels and capitalized on voters' fears of an uncontrolled increase in immigration, charging the Leave option with sufficient emotion to neutralize the economic fears of Brexit and clinch their victory.

Bringing together data on these dimensions shows that the Leave campaign dominated in all three. It is therefore not surprising that the late deciders, who did not make up their minds until the final days of the campaign, leaned toward a pro-Leave vote. In the next chapter we explore whether these campaign strategies had an impact on the eventual acceptance of the referendum outcome. Some Remain voters respected the result more than others did. The Leave side's de-risking strategy arguably neutralized the worries of a key group of Remain voters and made it easier for them to accept the Brexit choice.

6

Why Do Some Remain Voters Accept the Outcome and Some Do Not?

It is a very vigorous debate and I am not surprised by that for a moment. It raises very high passions, but we are a grown-up enough democracy that we can have this passionate debate, where the public, the people will decide, not the politicians, and then we accept the result.[1]

David Cameron

Campaign strategies may not only contribute to the referendum outcome but also go beyond it to influence whether or not that outcome is accepted. Although Prime Minister Cameron urged the public and politicians to accept the result, did everyone do so? What differentiated the Remain voters who accepted the outcome from those who did not? Did campaign strategies play a role in gaining their blessing?

The consent of the Remain voters after their defeat was far from inevitable, given that the referendum produced a close outcome with huge and likely irreversible consequences. In the aftermath of the Brexit vote, more than 4.1 million citizens signed a petition calling for a second referendum on EU membership, this time based on new rules in terms of the majority (60 per cent) and the turnout (75 per cent) required to act on the result (Harley 2016). Their hopes faded when the British government responded that the referendum held on 23 June 2016 was 'a once in a generation vote'. On the one hand, millions of citizens, most likely Remain supporters, were refusing to concede victory. On the other hand, the government ignored their request and made clear, especially to the Tory party base, that 'Brexit was going to happen' and that those 'who didn't like the result [of the referendum] had to respect it' (Shipman 2017, 3).

In this chapter we study the crucial phenomenon of losers' consent after the Brexit referendum. The rallying of a significant group of 'losers' after an electoral defeat is essential to ensuring the stability of democratic institutions (Nadeau and Blais 1993). 'Winners' will generally be satisfied with the system, which has just produced a result that is favourable to them. Much less obvious is the reaction of the 'losers', since their support requires the recognition of the legitimacy of a procedure that has produced an outcome deemed to be undesirable. Whether the British democracy is, to borrow David Cameron's words, 'grown-up' or not depends on its ability to secure the support of a substantial proportion of individuals who are displeased with the vote.

We argue that losers' consent is a fundamental yet overlooked aspect of the Brexit referendum. This crucial reservoir of support played a key role in consolidating the legitimacy of the Leave victory and in keeping the UK government on the path leading to Brexit. Below we first discuss the existing work on losers' consent. Second, using our survey data, we distinguish between the 'graceful' and 'sore' losers. Third, we examine the profiles of winners, graceful losers, and sore losers to gain a better understanding of their reactions after the Brexit vote. We find that losers' consent was driven by an interplay of emotions, cognition, and moderation. Those losers who recognized the legitimacy of the Brexit vote included two groups: sophisticated citizens capable of overcoming their frustration, and less-informed late deciders whose moderation contributed to their consent. Finally, we discuss the connection between these findings and the campaign. The habit of the British politicians of scapegoating the EU and the de-risking strategy of the Leave camp both facilitated the rallying of a group of losers. We conclude with the implications of our findings for the Brexit outcome and the sources of democratic regime stability.

LOSERS' CONSENT: WHAT DO WE KNOW WELL AND LESS WELL?

The concept of losers' consent is the focus of a significant body of literature. Some of these studies argue that the phenomenon expresses diffuse support for the electoral process and not necessarily for the winner of a particular election (Dahl 1989; Przeworski 1991; Esaiasson 2011). As Coleman (1988, 197) puts it, 'consenting to a process is not the same thing as consenting to the outcome of the process'.[2] Others study the contexts in which losers' consent would be easier to obtain (Anderson and Guillori 1997; Banducci and Karp 2003; Anderson et al. 2005; Curini, Jue, and Memoli 2011; Howell and Justwan 2013; Rich and Treece 2018), or where the absence of certain conditions could lead to challenging the electoral practices (Anderson and Tverdova 2001; Anderson and Mendes 2006; Moehler 2009). These studies imply that voters experience election outcomes with varying degrees of intensity depending on the institutional context. For instance, outcomes in more consensual, proportional regimes are experienced differently from those in presidential or majority regimes with a 'winner-takes-all' approach (Anderson and Guillori 1997; Anderson and LoTempio 2002; Anderson et al. 2005). Emerging democracies where the aftermath is sometimes uncertain are distinct from well-established ones where today's losers can be reasonably confident of being tomorrow's winners (Przeworski 1991; Anderson and Tverdova 2001; Anderson et al. 2005; Anderson and Mendes 2006; Moehler 2009; Rich 2015; Rich and Treece 2018). Having a narrowly decided winner is different from having a decisive winner (Howell and Justwan 2013). And finally, whether or not the victory is compensated for or amplified by a similar experience at the national or local/regional level makes a difference (Loewen and Blais 2006; Blais and Gélineau 2007; Singh, Karakoç, and Blais 2012).

The motivations of winners and losers also affect the degree of consent. A first approach explains the reaction of winners and losers in utilitarian terms. According to this logic, 'winners are happier because the parties that represent their views and interests are now in government and their preferences are likely to be enacted' (Singh, Karakoç, and Blais 2012, 202). From this perspective, the intensity of individuals' post-election reaction is related to their ideological distance from the winner (Anderson et al. 2005; Brunell and Buchler 2009; Curini, Jue, and Memoli 2011, Esaiasson 2011; Ezrow and Xezonakis 2011; Kim 2009; Singh, Lago, and Blais, 2012). A second approach is inspired by work that is grounded in people's key motivation to maintain consistency in their beliefs and attitudes (Anderson et al. 2005; Beggan and Allison 1993; Festinger 1957; Funder and Colvin 1991; Granberg 1993; McGuire 1968). The losers, in a state of 'post-election dissonance' (Cigler and Getter 1977; Frenkel and Doob 1976; Regan and Kilduff 1988; Joslyn 1998), re-establish a balance by devaluing the process that led to the rejection of their favourite candidate, while the winners find even more virtues in the process (Anderson and LoTempio 2002; Anderson et al. 2005; Craig et al. 2006). A third approach is based on the emotions generated by the experiences of victory and defeat. The experience of victory generates positive feelings (Atkinson 1957; McClelland 1987; Thaler 1994), whereas defeat produces negative emotions like anger and frustration (Anderson et al. 2005, 23–6; Esaiasson 2011; Singh, Karakoç, and Blais 2012). Therefore, a victory produces psychological benefits unrelated to policy considerations, which induces winners to show increased support for democratic institutions, while defeat incites the opposite reaction among the losers.

But there are limitations in this body of research. The first concerns the variable used to study the rallying of losers. As Rich (2015, 245) points out, there is little consensus on how to measure 'losers' consent other than the expectation of a divergence of opinion on democratic institutions between winners and losers'. (See also Rich and Treece 2018, 418.) Measures such as satisfaction with democracy or confidence in institutions are useful because they enable comparative studies to be carried out. (See here, in particular, Anderson et al. 2005.) Yet the central phenomenon remains the rallying of 'graceful' losers, which is crucial to ensure the stability of democratic institutions. More direct measures of this rallying should be used if we are to shed light on one of the most important phenomena in a democratic system.[3]

Another shortcoming of the existing work is the tendency to consider winners and losers as homogeneous groups. This practice is often justified by the shared experience of defeat or victory. However, it conceals the key phenomenon behind losers' consent. The fact that some studies have distinguished between different groups of winners and losers is a step in the right direction (Singh, Lago, and Blais 2011; Singh, Karakoç, and Blais 2012). Nonetheless, the main task is to distinguish the two groups of losers – those who recognize the legitimacy of a vote decision and those who challenge it – and to examine the profile and motivations of each group. In other words, we must return to the spirit of the question raised by Anderson and Mendes (2006, 92): 'Why are some losers more discontented than others to the point of contesting the legitimacy of an electoral outcome?'

A third weakness is that 'progress still needs to be made in identifying the individual-level processes that account for graceful or *voluntarily accepted* losing' (Craig et al. 2006, 579). While important work has been done on this issue, the focus remains on the study of contextual factors that may affect the magnitude of the winner-loser gap (e.g., Esaiasson 2011; Singh, Karakoç, and Blais 2012; Howell and Justwan 2013; Rich 2015; Rich and Treece 2018). The systematic study of the individual-level factors of losers' consent remains more limited. The effect of certain determinants such as emotions on losers' perceptions has been rarely studied, although it is often cited as a factor that may facilitate or hinder consent (Anderson et al. 2005, 25–6; Esaiasson 2011, 102–3; Singh, Karakoç, and Blais 2012).

A final limitation of the literature is privileging the 'normal' electoral context in a case study. This choice is easily justified. An election to choose the party or candidate who will run the government is the normal, if not essential, expression of the democratic process. For Przeworski (1991, 10), democracy is a 'system in which parties lose elections' and 'where competition creates periodic winners and losers'. It is this cyclical character that makes defeat more palatable and allows the losers to put the experience into perspective and mitigate its scope. Accepting defeat is more of a problem in emerging democracies, as has been demonstrated for Eastern Europe (Anderson and Tverdova 2001), Latin America (Anderson and Mendes 2006), Africa (Moehler 2009), and Asia (Rich 2015).

Brexit is one of those circumstances in which the rallying of the losers was difficult, as evidenced by the post-Brexit trauma that British politics has been experiencing. Very few studies have examined losers' consent in referendums. What is more, in the literature on EU referendums, this aspect has been only partially and indirectly brought up, in the context of its absence when national referendums are held selectively as opposed to EU-wide referendums (Rose and Borz 2013); in terms of the policy implications of these votes (Hobolt 2006a); in relation to the temporary politicization of the EU issue in referendum campaigns where voters quickly revert back to their previous opinions after the vote (Atikcan 2015a); and, finally, in the context of repeated referendums, where voters are asked to vote for a second time on the same question (Atikcan 2015b). No work has directly addressed this phenomenon despite the widespread consequences of EU referendums.

For these reasons, studying losers' consent in the Brexit referendum is particularly important. Our approach is guided by two hypotheses derived from the literature. First, it seems reasonable to believe that graceful losers hold more moderate views (or less intense preferences vis-à-vis the object of the vote decision) than do sore losers (Anderson et al. 2005; Brunell and Buchler 2009; Curini, Jou, and Memoli 2011; Esaiasson 2011; Ezrow and Xezonakis 2011; Kim 2009; Singh, Karakoç, and Blais 2012). Less intense or less passionate preferences should make consent easier and lead to higher levels of political support, since post-electoral dissonance is less pronounced among voters experiencing a lower loss of utility and lower level of anger. Second, it also seems reasonable to expect graceful losers to be more sophisticated than sore losers. Losers' consent is based on abstract principles (Coleman 1988; Dahl 1989; Esaiasson 2011; Przeworski 1991) that are more commonly shared among sophisticated individuals (Delli Carpini and Keeter 1996; Lupia and McCubbins 1998; Sniderman, Brody, and Tetlock 1991; Zaller 1992). The firmness and accessibility of sophisticated losers' views about democratic principles should facilitate their rallying after a defeat and contribute to maintaining their faith in democratic principles. Based on these expectations, we first determine if the level of satisfaction with democracy was indeed significantly higher for graceful losers than for sore losers after the Brexit referendum. We then look at whether the attitudinal profiles of these groups differ, with the expectation that graceful losers are more moderate and sophisticated than sore losers. Finally, we link these findings to the core argument of the book and explain why British politicians' habit of scapegoating the EU, along with the Leave camp's strategy of 'de-risking', may have facilitated the post-referendum rallying of a key group of losers.

DISTINGUISHING BETWEEN SORE AND GRACEFUL LOSERS

With the clear division of its camps and the irreversibility of its consequences, the Brexit referendum offers an interesting setting in which to study losers' consent. Added to these characteristics is the tightness of the result. The closeness of the referendum vote makes it even more difficult to rally the losers and easily lends support to disputing the result (Howell and Justwan 2013).[4]

Picking a good context is important, but picking the right question to study losers' consent is also crucial. Most studies focusing on winners and losers examine the attitudes of both groups toward democratic process and institutions following an election (Anderson et al. 2005). A second approach, much less used, is to ask respondents directly about the legitimacy of the winning camp's victory and then to examine the profile of 'graceful losers'.[5] To overcome the shortcomings of the existing work, we adopt this second approach.

The survey question used to measure the perception of the result's legitimacy is the following: 'Do you think that the government should accept the result of the referendum and that the UK should leave the

European Union or do you think that the government should not accept the result of the referendum and that a second referendum should be held on this question?'[6] Unsurprisingly, no less than 93 per cent of Leave supporters responded that the government should accept the result (table 6.1). But the most important finding lies in the reaction of the losers. The figures show that 37 per cent of losers believed the day after the Brexit referendum that the government had to accept the result and that the UK therefore had to leave the European Union (table 6.1). This means that almost two out of three losers refused to endorse the result, either because they objected to it (53 per cent) or were undecided (10 per cent) about it.[7]

The rallying of losers was particularly important in this instance because the Leave camp's support was only slightly higher (51.9 per cent) than the required (or procedural) majority to win. However, the democratic majority – in favour of accepting the result – reached 65 per cent (table 6.1) and far exceeded the procedural majority. Our data show that this figure comprised not only the massive coalition of winners (73 per cent of the democratic majority) but also a significant number of losers, who make up more than a quarter (27 per cent) of this group. It is clear that the stability of the UK's democratic regime is based much more on the expression of this majority and not only on the support expressed by the winners of the Brexit referendum, who are only slightly more numerous than its losers.

There are therefore not just two key groups after an election (i.e., 'winners' and 'losers') but rather three: 'winners', overwhelmingly satisfied with the result; 'sore losers', who refuse to recognize the legitimacy of the outcome; and 'graceful losers', who comply with the procedural rules.[8] The data in tables 6.2 and 6.3 indeed show the importance of distinguishing between these three groups. Grouping respondents into homogeneous blocks in table 6.2 leads to the oft-cited conclusion that satisfaction with democracy is higher among winners (52 per cent) than among losers (45 per cent). The results of table 6.3 change this interpretation by showing that the level of satisfaction with democracy among graceful losers (57 per cent) is not lower but in fact slightly higher than that of winners (52 per cent).[9] The twenty-point gap for the same variable (57 per cent versus 37 per cent) between 'sore' and 'graceful' losers is striking and confirms that the crucial distinction after an election is indeed between 'sore' and 'graceful' losers.

Does this distinction hold also in a multivariate model? The literature on the determinants of satisfaction with democracy offers

158 Framing Risky Choices

Table 6.1
Reactions to the Brexit referendum result

| | Vote | | *Government should accept the result?* | | |
			All	*Winners*	*Losers*
Leave	52	Yes	65	93	37
Remain	48	No/DK	35	7	63

Note: The vote column represents the official results (rounded) of the Brexit referendum.

Q: Do you think that the government should accept the result of the referendum and that the UK should leave the European Union or do you think that the government should not accept the result of the referendum and that a second referendum should be held on this question?

Table 6.2
Satisfaction with UK democracy and the Leave vote:
Losers versus winners

	Losers	*Winners*
Satisfied	45	52
Neither satisfied, nor unsatisfied	16	16
Unsatisfied	39	32
N	573	684
Pearson χ^2	12.33 (.015)	
Gamma	.13 (.003)	

Note: Entries are column percentages. Winners correspond to respondents who voted to Leave the EU; Losers correspond to respondents who voted to Remain in the EU and agree that the government should accept the result of the referendum or to those who voted to Remain in the EU and agree that the government should hold a second referendum or don't know.

Q: On a scale of 1 to 5, how satisfied are you with the way that democracy works in the UK (1 = very dissatisfied to 5 = very satisfied). Scores are categorized as follows: 1 and 2 = unsatisfied; 3 = neither satisfied nor unsatisfied; 4 and 5 = satisfied.

important insights into the specification of an adequate model for this variable. Previous studies show that, besides the winning/losing experience, satisfaction with democracy is linked to citizens' socio-demographic characteristics as well as to their evaluations of politicians' responsiveness (external efficacy) and their perceptions of the ability of the authorities to deliver favourable outcomes, particularly on the economic front (Anderson and Guillori 1997; Anderson et al. 2005; Blais, Morin-Chassé, and Singh 2017; Curini, Jou, and Memoli

Table 6.3
Satisfaction with UK democracy and the Leave vote: Sore/graceful losers versus winners

	Sore losers	*Graceful losers*	*Winners*
Satisfied	37	57	52
Neither unsatisfied nor satisfied	16	16	16
Unsatisfied	47	27	32
N	341	232	684
Pearson χ^2		39.95 (.000)	
Gamma		.15 (.000)	

Notes: Entries are column percentages.
Winners correspond to respondents who voted to Leave the EU; Graceful Losers to respondents who vote to Remain in the EU and agree that the government should accept the result of the referendum; and Sore Losers to those who voted to Remain in the EU and agree that the government should hold a second referendum or don't know.

2011; Ezrow and Xezonakis 2011; Howell and Justwan 2013; Nadeau and Blais 1993; Singh, Karakoç, and Blais 2012). Based on these findings, we use the following explanatory model:[10]

Satisfaction with democracy = f (age, gender, education, income, external efficacy, economic perceptions, winning/losing)

The dependent variable is measured on a five-point scale where 1 indicates being very dissatisfied with the way democracy works in the UK and 5 indicates being very satisfied (all variables are rescaled on a 0 to 1 interval). The results reported in figures 6.1 and 6.2 are based on OLS regressions. (The complete results are available in appendix table A3.2.) We use this technique for the sake of simplicity, but using more complex methods leaves our findings intact. The results of the model presented in figure 6.1 are in line with the existing work on the determinants of satisfaction with democracy. Political support is higher among the better-educated respondents and those expressing higher levels of external efficacy and economic optimism. Also consistent with previous research, the results show that being on the losing camp's side reduces the expressed level of satisfaction with democracy.

The most revealing results, however, are presented in figure 6.2. These results show that winners and graceful losers are not that different from one another when it comes to democratic satisfaction; the difference between the two groups is not statistically significant (coefficient = .01, t =.40). The opposite is true for winners and sore losers: these two groups are easily separable from one another. In this case, the difference in the level of satisfaction with democracy is noticeable (−.08) and statistically significant (t = 4.1). The magnitude of this impact is twice as important as the traditional winner-loser gap (−.08 vs. −.04). In other words, the real distinction is not between winners and losers but between winners and sore losers. This result underlines the importance of graceful losers for the stability of democratic institutions. Contrary to sore losers, graceful losers accept electoral outcomes and retain a high level of confidence in the democratic process. It is thus important to better understand who they are and why they comply gracefully with the democratic will after elections.

WHO ARE THE GRACEFUL LOSERS AND WHY DO THEY GRACEFULLY ACCEPT DEFEAT?

Once again, the extant literature on the reactions of winners and losers offers some clues on how to model the decision-making process of graceful losers. Socioeconomic variables are commonly found in such models and are included here as controls (e.g., Curini, Jue, and Memoli 2011; Howell and Justwan 2013; Rich 2015; Rich and Treece 2018; Singh, Karakoç, and Blais 2012). But our main interest lies in the impact of attitudinal and behavioural variables on losers' consent. Many studies have highlighted the impact of emotions on political behaviour (Marcus and MacKuen 1993; Marcus, Neuman, and MacKuen 2000; Nadeau, Niemi, and Amato 1995; Neuman et al. 2007). In particular, emotions caused by defeat are often presented as an important factor explaining voters' reactions after an election (Anderson et al. 2005, 25–6; Esaiasson 2011, 101; Singh, Karakoç, and Blais 2012, 202). Yet the link between emotions and losers' consent has not been clearly established to date. Following Anderson and colleagues (2005, 25), we agree that 'losing leads to anger' and include in our model a variable tapping into this emotional reaction with the expectation that graceful losers' emotional reaction to their defeat will be less intense than is the case for sore losers.

Previous work has also shown that losers' consent rests on the ability of individuals to make a distinction between the electoral process and the specific outcomes it produces (Dahl 1989; Esaiasson 2011; Przeworski 1991). Empirical work has shown that sophisticated citizens are more apt to handle this kind of distinction between abstract

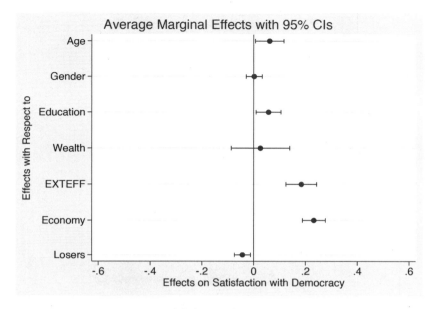

Figure 6.1 Linear regression models for satisfaction with democracy in the UK (losers and winners)

concepts like procedural fairness and concrete electoral outcomes. Since factual knowledge is recognized as the best indicator of citizens' level of political sophistication (Nadeau et al. 2008; Price and Zaller 1993; Zaller 1992), we expect that more politically cognizant losers will be better able to master the principles that drive the democratic process and hence will be more likely to accept defeat.

Losers' reactions similarly depend on individuals' perceived loss of utility and need to maintain consistency between their attitudes, opinions, and behaviours. Consequently, voters with moderate views (sharing part of their opponents' views) will more easily accept their defeat, as they will suffer a smaller loss of utility and find it easier to maintain cognitive consonance. In the Brexit case, moderate Remain supporters who are more attached to the UK than to Europe, or those who believe that the EU is too centralized, would be more likely to accept the Leave camp's victory. Another indicator of voters' moderation and ambivalence is the timing of their voting decision. A late voting decision is often related to an inability to decide between options that seem equally acceptable and thus remain in the balance until the very end of the campaign (Lavine 2001; Willocq 2019),

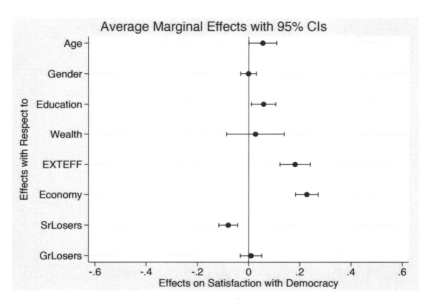

Figure 6.2 Linear regression models for satisfaction with democracy in the UK (sore losers, graceful losers, and winners)

something that is likely to make post-election rallying easier. A late decision can also reflect lesser interest vis-à-vis the electoral campaign and the issues being debated (Gopoian and Hadjiharalambous 1994). These two possible states of mind – ambivalence or indifference – can each explain why 'late deciders' may be more inclined to accept the referendum's outcome.

In brief, we hypothesize that graceful losers, compared to sore losers, would be less emotionally engaged in the Brexit debate, more politically sophisticated, more critical of the EU, and more inclined to make their voting decision close to polling day. The results presented in table 6.4, which offer descriptive information about the characteristics of winners, graceful losers, and sore losers, corroborate these expectations. To begin with, emotional reactions to the referendum outcome are measured on a scale from 1 to 5 (rescaled from 0 to 1) where the minimum value means being very angry about the result and the maximum means being very happy with it. The results in the first row of table 6.4 (Happy (Leave)) show the intense satisfaction of the winners and the profound anger of the sore losers. The figures also reflect the graceful losers' obvious disappointment after the defeat of the Remain campaign. The intensity of their emotional reaction, however, is less pronounced than that of the sore losers.

To assess whether graceful losers were indeed more politically sophisticated than sore losers, we used a factual knowledge scale including four items about the EU.[11] The results in the second row of table 6.4 (Information) show that graceful losers indeed stand out as more politically cognizant than sore losers (and slightly more so than winners). In terms of their feelings toward the EU, the figures in the third row (Attach UK-EU) measure voters' relative attachment to the UK and the EU and those in the fourth row (Centralization) tap into their opinion on whether too many issues are decided on by the European Union. As expected, the results in both cases show that graceful losers express more moderate opinions on these questions than do sore losers. Finally, concerning the timing of the vote decision, the higher score in the last row (Late deciders) confirms that graceful losers were more likely to make their decision later than the others (in the final week or on polling day).

To go beyond these descriptive statistics, we ran a multinomial regression, the most appropriate method to use with a categorical dependent variable (Greene 2003). Our model includes socio-demographic variables as well as our attitudinal and behavioural variables (Emotion, Information, Attachment (UK-EU), Centralization and Timing of Decision).[12] Given that our main interest lies in the comparison of the two groups of losers, the category 'sore losers' forms the omitted category in this estimation. The overall explanatory model can be expressed in equation form as follows:

Graceful losing = f (age, gender, education, income, emotion, information, centralization, attachment, late decision)

The value of the pseudo-R^2 (.73) indicates the good overall performance of the model (see table A3.3). Marginal average effects measuring the effect of explanatory variables on the probability of being winners, graceful losers, or sore losers are presented in figure 6.3. These results show that socioeconomic variables are not very useful in distinguishing between our three groups of voters,[13] but this is not the case for the other variables. Unsurprisingly, the strongest contrast is observed between winners and sore losers. The effects of the

Table 6.4
Descriptive statistics for winners, graceful losers, and sore losers

	Winners	Graceful losers	Sore losers
Happy (Leave)	.78 (.21)	.34 (.26)	.18 (.24)
Information (EU)	.56 (.27)	.57 (.28)	.50 (.28)
Attach (UK–EU)	.83 (.17)	.60 (.17)	.50 (.17)
EU too centralized	.96 (.14)	.74 (.29)	.56 (.28)
Late deciders	.30 (.29)	.35 (.30)	.25 (.26)
N	684	232	341

Note: Entries are means with standard errors in parentheses. See appendix for more details about the coding of the variable.

variables Emotion, Attachment, and Centralization tell us that these two groups are noticeably different from each other in terms of both their positions on the EU and their emotional reaction to the victory of the Leave option.

These findings stress the importance of distinguishing between graceful and sore losers to better understand the distribution of political support among the various groups of voters after Brexit. But why were the graceful losers more willing than sore losers to accept the outcome? The results presented in figure 6.3 offer interesting hints. It clearly appears that the emotional reaction of graceful losers to their defeat was less intense than was the case for sore losers. Furthermore, the results for the Information variable signal that graceful losers' higher level of sophistication may have propelled them to use democratic principles in forming their opinion about the legitimacy of the referendum's outcome and hence made them more likely to accept their defeat.

Finally, the last three variables imply that graceful losers were driven by contradictory feelings when faced with the options on the table. These variables may be interpreted as reflecting the state of mind of 'cross-pressured voters,' who were either ambivalent about the different options (Alvarez and Brehm 2002; Zaller 1992) or simply had a moderate opinion on the UK's membership in the EU. For instance, the positive effect for the Attachment and Centralization variables signals that graceful losers were less attached to the EU and more prone than the sore losers to think that it decides on too many issues. Holding these mixed, more moderate views about the EU may also explain why graceful losers made up their mind on this question later than sore losers did.[14]

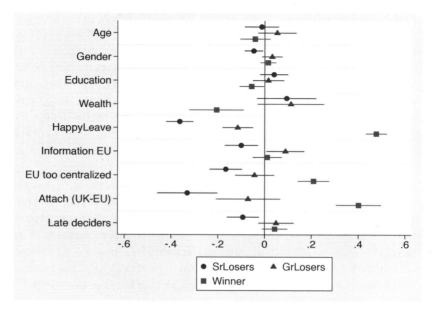

Figure 6.3 Average marginal effects of anchor variables, attitudes toward the EU, information, timing of decision, and emotions: model of winners, sore losers, and graceful losers

CONCLUSION: SCAPEGOATING, DE-RISKING, AND LOSERS' CONSENT

Did the campaign ground and the strategies of the two sides play any role in facilitating the losers' consent? The detailed profiles of the graceful and sore losers are important in answering this question. First, the tradition of scapegoating the EU for unpopular domestic measures has contributed to lukewarm attitudes toward European integration. In the Brexit campaign, the Leave side openly capitalized on these attitudes and the resentment toward the bureaucracy in Brussels. Second, the Leave side reframed the parameters of the debate by focusing on the political rather than economic risks of exiting the EU. This reframing was done via a good reading of public opinion, particularly on the issue of immigration and the resulting high appeal of their campaign arguments. As chapters 4 and 5 showed in detail, this political framing ultimately convinced a sufficient number of hesitant citizens to vote Leave. But this framing arguably had an impact even on some Remain voters, making defeat more acceptable to a significant proportion of losers. In other words, the campaign appears to have paved the way for the rallying of many losers by leading them to believe that the UK may not have lost so much by leaving the EU and perhaps may even gain something by taking the Brexit route. Our findings indeed show that some voters supported the Remain camp while expressing mixed feelings about the EU. More specifically, graceful losers have a limited attachment to the EU, and many dislike its excessive centralization. This reserve of moderate Remain voters undoubtedly explains why some people may have voted to remain in the EU but found the concept of Brexit potentially palatable.

This conclusion has implications for the existing studies of losers' consent. The winner-loser gap is traditionally theorized as representing the expression of post-electoral attitudes, suggesting that these reactions are mainly outcome driven. Our results reveal more factors at play. Both short-term factors such as the campaign process and long-term factors such as individuals' views on democratic principles shape these reactions. In terms of the campaign, consent was easier for 'soft' Remain supporters who were more critical of the EU, less emotionally engaged in the debate, and more optimistic about the consequences of a Leave victory, and were torn between the two options until the end of the campaign. But long-term factors also matter. Our findings show that graceful losers are politically involved, principled citizens who are more inclined to judge the merits of democracy in procedural terms. They will accept the result of a vote decision unless they have strong reasons to believe that the process that produced this outcome was flawed. For instance, it is revealing that the level of satisfaction with democracy for graceful losers is on par with the level observed for winners. The importance of this type of loser for the stability of democratic institutions cannot be overstated. The fact that a large number of voters ended up accepting their defeat is one comforting outcome of the Brexit referendum and a testament to the vitality of democratic principles in the British electorate.

Nonetheless, the phenomenon of losers' consent has become only more salient as Brexit negotiations have unfolded. The defeats in the House of Commons in 2019 of the exit deals of both Prime Minister May and Prime Minister Johnson were paralleled by an apparent rise in the number of people wishing for a second referendum – a second say on the matter. Based on this chapter's findings, it would make sense to expect that the degree of acceptance of the Brexit outcome since 2016 may have declined the most among ambivalent Remain supporters, especially those who were torn between the two options and were optimistic about the consequences of the Leave victory. These developments certainly underline the necessity in future research of studying the phenomenon of losers' consent not only as one grounded in long-standing adhesion to democratic principles but also as an ongoing process.

7

Arguing for and against Borders

Of all the talents bestowed upon men, none is so precious as the gift of oratory. He who enjoys it wields a power more durable than that of a great king ... A meeting of grave citizens, protected by all the cynicism of these prosaic days, is unable to resist its influence. From unresponsive silence they advance to grudging approval and thence to complete agreement with the speaker. The cheers become louder and more frequent; the enthusiasm momentarily increases; until they are convulsed by emotions they are unable to control and shaken by passions of which they have resigned the direction ... The climax of oratory is reached by a rapid succession of waves of sound and vivid pictures ... An apt analogy ... appeals to the everyday knowledge of the hearer and invites him to decide the problems that have baffled his powers of reason by the standard of the nursery and the heart. Argument by analogy leads to conviction rather than to proof, and has often led to glaring error.[1]

Winston Churchill

The argument for the "gift of oratory" is convincing coming from Winston Churchill, whose speeches during the Second World War 'mobilized the English language and sent it into battle'.[2] Our research for this book demonstrates that strategic arguments, even when they advocate drastic and costly change, can have an impact on public opinion. Voters usually resent change, and defenders of the status quo have won in most referendums to date. In spite of the split polls, everyone thought that this would be the outcome in the Brexit case as well and that the status quo bias would motivate enough voters for a narrow result in favour of remaining in the EU. Yet a critical group of the British public defied this rule and voted to take a major economic risk. The Remain side played its seemingly strong hand inefficiently, whereas the Leave side de-risked the change option and carried the public away from the expected 'safety' of the status quo. The pro-Leave arguments mobilized the British public with vivid imagery and analogies presenting Britain as 'shackled to the corpse of Europe', promising to reclaim the '£350 million' sent to Europe each week and urging the public to 'Take Back Control'. These arguments resonated with the 'everyday knowledge' of the public and touched a chord that was latent but already sensitive. In redefining whether or not the vote was risky, these arguments made it easier for a critical section of British society to vote for an uncertain future outside the EU.

Campaigns tend to affect voting behaviour more in referendums than in elections. For that reason, paying close attention to the political dynamics of referendums and campaign argumentation strategies is crucial in understanding referendum results. How does the way in which the Brexit campaign was run compare to that of other referendums? What did the Leave campaigners do differently? Relying on a unique dataset of over 150 face-to-face interviews with campaigners in Scotland and England and across Europe, and detailing the 'kit' of strategies most frequently used in EU and independence referendums, this book shows that the Brexit campaign decisions were primarily based on a simple referendum logic that included appealing to middle-ground undecided voters and activating or muting the status quo bias. Both the Remain and Leave campaigns tried to reach unsure soft voters and to appeal to voters' feelings about the risks of the choice. But the Leave side's specific *framing choices* saved them from mistakes that others have often made.

In comparison with EU referendum strategies, the Remain side ran its campaign on the economic costs of Brexit, which is the usual strength of pro-EU campaigns. But the Leave side responded exceptionally well to those arguments and placed diverse and potent risks of remaining in the EU on the agenda. They did so while maintaining a non-extremist profile, a typical difficulty for anti-EU campaigners. What is more, in EU referendums, the usual advantage of the No campaigners, when combined with the public's lack of information on the complexities of the European Union, can turn into a strong advantage for anti-EU campaigners. Our data demonstrate that the Leave side fully benefitted from these factors.

In comparison with the Scottish referendum, on the other hand, the key question is how the Leave side's campaign avoided the quintessential problem in independence referendums of economic fears trumping national identity. The Scottish referendum is especially comparable to the Brexit case because the Remain side pitched its campaign entirely on economic fears and was blamed for running 'Project Fear' – just as the Better Together campaign was. A few differences stand out in the interview data, however. While the Better Together campaign responded to the Yes Scotland campaign with a 'change' argument that proposed increased devolution, the Remain side did not adjust its strategy to counter the Leave campaign claims. Similarly, although the economic viability of Scotland remained a constant question in the minds of Scottish voters, the Leave campaigners were not bothered by the same concerns, since the UK had been an independent entity prior to its membership of the EU. The Leave side thus had an easier time in de-risking the Remain campaign's economic arguments than the Yes Scotland campaign did. A striking example here is the Leave camp's deliberate decision not to produce a detailed and concrete exit plan, in clear contrast with the Scottish government's strategy, which caused them much trouble in their pro-independence campaign. The importance of this particular decision was demonstrated by the difficulties both Prime Minister May and Prime Minister Johnson had in having their exit plans accepted by the House of Commons.

The book advances its argument step by step by employing a multi-method approach, relying on in-depth interviews, media content analysis, and a detailed post-referendum survey. The interview data are presented in two parts. First, the two sides began the campaign on an unequal footing. Given the tradition of *scapegoating the EU* in British politics, the Remain side was at a disadvantage from the outset. The Remain campaigners, a part of the British political elite who have never been enthusiastic toward the EU, did not feel comfortable promoting or defending it in a positive light. Conversely, this ambivalence offered the Leave camp an important shortcut – 'the undemocratic and costly Brussels'– which resonated instantly with the voters. This tradition set the stage for the campaign by structuring the choices available to the two sides. Second, as the campaign unfolded, the Leave camp effectively *de-risked a departure from the status quo*. The Leave campaign was more strategic in its choices, combining a core campaign on sovereignty and economy with a separate campaign on immigration. The Leave camp also successfully increased the number of dimensions in the debate, arguing that there would also be risks relating to remaining in the EU, including losing control of immigration policy and the NHS. The Remain side remained silent on these key issues and left the stage to the Leave side.

These strategies are also clearly visible in the media analysis. In line with the habit of *scapegoating the EU*, the Leave side was louder in the media than the Remain side. The Leave side was also very active in *de-risking the Brexit decision*. The two 'Project Fears', one on immigration and one on the economy, were mirrored in the news media. The data show that the pro-Leave sources not only ran their 'Project Fear' on the controversial issue of immigration but also became actively involved in the discussion on the economy, pitching their own 'Project Fear' on the topic. The pro-Remain sources were much less vocal in questioning the contentious issue of immigration.

The survey data in turn show that both the long-term scapegoating of the EU and the Leave side's specific campaign strategies to de-risk the Brexit decision had an impact on voting behaviour. The habit of scapegoating the EU reflected critical attitudes toward Europe in British public opinion and contributed to their spread. The Remain campaign could not promote or defend the EU in a positive light and chose instead to restrict itself to a negative frame on how leaving the EU would make things worse from an economic standpoint. The appeal of the pro-Remain arguments was also significantly undermined by their being advocated by actors such as Prime Minister Cameron, who until the last moment was very critical of the EU. The opposite was true for the Leave campaign; this tradition of presenting the EU in a negative light provided the Leave camp with the pre-existing and potent concept of 'undemocratic bureaucrats in Brussels'. Wrapping their campaign around this key theme helped the Leave camp considerably. To take a specific example, statistical analyses find that the Leave campaign was successful in persuading citizens holding moderate views on the EU to support the Brexit option, which the interview data show to be one of their core campaign strategies. For instance, 45 per cent of British voters believed that EU membership was globally beneficial for their country, compared to only 31 per cent holding the opposite view. Not surprisingly, support for the Remain option was massive among the first group (84 per cent) and very weak among the second group (8 per cent). But the real surprise came from the significant group of voters (25 per cent) holding mixed views about the contribution of the EU to their country. Among this key group, no less than 70 per cent chose to support the Leave option. Moreover, our data show that although long-term attitudes played a significant role in the voting decision of early deciders, these attitudes mattered less in explaining the decision of the pivotal group of late deciders, confirming the influence of the campaign on the referendum outcome.

The evidence is also overwhelming that the Leave side dominated the referendum campaign and *de-risked the choice*. Strongly confirming the interviews once again, detailed survey data demonstrate that the Leave side indeed reframed the choice and shifted the debate from the economy to sovereignty. Importantly, statistical analyses show that the Leave side prevailed over the Remain side in many aspects of the campaign: global perceptions of the campaign, opinions on the key campaign arguments, the image of the leaders, the role of emotions, and risk perceptions. The Leave side's messages on immigration and NHS funding provided a strong counterpoint to the Remain campaign's arguments on the economic costs of Brexit. Adding campaign-related variables to traditional voting models based on long-term factors increases their explanatory power. Our findings signal that these variables on campaign strategies were in fact more important for the vote choice of moderate/hesitant voters who made their choice later in the campaign – confirming the variables' contribution to the Brexit decision.

This research thus studies both how the long-term habit of scapegoating the EU set the stage for the campaign and how specific campaign strategies and arguments contributed to the final outcome. As such, instead of simply naming the long-term and short-term factors that affected the vote choice and listing the campaign as one of the variables, this book clarifies how these two sets of factors interacted in bringing about the Brexit decision. First and foremost, these two sets of factors affected the vote choice of early- and late-deciders differently. Moreover, long-term factors such as the existing Euroscepticism in the UK do not by themselves explain the referendum outcome. Campaigners determined which of these long-term views would become relevant for the vote choice and which would remain dormant. Nevertheless, the tradition of presenting the EU in a negative light and the resulting lukewarm public attitudes to the EU offered the Leave side an important toolkit, which it then fully mobilized.

Moving on to the question of the Brexit vote's legitimacy, which occupied the subsequent agenda as much as the result itself, this research also reveals why some Remain voters accepted the Brexit outcome and others did not. In the aftermath of the Brexit vote, more than 4.1 million citizens signed a petition calling for a second referendum on EU membership, based this time on new rules in terms of the majority (60 per cent) and the turnout (75 per cent) required to act on the result. Their hopes faded when the UK government declared the referendum of 23 June 2016 'a once in a generation vote'. Millions of citizens, most likely Remain supporters, refused to concede victory, yet the British government rejected the request for a second referendum, confident that a large majority of citizens, including a good proportion of the losers, would accept the referendum's outcome.

A close look at the profile and motivations of the crucial group of Remain supporters who accepted the Leave victory uncovers a critical and unstudied aspect of the Brexit outcome. Losers' consent was driven by the interplay of emotions, cognitions, and moderation; the losers who recognized the legitimacy of the Brexit vote consisted of both sophisticated citizens capable of overcoming their frustration and a group of less-informed late deciders whose moderation facilitated their rallying. Interestingly, this finding implies that the de-risking strategy of the Leave camp also facilitated the rallying of a group of losers.

UNCOVERING NEW THEORETICAL GROUND

A New Kind of Referendum

In asking the public directly about their country's membership in the EU, Brexit represented a new kind of referendum. Although there are two precedents, one in the UK in 1975 and another in Greenland in 1982, European integration has since changed drastically. Today, it resembles a state with decision-making powers on key issue areas such as immigration and currency. That is why in today's EU an exit referendum brings together two kinds of previously unconnected referendums: referendums on EU questions and those on independence.

The role of the Brexit campaign on the outcome has been examined time and time again. This book advances what we already know on the Brexit referendum by providing a comprehensive and nuanced understanding of how the campaign differed from previous referendum campaigns and how these differences likely contributed to its unexpected outcome. It makes four important contributions to the study of this new kind of referendum: by comparing the Brexit campaign to other kinds of similar referendums in the world, by paying close attention to the political dynamics of referendums, by assessing the impact of certain kinds of arguments, and by employing a multi-method approach using three different kinds of data.

First, placing the Brexit referendum within a comparative perspective allows us to grasp whether this new kind of vote is unique or not and to see exactly where its dynamics differed from those of EU and independence referendums. This understanding is crucial to building a more generalizable perspective in analysing this new kind of referendum. Second, referendums generate a specific type of campaign. This research delves deep into the political dynamics of referendums and extracts the most frequently used strategies in different kinds of referendums, while bringing together findings of the recent research on how successful these strategies were in shaping referendum results. This 'kit' will undoubtedly be valuable for future research on referendums. Third, some political arguments matter more than others, an insight of utmost importance when it comes to referendum campaigns, which are often more influential than election campaigns. By detailing the kinds of arguments that appeal to the public in different contexts, and by combining the findings on political psychology and social movements, this research offers a more complete understanding of the campaign framing process. Direct democracy is becoming more prominent in many countries and regions, making it all the more important that we understand the complexities of direct appeals in the context of referendums. Fourth, this research offers a systematic, multi-method analysis of the campaign, building its argument step by step, beginning with in-depth interviews with campaign strategists to reveal the reasoning behind the key campaign choices and messages, then moving on to media content analysis to assess the degree to which these messages were picked up by the news media, and concluding the analysis with survey data including experimental questions to understand how these messages contributed to the vote choice – a combination much needed in the literature. Future research could take this multi-method approach further by adding detailed measures of campaign exposure and survey experiments that compare the status of public opinion before and after the campaign.

By paying attention to these four overlooked aspects, this research advances our understanding of political campaigns in EU and non-EU referendums as well as in elections. The 'kit' of referendum strategies we develop has implications that go beyond EU campaigns. By comparing the different kinds of political communication strategies used by different camps (pro/anti-EU and pro/anti-independence) and their relative strength in different contexts, this analysis offers a valuable building block for similar analyses of other kinds of referendums and elections. What are the particular advantages of being in favour of or against the proposals? Which kinds of strategies are the winning ones in EU referendums? How do these strategies compare to the ones in independence referendums? To what extent have campaigners in independence referendums learned from the experience of EU referendums? Which kinds of factors matter for the success of these campaign strategies?

Moreover, in studying the political communication of an essential trade-off in today's globalizing world, the benefits of economic integration versus the loss of national decision-making power, this book encourages a conversation between nationalism and international political economy literatures. In an increasingly interdependent world, there will unquestionably be more referendums asking for the public's support for further international cooperation. Until what point can integration projects ask its members to cede national autonomy? Would the public's tolerance of such losses depend on the specific domain of international cooperation? Is the public genuinely having a shift of values and turning its back on globalization, or is this apparent shift a matter of political framing? These questions will undoubtedly form a fruitful research agenda in the near future.

A New Perspective on the Status Quo Bias

This book offers important insights into how voters make a choice when they face a decision invoking a significant degree of risk. Because of the apparent inclination of voters to err on the side of caution when confronted with these types of risky choices, scholars have paid a great deal of attention to the factors that explain why the status quo tends to prevail in high-stakes votes. The Leave camp's victory thus offers an opportunity for gaining greater insight into how and why proponents of radical political change can sometimes overcome the status quo bias and carry the day. Our core findings underline how the Leave camp was able to reorient the debate from the economic losses of leaving the EU to the political costs of staying in it, thereby neutralizing voters' natural aversion to uncertainty.

We also make a key point about the measurement of 'risk', just as we do on the measurement of 'wealth'. To our knowledge, previous research has conceptualized an individual's attitude toward risk as a single trait of personality, neglecting the possibility that the impact of risk-taking on political choices might be domain specific. Our results confirm that such risk aversion varies across different domains. Any future study of status quo bias in high-stakes elections or referendums should pay more attention to the framing of risky political choices and develop domain-specific measures to better understand political risk-taking.

Our research also uncovers new paths for future research by documenting how the interplay between emotions, reason, and moderation has driven the thinking of a critical segment of voters, leading them to vote against the status quo and even to recognize the legitimacy of the Brexit outcome. The role of emotions in the Brexit referendum cannot be overstated. The lack of enthusiasm for the European project, even among its supporters, contributed to the demobilization of its electorate and partly induced the Remain camp to focus its campaign on a narrow, uninspiring, and essentially negative message about the detrimental economic consequences of a departure from the EU. Our data show that this strategic choice proved insufficient for victory. Negative emotions like fear may not always be sufficient to enable the status quo to prevail; positive emotions may also play a role in sustaining voters' desire to keep things as they are. In other words, our results imply that the status quo bias may not necessarily prevent voters from backing radical projects if the campaign representing continuity does not raise deep and intense positive sentiments, at least among a significant segment of the electorate. Future studies should thus consider the limits of the status quo bias in preventing voters from making risky choices when the status quo bias is not reinforced by a certain amount of passion. The Remain camp evidently failed to stir this kind of passion among British voters.

This was not the case for Leave campaigners, who strategically tapped into three types of emotions: positive feelings toward the UK and its political sovereignty, fear of mass immigration, and anger toward the bureaucrats in Brussels. Many interviewees, as well as many observers of the campaign, noted that there was more enthusiasm and hope in pro-Leave arguments than in pro-Remain ones. The Leave side invited voters to 'Take Back Control' of their country; Boris Johnson called on them to celebrate 'Independence day'.[3] Negative sentiments like fear and anger played a role in the Leave camp's victory as well. Our findings provide overwhelming evidence that the fear of further immigration was highly potent for many voters and that the negative sentiments toward 'Brussels bureaucrats' reflected the sheer anger among many voters. As Lerner and Keltner (2001, 146) famously put it, 'angry people express optimistic risk estimates and risk-seeking choices'. In 2015, in a survey asking respondents to choose up to four sentiments they felt toward the EU, almost one person in four (23 per cent) said they were angry or disgusted (Wagner and Vasilopoulou 2016).[4] This important reservoir of voters with extremely negative sentiments toward the EU unquestionably formed a pivotal group in explaining the Brexit outcome.

The status quo bias did not, however, depend on emotions alone; rational arguments were also central to the vote choice. We have documented how the Leave camp was successful in adding dimensions to the Brexit debate. Anti-EU campaigners often benefitted from using *heresthetic*, the art of political strategy (Riker 1986), and thereby gained an important advantage in setting the campaign agenda. The Leave camp was highly strategic in framing the risks attached to the vote, highlighting those concerning immigration and the NHS while diluting those concerning the economy. The success of this framing strategy calls for future research on the clash of similar arguments in other high-stakes elections and referendums. The British electorate worried less about economic risk than voters typically do in independence referendums. In both Quebec and Scotland, voters had to weigh the advantage of more sovereignty for their region against not only the eventual economic costs (not to mention the uncertainty of sharing the same currency with a 'foreign country') but also the disadvantages of no longer being part of a large country and the prestigious G7 international network. The fact that in the British debate the EU was not perceived to provide these benefits may also explain why a critical section of the society ultimately made the calculation that that the UK did not have much to lose by choosing the Brexit route.

The Leave campaign's success in moderating risk perceptions also played an important role in explaining a crucial yet neglected episode of the Brexit story: the rallying of the losers in the aftermath of their defeat. The post-referendum support of the losers was crucial, especially because the Leave side's support was only slightly higher (51.9 per cent) than the required (or procedural) majority (50 per cent + 1) to win. However, a second, much larger majority emerged as soon as the results were announced. The democratic majority in favour of accepting the result brought together 65 per cent of the voters. This group was formed by the quasi-unanimous group of winners (93 per cent) and, more importantly, by a significant proportion of the losers (37 per cent). The Leave camp's particular framing, neutralizing the economic risks of departure from the EU, had an impact on rallying this important segment of moderate Remain supporters and thus consolidating its narrow victory.

A New Perspective on Accepting Democratic Outcomes

Our findings on losers' consent have implications for democratic theory. The literature on voters' post-electoral reactions has largely focused on the distinction between winners and losers. We argue that the critical distinction is not between winners and losers but between graceful and sore losers. After all, losers may or may not choose to recognize the legitimacy of a procedure that has produced an undesirable outcome. As Nadeau and Blais (1993, 553) put it, 'The viability of electoral democracy depends on its ability to secure the support of a substantial proportion of individuals who are displeased with the outcome of an election.' Our research suggests that satisfaction with democracy is not necessarily driven by election outcomes; graceful losers choose to support political institutions on the basis of their commitment to the electoral process.

The profile and attitudes of the graceful losers presented in this book reflect the image of the ideal citizen: informed, sophisticated, and able to overcome frustrations after a defeat in the name of their principles. However, our results also show that this idyllic portrait needs to be nuanced. The stability of democracy depends equally on voters who are indecisive, hesitant, torn, and above all, moderate. Understanding losers' consent as a mix of emotions, reason, and moderation sheds light on the question of why a democratic majority emerged in the aftermath of the Brexit victory. This finding also offers a powerful reminder that parties must try to accomplish two tasks when they campaign: to win but also to do so in a manner that facilitates the rallying of a significant proportion of losers after their defeat. The results presented in this book suggest that the Leave camp succeeded on both counts.

MOVING TOWARD A NEW KIND OF POLICY DEBATE

An extremely important aspect of this research is the insights it provides into the core of what we call 'post-truth' politics. In today's world, populism and post-truth politics pose a serious challenge to liberal democracy. The strength of a frame lies in its appeal to the public, not in its intellectual or moral content (Chong and Druckman 2007b, 111; Hopkin and Rosamond 2017). The frame analysis in this book therefore separates considerations of fairness from those of resonance. A frame is not strong because it is accurate, valid, or based on scientific evidence; a strong frame may very well exaggerate the situation, mislead the audience, or capitalize on the public's emotions and fears. As the Brexit campaign shows perfectly, strong frames often involve symbols rather than direct information on the substance of a policy. Insights into the effect and influence of referendum campaigns are particularly pertinent at a time when populism and post-truth politics are observed all across the globe.

The idea of post-truth politics came up often during the Brexit campaign. Despite charges by 'experts' that the Leave camp was misleading the public, the arguments of the Leave campaign were stronger, closely matching voters' existing worries with key themes such as immigration, loss of control in a globalizing world, and deterioration of the NHS. Only a month before the referendum, the House of Commons Treasury Select Committee complained that 'the public debate is being poorly served by inconsistent, unqualified and, in some cases, misleading claims and counter-claims' (Renwick, Flinders, and Jenning 2016).[5] The committee emphasized that members of both the Leave and Remain campaigns were responsible for such misleading claims. Former prime minister Sir John Major similarly stated that he was 'angry about the way the British people are being misled'. A public letter signed by over 250 leading academics suggested that the level of misinformation in the referendum campaign was so great that the democratic legitimacy of the final vote might be questioned (ibid.).

Yet post-truth politics is neither new nor temporary. Politics is all about appealing to the emotions of the public and, as Churchill's quote neatly puts it, often 'leads to conviction rather than to proof'. This book demonstrates why this dynamic happens, how it happened in the Brexit case, and how it compares to similar dynamics in other parts of the world. What is more, it explains the mechanisms of post-truth politics on a core issue in a globalizing world. The Brexit campaign unfolded around the dilemma of open versus closed borders. Increasingly, a choice is being presented between the benefits of economic globalization and the protection of national sovereignty, as was the case in the most recent US and French elections. Although 'taking back control' is unrealistic in a world of complex economic, social, and political interdependence, its appeal is extraordinary for the public. Politicians often provide 'alternative facts' and use strong appeals to emotions, especially when they are discussing the controversial issue of open or closed borders. The Leave side's strategies, in line with contemporary politics on closed borders, played a remarkable role in framing the choice. Our findings are therefore highly generalizable to referendums and elections around the world, having significant implications for all kinds of international regimes and states' faith and participation in them.

In arguing for and against borders, politicians who opt for a certain kind of language tend to have an advantage over others. Framing theory indicates that arguments that match the public's immediate reality and that are vivid, emotional, catchy, and negative will have considerably more success than arguments that highlight distant benefits and abstract ideals. Voters are inclined to prefer simple and often empirically inaccurate answers over complex but empirically accurate ones.

This tendency was important for Remain campaigners. The chief campaign spokesperson of the Remain side, James McGrory, argued that in the face of the Leave camp's simplistic argument that 'we should control everything', the Remain side had to argue that 'it was not that simple in the modern world'.[6] The concept of sovereignty is particularly difficult to simplify for voters, McGrory observed:

> If you follow the idea that you are sovereign as a nation because you choose to do things entirely on your own, then the most sovereign nation is North Korea. But Britain has been an enthusiastic signer-up to international treaties. Does the signing up to the international defence against torture make us less sovereign? No ... How about signing up to NATO? That is pooling of sovereignty ... The idea that we are somehow a more sovereign nation because we do not collectively pool interests with others when it is in our interests is ... a joke.

Labour MP Alan Johnson similarly noted that while the Remain side had the complex task of explaining why Britain had not lost its sovereignty within the EU, the Leave side was able to respond with a very potent slogan of merely three words:[7]

You had to sit down for half an hour to explain, 'Look, every country cedes some sovereignty for the greater good'... We had to take them through the whole course of history from the Second World War – whereas all they had to say was 'Take Back Control' ... They talked about unelected people running Brussels. And then you would say 'every decision made by the EU is made by ministers of elected government'. And you have to explain that if you elected the Commissioners, then it would be like another country. The whole point of the system is that it is not another country, it is an umbrella group to bring countries together. And so, all of that was quite complex.

McGrory generalized this pattern to the "progressive camp" across the world:[8]

The progressive camp makes quite complex, quite high-minded arguments because they appreciate the world is extremely complicated. The people on the other side of the argument peddle easy answers to extremely complicated questions. So Trump – build a wall. How is that going to help anybody? In the Brexit referendum it is 'Take Back Control. I want my country back.' From where? From whom? To do what? How do people on my side of the argument do this? What are our arguments to respond to that? Everywhere we look, we are being beaten back, whether it's Trump or Le Pen. Everywhere in the Western world, my argument is losing. Until we find a way of connecting with regular people again, I am genuinely fearful for progressive values in the Western world.

In the past, pro-EU politicians designed various strategies to deal with this kind of imbalance between simplicity and complexity (Atikcan, 2015b). Danish voters rejected the Maastricht Treaty in a referendum, and Irish voters did the same with the Nice and Lisbon treaties; their pro-EU governments, however, decided to go back to the EU, and after securing 'guarantees' on the most controversial themes of the referendum campaigns, asked the public the same question again. Some of these guarantees were on actual issues from the treaties, but some were perceptions fuelled by the anti-EU campaigns mounted against the supposed creation of a United States of Europe or interference into military neutrality or abortion laws – campaigns that in their dynamics closely resembled those of the Brexit campaign. Regardless of the nature of public concerns, whether they originated from the text of the treaties or the claims of the campaigners, the EU guarantees served to redefine the agenda. Having removed these contentious themes from the table, the Danish and Irish governments put the question to the public again in second referendums. In these second rounds, the pro-EU actors made the campaign entirely about the economic benefits of EU membership, much as the Remain camp did. Nonetheless, there was an important difference. With the guarantees, the pro-EU Danish and Irish actors were now able to restrain the opposition and had the stage to themselves – whereas the Brexit campaign did not see any such guarantees. Yet that option was available to the Remain campaign at the outset. David Cameron secured a deal with the EU before the Brexit referendum precisely to block the Leave side from advancing the types of arguments it did. But as our data have shown, that deal was not seen as a substantial one and remained invisible in the campaign. The campaign ground in a potential referendum on the final 'Brexit deal' *after* exit negotiations could yet be very similar to those in the repeat referendums in Denmark and Ireland, since the range of available Leave arguments would decrease significantly once the terms of the deal were known. For better or for worse, these kinds of 'deals' from the EU or other international cooperation schemes might become the norm for politicians advocating open borders, as they would serve to limit the arguments on the table and remove from the discussion the tangible and immediate losses that the public fears.

There seems to be an additional issue, however. While the economic aspect of the borders issue (the economic advantages or disadvantages of an international agreement) lends itself reasonably well to debate, the autonomy aspect (the advantages or disadvantages of pooling sovereignty) does not. In other words, campaigners do not seem to have difficulty in generating economic arguments when they are arguing for or against borders, but when it comes to arguments on losing national autonomy, only the side that advocates closed borders appears to be vocal. In the Brexit referendum, the Remain side felt that every minute spent talking about immigration was a 'wasted minute' because they foresaw losing that argument.[9] In Blair Jenkins's words, 'The only response the Remain side had was "you are right, we do not like them either, but we have to be in this club because it is the only way of getting the economy going".'[10]

But is it truly impossible to make a direct case for *not* 'taking back control'? Can the advocates of open borders only resort to strategies that would block the other side's arguments on autonomy, as happened with EU guarantees, rather than attacking the issue directly? Is their perceived limitation due to the fact that arguments on autonomy are inherently more emotional than those on economy? The answers to these questions depend on the political elite, specifically those advocating open borders, and whether they will choose to discuss the issue and find simple and emotional arguments to make their case. Labour MP Alan Johnson thought that there could have been an answer to 'Take Back Control': 'I think there was an answer to it. I think we could have made an argument that actually leaving the EU would mean we lose control ... we lose the Dublin regulation [on the entry of asylum-seekers].'[11] Whether or not these types of arguments are advanced will determine the future of international cooperation. And for a project like the European Union, whose foundations rest on the very idea of open borders, it will be a question of existence.

APPENDICES

APPENDIX ONE

Interviews

Özlem Atikcan conducted field research in France, Spain, the Netherlands, and Luxembourg in 2008 on the European Constitution referendums, in Denmark and Ireland in 2011 on the Nice, Maastricht, and Lisbon Treaty referendums, in Ireland again in 2015 on the Fiscal Compact referendum, and in the UK in 2017 on the Brexit and Scottish independence referendums. In addition, she has extensively interviewed senior officials working in EU institutions regarding the EU's communication strategy. Her dataset thus includes in-depth data from over 180 interviews with EU officials and campaigners from all political parties and civil society groups that were active in the campaigns. These interviews were face to face and semi-structured, based on opportunity and snowball sampling.

INTERVIEW QUESTIONNAIRE

1. What were the main issues/arguments raised in your campaign (and second campaign if a repeat referendum)?
2. Why did you specifically choose these issues and arguments?
3. Did your party/organization have a campaigning strategy (and did your party/organization change its campaign strategy in the second referendum if a repeat referendum)?
4. How did you organize your campaign (and was your preparation different for the second referendum if a repeat referendum)?
5. What were the main challenges you faced during your campaign?
6. How well do you think the other side has performed?

Appendix One

7. What would you say were the main challenges the other side faced?
8. Did you have specific strategies to appeal to the emotions of the voters?
9. Which campaign do you think used a more emotional language?
10. Did you have specific strategies to appeal to risk aversion?
11. Which campaign do you think has controlled the risk factor?

LIST OF INTERVIEWEES

United Kingdom

o Ryan Coetzee (director of strategy of the Remain campaign)
o James McGrory (chief campaign spokesperson of the Remain campaign)
o Lord Rose (chair of the Remain campaign)
o Alan Johnson (Labour MP, Remain campaign)
o Matthew Elliott (chief executive of the Vote Leave campaign)
o Gisela Stuart (Labour MP, chair of the Vote Leave campaign)
o Richard Tice (co-founder of Leave.EU campaign)
o Matthew Ellery (Get Britain Out campaign)

Scotland

o Blair Jenkins (chief executive of the Yes Scotland campaign)
o Kevin Pringle (strategic communications director of the Scottish National Party–Yes Scotland campaign)
o Robert Shorthouse (director of communications of the Better Together campaign)
o Phil Anderton (board member of the Better Together campaign)

Spain

o Juan Fernando López Aguilar (PSOE, Partido Socialista Obrero Español/Party of European Socialists Group, MP, minister of justice and interior affairs)
o Juan Moscoso del Prado Hernández (PSOE, MP)
o Enrique Baron Crespo (PSOE, MEP; PSOE chairman, European Parliament, 1999–2004)

Interviews

o Orestes Suárez Antón (PSOE, international secretary)
o Alejando Muñoz Alonso (PP, Partido Popular/People's Party, senator)
o Ignacio Cosidó Gutiérrez (PP, MP)
o Jordi Xuclà i Costa (CiU, Convergència i Unió/Convergence and Union, MP)
o José Ramón Beloki Guerra (PNV, Partido Nacionalista Vasco/ Basque Nationalist Party, MP)
o Carles Llorens I Vila (CDC, Convergència Democràtica de Catalunya, international secretary)
o José Manuel Fernández Fernández, IU, Izquierda Unida/United Left], coordinator of the Parliamentary Group, and mayor of Bustarviejo)
o Joaquim Puig Vilamala (European Research Council, coordinator
o Oriol Duran Torres (spokesperson of ERC Parliamentary Group)
o Marc Giménez Villahoz (ICV, Iniciativa per Catalunya Verds/ Initiative for Catalonia Greens, European politics coordinator)
o Mikel Irujo Amezaga (EA, Eusko Alkartasuna, MEP)
o Jaime Pastor (IU, ATTAC España, Association pour la Taxation des Transactions financières et pour l'Action Citoyenne; Alternative Space)
o Ricardo Gómez Muñoz (IU, ATTAC España)
o Carlos Girbau Costa (IU, Social Forum)
o Luis González Reyes (Ecologists in Action)
o *José* Ignacio *Torreblanca* (senior analyst for EU Affairs, Elcano Royal Institute for International Affairs)
o Jordi Vaquer i Fanés (European program coordinator, CIDOB, Barcelona Centre for International Affairs)

France

o Olivier Ubéda (UMP, Union pour un mouvement populaire, deputy director of communications and European affairs delegate)
o Alain Bergounioux (PS, Parti socialiste, secretary general of the PS Scientific Council)
o Pierre Kanuty (PS, International and European affairs political assistant)

190 Appendix One

- Patrick Farbiaz (The Greens/Les Verts, international secretary)
- Isabelle Sicart (UDF, Union pour la Démocratie Française)
- Nicolas Dupont-Aignan (UMP, MP)
- Jacques Myard (UMP, MP)
- Jacques Généreux (PS)
- Francine Bavay (Greens executive committee member; vice-president of the Regional Council of Île-de-France)
- Daniel Cirera (PCF, Parti communiste français, international secretary)
- Dominique Touraine (PCF)
- Alain Krivine (LCR, Ligue communiste révolutionnaire)
- Catherine Salagnac (National Rally/Rassemblement national)
- Yves Salesse (co-president of Copernic Foundation; Conseil d'État member; co-initiator of the Appeal of 200)
- Claude Debons (CGT, General Workers' Confederation, co-initiator of the Appeal of 200)
- Pierre Khalfa (ATTAC France, and SUD, Solidarity-Unity-Democracy)
- Susan George (ATTAC France)
- Aurélie Trouvé (ATTAC France)
- Maxime Combes (ATTAC France)
- Christophe Beaudouin (secretary general of the Group for a Confederation of the States of Europe, campaigned with the MPF, Mouvement pour la France)
- Raoul-Marc Jennar (member of the No Committee)
- Gaëtane Ricard-Nihoul (secretary general of Notre Europe)

The Netherlands

- Atzo Nicolaï (VVD, Volkspartij voor Vrijheid en Democratie, MP, minister of European affairs)
- Jan Jacob van Dijk (CDA, Christen-Democratisch Appèl, MP)
- Marije Laffeber (PvdA, Partij van de Arbeid, international secretary)
- Bas Eickhout (GreenLeft/GroenLinks, delegate of the European Green Party)
- Gerben-Jan Gerbrandy (D66, Democraten 66, secretary of D66 Parliamentary Group)
- Michiel van Hulten (director of Foundation for a Better Europe)

Interviews 191

o Hilde Laffeber (Ministry of Foreign Affairs; member of the Yes campaign team)

o Delphine Pronk (Ministry of Foreign Affairs; head of the EU Communications Unit)

o Marco Pastors (political leader of the local party Liveable Rotterdam; member of the City Council, and deputy mayor of Rotterdam)

o Otto Ter Haar (The Greens/De Groenen, international secretary)

o Harry van Bommel (SP, Socialistische Partij, MP)

o Renske Leijten (SP, leader of the ROOD, SP's youth organization)

o Hans van Heijningen (SP, secretary general)

o Esme Wiegman (CU, MP)

o Mat Herben (LPF, Lijst Pim Fortuyn, now defunct, chairman)

o Alexander van Hattem (Young Fortuynists, youth organization of the LPF)

o Willem Bos (president of ConstitutionNo, and ATTAC Netherlands)

o Erik Wesselius (ConstitutionNo)

o Wim van de Donk (president of the WRR, Scientific Council for Government Policy)

o Monica Sie Dhian Ho (WRR)

o Patrick van Schie (director of the Liberal think tank related to the VVD)

Luxembourg

o François Biltgen (CSV, Chrëschtlech Sozial Vollekspartei, MP, chairman and minister of labor and employment)

o Laurent Mosar (CSV, MP)

o Ben Fayot (LSAP, Lëtzebuerger Sozialistesch Aarbechterpartei, MP, president of the Parliamentary Group)

o Charles Goerens (DP, Demokratesch Partei, MP, Minister of Foreign Affairs)

o Abbes Jacoby (The Greens/Déi Gréng, secretary general of the Parliamentary Group)

o Dan Michels (The Greens, parliamentary attaché)

o Jacques-Yves Henckes (ADR, Alternativ Demokratesch Reformpartei, MP)

Appendix One

- o Henri Wehenkel (The Left/Déi Lénk)
- o André Kremer (coordinator and leader of the No Committee)
- o Pierre *Gramegna* (director general of the Chamber of Commerce)
- o Nico Clement (OGBL, Confederation of Independent Trade Unions of Luxembourg)
- o Nico Wennmacher (president of the Railways Trade Union FNCTTFEL-Landesverband)
- o Tom Graas (director of national RTL TV News)
- o Marc Linster (director of national RTL Radio)
- o Anne-Marie Berny (ATTAC Luxembourg)
- o Adrien Thomas (UNEL, Union national des étudiantes du Luxembourg)
- o Frédéric Krier (UNEL)
- o Alfred Groff (Luxembourg Social Forum)
- o Jürgen Stoldt (political communication expert; editor of *Forum*)
- o Thomas Rupp (Organizer of European No Campaign)

Denmark

- o Uffe Ellemann-Jensen (Liberal Party, minister of foreign affairs, 1992, and leader)
- o Niels Helveg Petersen (Social Liberal Party, minister of foreign affairs, 1993, and MP)
- o Mogens Lykketoft (Social Democrat MP)
- o Jacob Buksti (Social Democrat MP)
- o Charlotte Antonsen (Liberal Party MP)
- o Jørgen Ørstrøm Møller (Ministry of Foreign Affairs, state secretary)
- o Holger K. Nielsen (leader of the Socialist People's Party, MP)
- o Steen Gade (Socialist People's Party, MP)
- o Søren Krarup (Progress Party)
- o Kenneth Kristensen Berth (Danish People's Party)
- o Ole Krarup (president of the People's Movement against the EU)
- o Jens-Peter Bonde (president of the June Movement)
- o Erik Boel (president of the European Movement)

Ireland

- o Dick Roche (Fianna Fáil, MP, minister of European affairs)

Interviews

- Timmy Dooley (Fianna Fáil, MP) (two interviews, 2011 and 2015)
- David Harmon (Fianna Fáil, director of press and communications)
- Seán Dorgan (Fianna Fáil, general secretary)
- Lucinda Creighton (Fine Gael, MP)
- Tom Curran (Fine Gael, general secretary)
- Terry Murphy (Fine Gael, Dublin director) (two interviews, 2011 and 2015)
- Joe Costello (Labour Party, MP) (two interviews, 2011 and 2015)
- Thomas Broughan (Labour Party, MP)
- Déirdre de Búrca (Green Party, MP)
- Mary Lou McDonald (Sinn Féin, MP)
- Eoin Ó'Broin (Sinn Féin, campaign director) (two interviews, 2011 and 2015)
- Killian Forde (Sinn Féin, director of strategy, Lisbon1)
- Joe Higgins (Socialist Party, MP)
- Paul Murphy (Socialist Party, MP)
- Padraig Mannion (Workers' Party, campaign director)
- Declan Ganley (Libertas, president)
- Naoise Nunn (Libertas, executive director)
- John McGuirk (Libertas, communications director)
- Scott Schittl (Cóir, campaign director)
- Ben Conroy (Iona Institute)
- Anthony Coughlan (National Platform, president) (two interviews, 2011 and 2015)
- Peter Lacey (People's Movement)
- Roger Cole (Peace and Neutrality Alliance, president) (two interviews, 2011 and 2015)
- Brendan Kiely (Irish Alliance for Europe, chief executive)
- Karen White (Irish Alliance for Europe)
- Pat Cox (Ireland for Europe, campaign director)
- Brendan Halligan (Ireland for Europe, national campaign coordinator) (two interviews, 2011 and 2015)
- Brigid Laffan (Ireland for Europe, chair)
- Caroline Erskine (Ireland for Europe, communications director)
- Anthony Brown (Ireland for Europe, director of research)
- Michelle O'Donnell Keating (Women for Europe, co-founder)
- Jillian van Turnhout (Ireland for Europe)
- Billie Sparks (Women for Europe)

- o Blair Horan (Charter Group) (two interviews, 2011 and 2015)
- o Dan O'Brien (economist, Institute of International and European Affairs)
- o Michael Taft (economist, Unite)
- o Andy Storey (university professor and No campaigner)
- o Paul Hand (press liaison officer to the Parliamentary Sub-Committee on Fiscal Compact)
- o Ciarán Toland (civil society Yes campaigner in the Nice Treaty referendums)

APPENDIX TWO

Data and Variables

DATA

The opinion results of this study are based on an online survey conducted by the polling firm Survation between 1 July and 5 July 2016, with 1,514 respondents. This survey was designed by an academic research team that included the authors of this book. The survey used a representative quota-based sampling approach using the online panels of the polling firm. Respondents were targeted according to their age band, sex, and region. The survey was weighted according to the demographic targets of the UK to correct for sample imbalance. The weighting targets are based on mid-year estimates for 2015 of the 2011 Census.

Table A2.1
Variables

Dependent Variables		
Leave	Dummy	1 = respondents who voted to Leave the EU 0 = respondents who voted to Remain in the EU
Satisfaction	5-point scale	On a scale of 1 to 5, respondents state how satisfied they are with the way democracy works in the UK (0 = very dissatisfied to 5 = very satisfied). Scores are rescaled from 0 to 1.
Losers' consent	Multinomial	Three groups are created: Sore losers = respondents who voted for the Remain option AND agree that the UK government should hold a second referendum about British membership in the European Union Graceful losers = respondents who voted for the Remain option AND agree that the UK government should accept the result Winners = respondents who voted for the Leave option in the EU Referendum

Sociodemographic Variables

Age	Scale	Age of respondents, rescaled from (0) to (1)
Gender	Dummy	1 = male; 0 = female

Socioeconomic Variables and Ideology

Education	7-point scale	Level of educational qualifications completed by the respondents (1 = no qualifications or a formal apprenticeship to 7 = degree/postgraduate degree), rescaled from 0 to 1.
Wealth	11-point scale	Average scores for Income and Patrimony Income = respondents' household income from lowest income (1 = less than £10,000) to highest income (11 = £90,000 or more), rescaled from 0 to 1. Patrimony = number of a total of 4 property items (home, savings, enterprise, stocks), rescaled from (0) to (1).
Ideology	11-point scale	On a scale of 0 to 10, where 0 is the most left and 10 is the most right, respondents say where they would place their own political views. Scores are rescaled from 0 to 1.

Risk Perception Variables

POLRISK	11-point scale	On a scale of 0 to 10, respondents state how willing they are to take risks in making political choices (0 = unwilling to take risks to 10 = fully prepared to take risks). Scores are rescaled from 0 to 1.
ECNRISK	11-point scale	On a scale of 0 to 10, respondents state how willing they are to take risks in financial matters (0 = unwilling to take risks to 10 = fully prepared to take risks). Scores are rescaled from 0 to 1.
GENRISK	11-point scale	On a scale of 0 to 10, respondents state how willing they are to take risks in general (0 = unwilling to take risks to 10 = fully prepared to take risks). Scores are rescaled from 0 to 1.

Data and Variables

Opinion and Attitude Variables

Information (EU)	5-point scale	Number of correct answers for the following items: 1. Switzerland is a member of the EU (*false*). 2. Every country in the EU elects the same number of representatives to the European Parliament (*false*). 3. The Netherlands holds at the moment the presidency of the Council of the European Union (*true*). 4. The European Union has 15 Member States (*false*). Scores are rescaled from 0 to 1.
Happy (Leave)	5-point scale	Emotion scale (1 = very angry to 5 = very happy) measuring feelings about the Leave victory. Scores are rescaled from 0 to 1.
Attach (UK-EU)	Scale	Difference between AttachUK and AttachEU, scores rescaled from 0 to 1. AttachUK = respondents' level of attachment to the UK varying from 0 (not at all attached) to 5 (very attached), rescaled from 0 to 1. AttachEU = respondents' level of attachment to the EU varying from 0 (not at all attached) to 5 (very attached), rescaled from 0 to 1.
Evaluation EU	5-point scale	On a scale of 1 to 5, respondents state if on balance the UK has benefited or not from being a member of the EU (1 = not benefitted to 5 = strongly benefitted). Scores are rescaled from 0 to 1.
EU too centralized	3-point scale	1 = respondents say that too many issues are decided by the EU .5 = respondents say that the number of issues decided by the EU at present is about right or don't know 0 = respondents say that more issues should be decided on by the EU
Late deciders	4-point scale	'If you voted, when did you make up your mind on how you would vote in the referendum on British membership of the European Union?' 1 = on the referendum day itself .67 = in the final week of the campaign .33 = fairly early during the campaign 0 = at the time the referendum was announced

External efficacy	5-point scale	Respondents state how strongly they agree (1 = strongly agree) or disagree (5 = strongly disagree) with the statement 'Politicians don't care about what people like me think.' Scores are rescaled from 0 to 1.
Economic perceptions	3-point scale	'Would you say that over the last twelve months, the state of the economy in the UK has gotten better, stayed the same, or gotten worse?' 1 = it has gotten better .5 = it stayed the same OR don't know 0 = it has gotten worse
Losers	Dummy	1 = respondents who voted to Remain in the EU 0 = otherwise
Sore Losers	Dummy	1 = respondents who voted to Remain in the EU AND agree that the UK government should hold a second referendum about British membership in the European Union 0 = otherwise
Graceful Losers	Dummy	1 = respondents who voted to Remain in the EU AND agree that the UK government should accept the result 0 = otherwise

Issue Variables

ARG Jobs	5-point scale	On a scale of 1 to 5, respondents state how likely there would be loss of jobs, trade and investment, in a UK outside the EU (1 = very unlikely to 5 = very likely). Scores are rescaled from 0 to 1.
ARG Imm	5-point scale	On a scale of 1 to 5, respondents state how likely the level of immigration to the UK would decrease, in a UK outside the EU (1 = very unlikely to 5 = very likely). Scores are rescaled from 0 to 1.
ARG NHS	5-point scale	On a scale of 1 to 5, respondents state how likely the National Health System (NHS) would be protected, in a UK outside the EU (1 = very unlikely to 5 = very likely). Scores are rescaled from 0 to 1.

Data and Variables

Popularity Variables

POPCVCameron	Scale	Interaction between POPCameron and CVCameron POPCameron = feelings about David Cameron, on a scale going from 0 (really dislike) to 10 (really like him), scores rescaled from 0 to 1. CVCameron: 1 = convincing campaign; 0 = unconvincing campaign
POPCVJohnson	Scale	Interaction between POPJohnson and CVJohnson POPJohnson = feelings about Boris Johnson, on a scale going from 0 (really dislike) to 10 (really like him), scores rescaled from 0 to 1. CVJohnson: 1 = convincing campaign; 0 = unconvincing campaign
POPCVFarage	Scale	Interaction between POPFarage and CVFarage POPFarage = feelings about Nigel Farage, on a scale going from 0 (really dislike) to 10 (really like him), scores rescaled from 0 to 1. CVFarage: 1 = convincing campaign; 0 = unconvincing campaign
POPCVCorbyn	Scale	Interaction between POPCorbyn and CVCorbyn POPCorbyn = feelings about Jeremy Corbyn, on a scale going from 0 (really dislike) to 10 (really like him), scores rescaled from 0 to 1. CVCorbyn: 1 = convincing campaign; 0 = unconvincing campaign

APPENDIX THREE

Tables

Table A3.1
Logistic regression models for a vote in favour of leaving the EU

	(1)	(2)	(3)	(4)	(5)	(6)
Age	1.41**	−.72*	−1.04*	−.84	−1.30*	−1.45*
	(.23)	(.36)	(.42)	(.44)	(.58)	(.67)
Gender (male)	.08	.33	.47*	.35	.31	.33
	(.13)	(.19)	(.23)	(.24)	(.29)	(.32)
Education	−.74**	−.52	−.83*	−.90*	−1.24**	−1.24**
	(.20)	(.31)	(.36)	(.37)	(.45)	(.50)
Wealth	−2.17**	−1.54*	−.96	−1.07	−.45	−.59
	(.48)	(.71)	(.81)	(.82)	(1.02)	(1.03)
Ideology	1.37**	.34	−.40	−.64	−.53	−1.06
	(.24)	(.37)	(.43)	(.45)	(.63)	(.74)
Attach (UK-EU)	−	5.72**	4.13**	4.22**	5.37**	4.97**
		(.64)	(.75)	(.77)	(.99)	(1.08)
Evaluation EU	−	−4.34**	−3.59**	−3.60**	−3.35**	−3.24**
		(.42)	(.51)	(.52)	(.63)	(.77)
EU too centralized	−	3.59**	3.20**	3.14**	2.62**	1.99**
		(.45)	(.51)	(.51)	(.60)	(.65)
ARG Jobs	−	−	−3.53**	−3.68**	−2.30**	−1.25
			(.51)	(.53)	(.60)	(.67)
ARG Imm	−	−	2.44**	2.33**	1.74**	1.04
			(.51)	(.52)	(.66)	(.74)
ARG NHS	−	−	2.66**	2.48**	2.60**	1.86*
			(.52)	(.52)	(.67)	(.77)
POLRISK	−	−	−	1.67**	.84	−.28
				(.66)	(.80)	(.95)
GENRISK	−	−	−	−.48	−.09	−.08
				(.71)	(.84)	(.92)
ECNRISK	−	−	−	.47	.10	−.25
				(.74)	(.88)	(.98)
POPCV Cameron	−	−	−	−	−2.58**	−2.56**
					(.45)	(.49)

Tables

POPCV Johnson	–	–	–	–	1.77** (.48)	1.04* (.54)
POPCV Farage	–	–	–	–	1.90** (.51)	1.99** (.56)
POPCV Corbyn	–	–	–	–	–.35 (.47)	–.33 (.49)
Angry(Leave)	–	–	–	–	–	–4.99** (.75)
Constant	–.69** (.18)	–3.99** (.60)	–3.34** (.81)	–3.81** (.84)	–4.45** (1.06)	.18 (1.33)
N	1,159	1,159	1,159	1,159	1,015	1,015
Nagelkerke pseudo-R^2	.13	.70	.79	.80	.85	.88
% correctly predicted	64	87	91	91	93	94

Note: Entries are logistic regression coefficients with standard error in parentheses. * p < .05; ** p < .01 (two-tailed tests).

Table A3.2
Linear regression models for satisfaction with democracy in the UK

	(1)	(2)
Age	.06* (.03)	.06* (.03)
Gender (male)	.00 (.02)	–.00 (.02)
Education	.06* (.03)	.06** (.02)
Wealth	.03 (.06)	.03 (.06)
External efficacy	.18** (.03)	.18** (.03)
Economic perceptions	.23** (.02)	.23** (.02)
Losers	–.04** (.02)	–
Sore losers	–	–.08** (.02)
Graceful losers	–	.01 (.02)
Constant	.31** (.02)	.32** (.03)
N	1,260	1,260
R-square	.14	.15

Note: Entries are linear regression coefficients with standard error in parentheses. * p < .05; ** p < .01 (two-tailed tests). For more details about variables in the model, see our appendix.

Table A.3.3
Multinomial regression model of winners, sore losers, and graceful losers

	Winners (1)	Graceful losers (2)
Age	−.37 (.52)	.27 (.38)
Gender (male)	.50 (.27)	.44* (.21)
Education	−.91* (.42)	−.23 (.31)
Wealth	−2.99** (.95)	−.28 (.66)
Happy (Leave)	7.98** (.60)	2.17** (.41)
Information (EU)	.83 (.50)	1.01** (.38)
EU too centralized	3.55** (.57)	1.03** (.38)
Attach (UK-EU)	6.89** (.90)	2.10** (.70)
Late deciders	1.15** (.46)	.83* (.37)
Constant	−10.70 (.81)	−3.72** (.48)
N	1,088	
Nagelkerke pseudo-R^2	.73	

Note: Entries are multinomial regression coefficients with standard errors in parentheses. The reference category is Sore losers.
* p < .05; ** p < .01 (two-tailed tests).

Notes

CHAPTER ONE

1 Chief campaign spokesperson of the Remain campaign, interview, 8 November 2016.

2 The online survey was conducted between 24 May and 2 June 2016.

3 The authors warn that the pro-Leave arguments would already be 'priced in' due to the existing Euroscepticism in the UK. We make a similar claim by arguing that the Leave camp benefitted from the tradition of scapegoating the EU. We make two further claims, however. First, we argue that such scapegoating would actually weaken pro-EU frames, as they would likely be perceived as contradicting the dominant long-term rhetoric on the topic. Second, comparing the Brexit case to the previous EU referendums, we argue that the Leave side would benefit from the typical agenda-setting advantage of anti-EU campaigners. Please see chapters 2 and 3 for a discussion of these dynamics.

4 Theoretically, the status quo bias is attributed to risk aversion, and risk aversion is theorized to act as the intervening variable for confusion or uncertainty. Lengths of the ballot, ballot summary, or ballot title, seen as proxies for confusion, are shown to be influential. The longer these elements are, the more people vote negatively (Bowler and Donovan 1998; Hyink 1969; Magleby 1984). Christin, Hug, and Sciarini (2002) similarly find some evidence that poorly informed voters often reject new proposals. Nevertheless, more recent research demonstrates that when one tests the individual basis of this theoretical idea, the effect of confusion on voting negatively is much smaller than that of partisanship or issue preference (Binder 2010). Therefore,

204   Notes to pages 13–19

what is highly interesting from the point of view of this research is not the confusion but the campaign cues and elite endorsements that shape the status quo bias.

5   The authors add, nonetheless, that only in one referendum, the Maltese referendum on divorce in 2011, has the public supported change when their prime minister advised against it.

6   The authors warn about the unreliability of this figure.

7   For instance, first, following the types of referendums proposed by LeDuc (2002), in cases where the issue is something highly familiar to the public, the volatility in opinion might be very low, as happened in the Scottish devolution referendum in 1997. Second, the support for change may not go down, because the reversion point (i.e., what follows a No vote or the status quo) might be painted by the campaign as unsustainable, as was the case in EU accession referendums in 1994. Third, the support for change might receive important support in non-decisive referendums if the entire establishment supports the proposal and the voters are in an anti-establishment mood, as in the New Zealand referendum on electoral reform in 1992.

8   Another type of framing effect, the equivalency or valence framing effect, occurs when different but *logically equivalent* phrases cause individuals to alter their preferences. For this type, see Tversky and Kahneman (1990).

9   The core idea of this body of literature is that individuals process campaign messages differently depending on their emotional mood (Schwarz 2000). Some of this work has focused on the use of images and music in campaign messages (Brader 2006; Huddy and Gunnthorsdottir 2000). In another example, campaign messages cueing fear are shown to stimulate persuasion, whereas messages evoking enthusiasm encourage individuals to stay loyal to their pre-existing preferences (Brader 2005, 2006).

10   In a similar perspective, individuals are shown to have a strong need to believe in a just world (Hafer and Bègue 2005). When this view is threatened, they tend to employ defensive responses, such as dismissal or rationalization of the information that threatens their view. For instance, in their study investigating the impact of various frames on attitudes toward global warming, Feinberg and Willer (2011) find that the scarier the message, the more people who are committed to viewing the world as fundamentally stable and fair are motivated to deny it. The authors recommend that scientists and advocates communicate their findings in less apocalyptic ways and present solutions to global

warming. Their conclusion is that fear-based appeals, especially when not coupled with a clear solution, can backfire and undermine the intended effects of messages.

11 http://www.dailymail.co.uk/debate/article-2140532/Francois-Hollande-French-president-Britain-shackled-corpse-Europe.html.

12 The slogan 'Take Back Control' also speaks to the popular marketing strategy 'call to action,' in that it sought to provoke an immediate response from voters.

13 Interview, 8 November 2016.

CHAPTER TWO

1 Strategic communications director of the Scottish National Party, interview, 7 April 2017.

2 Atikcan conducted these interviews between 2008 and 2017. The interviews were face to face and semi-structured, based on opportunity and snowball sampling. Please see the appendix for the detailed list of interviewees and the questionnaire used.

3 An equally interesting discussion is taking place in the literature on EU attitudes, making a strong case for studying ambivalent and indifferent citizens instead of focusing exclusively on consenters and dissenters (e.g., van Ingelgom 2014).

4 For a detailed discussion of the political costs of being excluded from mainstream politics, see Evans and Ivaldi's (2005) analysis of the National Front in France.

5 Interview, 19 September 2008.

6 Interview, 24 September 2008.

7 Interview, 15 October 2008.

8 Interview, 17 November 2008.

9 Interview, 26 April 2011.

10 Interview, 18 April 2011.

11 Interview, 12 April 2011.

12 Interview, 14 April 2011.

13 Interview, 14 April 2011.

14 Interview, 28 April 2011.

15 Interview, 29 April 2011.

16 Interview, 11 April 2008.

17 Interview, 5 November 2008.

18 Interview, 6 November 2008.

19 Interview, 11 April 2011.

20 Interview, 23 October 2008.

21 Interview, 29 October 2008.

22 Interview, 22 October 2008.

23 Interview, 12 November 2008.

24 Interview, 10 November 2008.

25 Interviews, 8 April 2008 and 31 October 2008.

26 Interview, 16 October 2008.

27 Interview, 14 November 2008.

28 Interview, 8 September 2008.

29 Interview, 9 September 2008.

30 Interview, 28 April 2011.

31 Interview, 27 April 2011.

32 Interview, 29 April 2011.

33 Interview, 19 April 2011.

34 Interview, 28 April 2011.

35 Interview, 12 April 2011.

36 Interview, 20 April 2011.

37 Interview, 14 November 2008.

38 Interview, 28 April 2011.

39 Interview, 29 October 2008.

40 Interview, 29 October 2008.

41 Interview, 24 September 2008.

42 Interview, 29 October 2008.

43 In their discussion of Quebec politics, they identify two potential worst outcomes, the first the possibility of a serious economic crisis during the transition period leading to sovereignty, and the second related to the fate of linguistic communities.

44 Interview, 6 April 2017.

45 Interview, 7 April 2017.

46 Interview, 7 April 2017.

47 Interview, 13 April 2017.

48 Interviews, 6–7 April 2017.

49 Interview, 7 April 2017.

50 Interview, 7 April 2017.

51 Interview, 6 April 2017.

52 Interview, 7 April 2017.

53 Interview, 6 April 2017.

54 Interview, 7 April 2017.

55 Interview, 7 April 2017.

56 Interview, 13 April 2017.

Notes to pages 63–80

57 Interview, 6 April 2017.
58 Interview, 8 November 2016.
59 Interview, 5 May 2017.
60 Interview, 18 April 2017.
61 Interview, 7 April 2017.
62 Interview, 8 November 2016.
63 Interview, 7 April 2017.
64 Interview, 7 April 2017.
65 See http://www.bbc.co.uk/news/uk-scotland-scotland-politics-26791763.
66 Interview, 6 April 2017.
67 Interview, 7 April 2017.
68 Interview, 6 April 2017.
69 Interview, 13 April 2017.
70 Interview, 7 April 2017.
71 Interview, 6 April 2017.
72 Interview, 13 April 2017.
73 Interview, 7 April 2017.
74 Interview, 7 April 2017.
75 Interview, 6 April 2017.

CHAPTER THREE

1 Chief executive of the Yes Scotland campaign, interview, 6 April 2017.
2 Interview, 6 April 2017.
3 Interview, 8 November 2016.
4 Interview, 16 August 2017.
5 Interview, 8 November 2016.
6 Interview, 16 August 2017.
7 Interview, 10 March 2016.
8 Interview, 5 June 2017.
9 Interview, 8 November 2016.
10 Interview, 10 March 2016.
11 Interview, 18 April 2017.
12 Interview, 8 November 2016.
13 Interview, 5 May 2017.
14 Interview, 8 November 2016.
15 Interview, 16 August 2017.
16 Interview, 8 November 2016.
17 Interview, 5 June 2017.

208 Notes to pages 80–90

18 Interview, 9 November 2016.
19 Interview, 8 November 2016.
20 Interview, 16 August 2017.
21 Interview, 8 November 2016.
22 Interview, 10 March 2016.
23 Interview, 5 June 2017.
24 Interview, 16 August 2017.
25 Interview, 9 November 2016. For Cameron's statement, see http://www.mirror.co.uk/news/uk-news/brexit-could-trigger-world-war-7928607.
26 Interview, 5 May 2017.
27 Interview, 8 November 2016.
28 Interview, 10 March 2016.
29 Interview, 8 November 2016.
30 Interview, 18 April 2017.
31 Interview, 8 November 2016.
32 Interview, 9 November 2016.
33 Interview, 16 August 2017.
34 Interview, 8 November 2016.
35 Interview, 5 May 2017.
36 Interview, 8 November 2016.
37 Interview, 5 June 2017.
38 Interview, 8 November 2016.
39 Interview, 5 May 2017.
40 Interview, 18 April 2017.
41 Interview, 8 November 2016.
42 Interview, 16 August 2017.
43 Interview, 5 June 2017.
44 Interview, 9 November 2016.
45 Interview, 5 June 2017.
46 Interview, 5 May 2017.
47 Interview, 18 April 2017.
48 Interview, 16 August 2017.
49 Interview, 5 May 2017.
50 Interview, 5 June 2017.
51 Interview, 16 August 2017.
52 Interview, 18 April 2017.
53 Media analysis of Loughborough University (Centre for Research in Communication and Culture 2016). This is a study of the news coverage of the EU referendum produced on weekdays (i.e., Monday to

Friday) between 6 May and 22 June 2016 from the following news outlets: television, *Channel 4 News* (7 p.m.), *Channel 5 News Tonight* (6.30 p.m.), *BBC1 News at 10*, *ITV1 News at 10*, *Sky News* (8–8.30 p.m.); press, *Guardian, Times, Daily Telegraph, Financial Times, Daily Mail, Daily Express, Daily Mirror, Sun, Star, I.*

54 Interview with James McGrory, 8 November 2016.

55 Interview, 6 April 2017.

56 This study examines all relevant articles published online over the official ten-week campaign (from 15 April to 23 June) by the following sources: broadcasters: *BBC, ITV, Channel 4, Sky News*; newspapers, *Daily Mail, Daily Express, Daily Mirror, Daily Star, Daily Telegraph, Financial Times, Guardian and Observer, Independent, Times, Sun*; news magazines, *Economist, New Statesman, Spectator*; digital only, *Buzzfeed UK, Huffington Post UK, Vice UK*.

57 Detailed studies of social media activity confirm similar trends. Usherwood and Wright (2017), drawing on a dataset covering the six months prior to the Brexit vote, find that both sides in their Twitter campaigns used emotional language and framing, but that the Leave side had superior agenda-setting skills, shaping the debate.

CHAPTER FOUR

1 Chief executive of the Vote Leave campaign, interview, 8 November 2016.

2 In line with the Michigan model tradition stating that voting choices depend on long-term and short-term factors (see Campbell et al. 1960; Lewis-Beck et al. 2008), we posit that attitudes toward the EU, alongside individuals' socioeconomic profile, belong to the first category, whereas the variables examined in chapter 5, namely, campaign arguments and leaders' images, belong to the second.

3 This dataset is created from a dyad ratios algorithm based on fourteen survey items.

4 The item used reads as follows: 'Generally speaking, do you think that your country's membership of the European Union is a good thing, a bad thing or neither good nor bad?' The Eurobarometer is a series of cross-national longitudinal surveys conducted regularly on behalf of the European Commission since 1973 and designed to compare and gauge trends within member states of the EU. Detailed description of these surveys can be found on the website of the European Commission's Directorate-General Communication. A detailed

Notes to pages 97–105

account of the depth of Euroscepticism sentiment among the British public compared to the rest of the EU one year before the referendum on Brexit can be found in the report based on the results of the Eurobarometer conducted in the spring of 2015 (see *Public Opinion in the European Union*, Standard Eurobarometer 83/ Spring 2015 – TNS opinion and social, https://ec.europa.eu/commfrontoffice/publicopinion/indexb_en.htm.

5 See John Curtice (2015), table 6, 11. Available at https://whatukthinks.org/eu/wp-content/uploads/2016/02/Analysis-paper-5-How-deeply-does-Britains-Euroscepticism-run.pdf.

6 Ibid., table 2, 6.

7 Fox and Pearce (2018) further show that British Euroscepticism partly overlaps with a generational divide, with the youngest generation being less Eurosceptical than older age groups – a consequence of young Britons being less nationalist and more open to diversity and having greater access to education.

8 Examining public opinion change on the EU issue over the 1983–2004 period, Evans and Butt (2007, 188) conclude that elites followed opinion more than they led it. However, as the authors note, this trend is mainly attributable to political parties having switched positions on this issue over that period and thus having sent mixed signals to the public. Since their study does not cover the mass-elite relationship during the previous three decades, it is difficult to draw from their analysis definitive conclusions about the direction of causality.

9 The survey was weighted to demographic targets of the UK population (age, gender, region) to correct for sample imbalance. These weighting targets are based on mid-year estimates for 2015 in the 2011 Census. Weighting targets also included the 2015 Westminster vote and the Brexit referendum vote. Please see the appendix for further details.

10 Household income is a scale based on income brackets expressed in sterling pounds. Assets include owning a home or apartment, a country house, a savings account, a business, rental properties, and stocks.

11 These results come from a split-sample question-wording experiment, whereby a random half of our sample was asked one version of the question (version A, which referred to 'the European Union' intervening too much in the affairs of the UK) and the other random half was asked another version (version B, which referred to 'the bureaucrats in Brussels' intervening too much in the affairs of the UK). As can be seen in table 4.6, both the control group (A) and the experimental group

(B) agree with the statement about there being too much intervention. That said, the statistical test indicates that the experimental group is even more in agreement with the statement (tau-b = 0.06, p<0.02), thus showing that the idea of 'the bureaucrats in Brussels' elicits even more negative views about the EU's level of intervention in UK affairs.

12 Note that the treatment has no significant impact on the relationship between this item and referendum vote choice (p=0.639 in a logistic regression).

13 Answers to this question correlate moderately with those given to the question about EU/bureaucrats in Brussels intervening too much in the affairs of the UK (table 4.6) and the questions about whether the European integration project has gone too far in the domains of free trade and immigration (table 4.8). Pearson's R are 0.69, 0.26, and 0.39, respectively.

CHAPTER FIVE

1 Chief executive of the Vote Leave campaign, interview, 8 November 2016.

2 Most scholarly work assumes that issues and arguments precede leaders' images and emotions in the funnel of causality going from the most remote to the more proximate determinants of the vote (Lewis-Beck et al. 2008; Nadeau et al. 2012; Kritzinger et al. 2013).

3 This was the case during the Quebec referendum campaign in 1995. Even though the pro-independence side lost the referendum, observers and analysts recognize that the OUI camp led a much better campaign than the victorious NON camp (Martin and Nadeau 2001). Vavreck (2009) has also shown that some presidential candidates ended up winning after running suboptimal campaigns.

4 Focusing on the main spokespersons for the Remain and Leave camps appears to be a reasonable approach given their high visibility during the Brexit campaign. This stategy is also consistent with that adopted by scholars who have analysed individual voting decisions in referendum campains (see Clarke and Kornberg 1994, 1996; Martin and Nadeau 2002; Clarke, Goodwin, and Whiteley 2017).

5 This five-point difference is in the expected direction (Gamma = .10) and approaches the .05 threshold of statistical significance ($\chi2$ = 2.25, p <.076, one-tailed test). Furthermore, a logistic regression using the vote choice as the dependent variable (taking the value of 1 for Leave supporters and 0 otherwise) and including five controls (age, gender,

education, income, and ideology) as well as a 'late decider' item (which equals 1 for late deciders and 0 otherwise) shows that the coefficient associated with this latter variable is of the expected sign and statistically significant at the .003 level (two-tailed test; the coefficient is 0.47 with a standard deviation of .15). This result confirms the idea that late deciders leaned more toward the Leave option.

6 The Remain side would have received 50.6 per cent of the vote if the late deciders (22 per cent of the sample) gave a five-point lead to this option.

7 As discussed in detail in chapter 2, strategists working on Quebec and Scottish independence made great efforts to reassure voters by insisting that a sovereign Quebec and Scotland would retain political, economic, and commercial ties with their host countries, including sharing the same currency.

8 The difference between the two groups is significant at p < .02.

9 The difference between the two groups is significant at p < .03.

10 To better measure the effect of leader image on vote choice, we included interaction effects in the model, where the popularity of the leaders (table 5.11) is multiplied by perceptions about their performance during the campaign (i.e., convincing or not; see table 5.4).

11 If these attitudes were more widespread among the population, the percentage of respondents disappointed with the result would have been higher than those who were happy.

12 See Gopian and Hadjiharalambous (1994), Chaffee and Rimal (1996), Fournier et al. (2001), and Cattelini and Alberici (2012).

13 The questions used to measure individuals' attitudes toward risk are as follows: Where would you place yourself on a scale going from 0 to 10, where 0 means being unwilling to take risks and 10 means being fully prepared to take risks in general? (GENRISK). In financial matters? (ECNRISK). In making political choices? (POLRISK).

14 Scholars are still debating if risk-taking is a general disposition or mainly domain specific (Blais and Weber 2006; Figner and Weber 2011; Highhouse et al. 2017). This is why we have included in the analyses both general and domain-specific measures of individuals' disposition toward risks.

15 These results are not related to the simultaneous presence of the three risk variables in the model. Analyses that include these variables one at a time are similar to those in figure 5.7. The coefficients of the GENRISK, ECNRISK, and POLRISK variables change very little when compared to a model where they are all included simultaneously.

Only the political risk measure is significantly related to referendum vote choice.

16 Results from uncertain voters on the economic consequences of Brexit shed further light on the effects of the Leave campaign. They show that this group of moderate voters has been particularly sensitive to arguments that the withdrawal of the UK from the EU would reduce immigration and better fund the NHS.

CHAPTER SIX

1 Prime minister of the UK, 2010–16, interview with ITV, "Good Morning Britain," 3 June 2016.

2 According to Esaiasson (2011, 102), 'Citizens' reactions to elections … are shaped by two different processes. In one process, elections are associated with favourable and unfavourable outcomes of a power struggle (Anderson et al. 2005). In the other process, elections are associated with a legitimate procedure for conflict resolution (e.g., Dahl 1989).'

3 As stated by Rich (2015, 245), 'Democracy at its core requires the continued support of those displeased with election results (Nadeau and Blais 1993, 553), which in many cases outnumber winners.'

4 Howell and Justwan (2013) limited their study to elections held in presidential and parliamentary systems precisely to obtain the strongest contrasts between winners and losers.

5 Nadeau and Blais (1993) measured the legitimacy of the victory of the winning party in the 1988 Canadian federal election using the question 'As a result of this election, did the Canadian people give the Conservative government the right to implement the Free Trade Agreement?' Not surprisingly, the overwhelming majority of those on the winning side (93 per cent) responded in the affirmative, whereas only 58 per cent of those on the losing side recognized the legitimacy of the Conservative Party's victory and its right to go ahead with the signing of the free trade agreement with the United States.

6 The Brexit referendum was not legally binding. However, because the question of the non-binding character of the referendum was virtually absent in the campaign and in the media (Jackson, Thorsen, and Wring 2016) we believe that it is unlikely to have affected losers' decision whether or not to accept the result.

7 The 37 per cent rallying figure in the case of the Brexit referendum is lower than that of the 1988 'free trade election' in Canada. This is not surprising, given the different scope of the two plebiscites. The 1988

214   Notes to pages 159–68

election was about joining an economic free trade agreement, while the 2016 referendum was about withdrawing from a much larger economic and political partnership.

8 It may be possible to think of abstainers as having been the real losers of Brexit. Yet as much as 46 per cent of the abstainers we surveyed expressed a neutral position on our Emotion scale, and about half of them said that the UK government should accept the referendum's result. These figures do not lend much support to the idea of abstainers having been deeply disappointed with the outcome.

9 Satisfaction with democracy is measured on a five-point scale where 1 is being very dissatisfied with the way democracy works in the UK and 5 is very satisfied. The percentages of satisfaction reported in tables 6.2 and 6.3 represent the proportions of respondents who picked categories 4 (satisfied) or 5 (very satisfied) on this scale.

10 See appendix 2 for the coding of the variables.

11 The battery is formed of the following four statements to which respondents were asked to answer true or false: 1) "Switzerland is a member of the EU" (false); 2) "Every country in the EU elects the same number of representatives to the European Parliament" (false); 3) "The Netherlands hold at the moment the presidency of the Council of the European Union" (true); 4) "The European Union has 15 Member States" (false).

12 All the details about the coding of the variables are included in appendix 2.

13 Adding regional dummy variables to this model further indicates that there is no significant relationship between individuals' region of residence and the likelihood of their accepting the referendum's outcome.

14 The fact that winners seem to have made their decision later than sore losers reflects the shift toward the Leave option during the campaign. Moreover, the average marginal effects displayed in the appendix table A3.2 round out the picture. These results also neatly suggest that graceful losers expressed more moderate and informed views than sore losers (and winners).

CHAPTER SEVEN

1 'The Scaffolding of Rhetoric', unpublished essay by Churchill, 1897. Text available at http://www.winstonchurchill.org/wp-content/uploads/2016/06/THE_SCAFFOLDING_OF_RHETORIC.pdf.

2 Speech by President John F. Kennedy, 9 April 1963, quoting the words of American broadcast journalist Edward R. Murrow, 1954.
3 See https://www.independent.co.uk/news/uk/politics/eu-referendum-boris-johnson-independence-day-live-debate-bbc-vote-leave-brexit-remain-a7094531.html.
4 A similar dynamic is observable in independence referendums. Empirical work on Quebec political dynamics has shown that the level of support for political independence reached its peak in the early 1990s when Quebeckers were infuriated about the rejection of a constitutional agreement (the Meech Lake Accord) between their province and the rest of Canada (see Nadeau 1992; Blais and Nadeau 1992; Yale and Durand 2011).
5 The full report is available at http://www.publications.parliament.uk/pa/cm201617/cmselect/cmtreasy/122/122.pdf.
6 Interview, 8 November 2016.
7 Interview, 16 August 2017.
8 Interview, 8 November 2016.
9 Interview with chief campaign spokesperson of the Remain side, James McGrory, 8 November 2016.
10 Interview, 6 April 2017.
11 Interview, 16 August 2017.

Bibliography

Aarts, Kees, and Hen van der Kolk. 2006. 'Understanding the Dutch "No": The Euro, the East, and the Elite.' *PS: Political Science and Politics* 39, no. 2: 243–6.

Aimer, Peter, and Raymond Miller. 2002. 'Partisanship and Principle: Voters and the New Zealand Electoral Referendum of 1993.' *European Journal of Political Research* 41, no. 6: 795–809.

Altman, David. 2010. *Direct Democracy Worldwide*. Cambridge: Cambridge University Press.

Alvarez, R. Michael, and John Brehm. 2002. *Hard Choices, Easy Answers: Values, Information, and American Public Opinion*. Princeton: Princeton University Press.

Anderson, Christopher J., and Christine A. Guillori. 1997. 'Political Institutions and Satisfaction with Democracy.' *American Political Science Review* 91, no. 1: 66–81.

Anderson, Christopher J., and Jason D. Hecht. 2018. 'The Preference for Europe: Public Opinion about European Integration since 1952.' *European Union Politics* 19, no. 4: 617–38.

Anderson, Christopher J., and Andrew J. LoTempio. 2002. 'Winning, Losing and Political Trust in America.' *British Journal of Political Science* 32, no. 2: 335–51.

Anderson, Christopher J., and Silvia M. Mendes. 2006. 'Learning to Lose: Election Outcomes, Democratic Experiences and Political Protest Potential.' *British Journal of Political Science* 36, no. 1: 91–111.

Anderson, Christopher J., and Yuliya Tverdova. 2001. 'Winners, Losers, and Attitudes about Government in Contemporary Democracies.' *International Political Science Review* 22, no. 4: 321–38.

Bibliography

Anderson, Christopher J., André Blais, Shaun Bowler, Todd Donovan, and Ola Listhaug. 2005. *Losers' Consent: Elections and Democratic Legitimacy*. Oxford: Oxford University Press.

Anker, Hans. 2006. 'The Netherlands, Referendum on the European Constitution, June 1: A Referendum on the Gap between the Citizens and the Political Establishment.' In *Election Time 2005: The European Yearbook of Political Campaigning 2005*, edited by S. Hartinger. European Association of Political Consultants and Hartinger Consulting Communications.

Atikcan, Ece Özlem. 2015a. *Framing the European Union: The Power of Political Arguments in Shaping European Integration*. Cambridge: Cambridge University Press.

– 2015b. 'The Puzzle of Double Referendums in the European Union.' *Journal of Common Market Studies* 53, no. 5: 937–56.

– 2018. 'Agenda Control in EU Referendum Campaigns: The Power of the Anti-EU Side.' *European Journal of Political Research* 57, no. 1: 93–115.

Atkinson, John W. 1957. 'Motivational Determinants of Risk-Taking Behavior.' *Psychological Review* 64, no. 6: 585–91.

Banducci, Susan A., and Jeffrey A. Karp. 2003. 'How Elections Change the Way Citizens View the Political System: Media Effects and Electoral Outcomes in Comparative Perspective.' *British Journal of Political Science* 33, no. 3: 443–67.

Banks, Arron. 2016. *The Bad Boys of Brexit: Tales of Mischief, Mayhem and Guerrilla Warfare in the EU Referendum Campaign*. London: Biteback Publishing.

Bartels, Larry M. 1992. 'The Impact of Electioneering in the United States.' In *Electioneering: A Comparative Study of Continuity and Change*, edited by David E. Butler and Austen Ranney, 245–77. Oxford: Clarendon Press.

Becker, Sascha O., Thiemo Fetzer, and Dennis Novy. 2017. 'Who Voted for Brexit? A Comprehensive District-Level Analysis.' *Economic Policy* 32, no. 92: 601–51.

Beggan, James K., and Scott T. Allison. 1993. 'The Landslide Victory That Wasn't: The Bias toward Consistency in Recall of Election Support.' *Journal of Applied Social Psychology* 23, no. 8: 669–77.

Bélanger, Éric, Richard Nadeau, Ailsa Henderson, and Eve Hepburn. 2018. *The National Question and Electoral Politics in Quebec and Scotland*. Montreal and Kingston: McGill-Queen's University Press.

Bennett, Owen. 2016. *The Brexit Club: The Inside Story of the Leave Campaign's Shock Victory*. London: Biteback Publishing.

Binder, Michael. 2010. 'Getting It Right or Playing It Safe? Confusion, the Status Quo Bias and Correct Voting in Direct Democracy.' PhD diss., University of California. UC San Diego Electronic Theses and Dissertations.

Blais, André, and François Gélineau. 2007. 'Winning, Losing and Satisfaction with Democracy.' *Political Studies* 55, no. 2: 425–41.

Blais, André, Pierre Martin, and Richard Nadeau. 1995. 'Attentes économiques et linguistiques et appui à la souveraineté du Québec.' *Canadian Journal of Political Science* 28, no. 4: 637–57.

– 1998. 'Can People Explain Their Own Vote? Introspective Questions as Indicators of Salience in the 1995 Quebec Referendum on Sovereignty.' *Quality and Quantity* 32, no. 4: 355–66.

Blais, André, Alexandre Morin-Chassé, and Shane Singh. 2017. 'Election Outcomes, Legislative Representation, and Satisfaction with Democracy.' *Party Politics* 23, no. 2: 85–95.

Blais, André, and Richard Nadeau. 1992. 'To Be or Not to Be Sovereignist: Quebeckers' Perennial Dilemma.' *Canadian Public Policy* 18, no. 1: 89–103.

Blais, Ann-Renée, and Elke U. Weber. 2006. 'A Domain-Specific Risk-Taking (DOSPERT) Scale for Adult Populations.' *Judgment and Decision-Making* 1, no. 1: 33–47.

Bølstad, Jørgen. 2015. 'Dynamics of European Integration: Public Opinion in the Core and Periphery.' *European Union Politics* 16, no. 1: 23–44.

Bowler, Shaun, and Todd Donovan. 1998. *Demanding Choices: Opinion, Voting, and Direct Democracy*. Ann Arbor: University of Michigan Press.

Brader, Ted. 2005. 'Striking a Responsive Chord: How Political Ads Motivate and Persuade Voters by Appealing to Emotions.' *American Journal of Political Science* 49, no. 2: 388–405.

– 2006. *Campaigining for Hearts and Minds: How Emotional Appeals in Political Ads Work*. New York: Cambridge University Press.

Brader, Ted, and George Marcus. 2013. 'Emotions and Political Psychology.' In *The Oxford Handbook of Political Psychology*, edited by L. Huddy, D. Sears, and J. Levy. Oxford: Oxford University Press.

Brady, Henry, Richard Johnston, and John Sides. 2006. 'The Study of Political Campaigns.' In *Capturing Campaign Effects*, edited by H. Brady and R. Johnston. Ann Arbor: University of Michigan Press.

Bibliography

Breton, Charles, Fred Cutler, Sarah Lachance, and Alex Mierke-Zatwarnicki. 2017. 'Telephone versus Online Survey Modes for Elections Studies: Comparing Canadian Public Opinion and Vote Choice in the 2015 Federal Election.' *Canadian Journal of Political Science* 50, no. 4: 1005–36.

Brouard, Sylvain, and Nicolas Sauger. 2005. 'Comprendre la victoire du "Non": Proximité partisane, conjoncture et attitude à l'égard de l'Europe.' In *Le référendum de ratification du Traité constitutionnel européen du 29 mai 2005: Comprendre le 'Non' français*, edited by A. Laurent and N. Sauger. Paris: CEVIPOF.

Brunell, Thomas J., and Justin Buchler. 2009. 'Ideological Representation and Competitive Congressional Elections.' *Electoral Studies* 28, no. 3: 448–57.

Butler, David, and Austin Ranney, eds. 1994. *Referendums around the World: The Growing Use of Direct Democracy.* Washington, DC: American Enterprise Institute for Public Policy Research.

Butler, David, and Uwe Kitzinger. 1996. *The 1975 Referendum.* 2nd ed. Basingtoke, UK: Palgrave Macmillan.

Campbell, Angus, Phillip E. Converse, Warren E. Miller, and Donald E. Stokes. 1960. *The American Voter.* New York: John Wiley & Sons.

Carey, Sean. 2002. 'Undivided Loyalties: Is National Identity an Obstacle to European Integration?' *European Union Politics* 3, no. 4: 387–413.

Catellani, Patrizia, and Augusta Isabella Alberici. 2012. 'Does the Candidate Matter? Comparing the Voting Choice of Early and Late Deciders.' *Political Psychology* 33, no. 5: 619–34.

Centre for Research in Communication and Culture. 2016. *Media Analysis of the Brexit Referendum Campaign.* Loughborough: Loughborough University.

Chaffee, Steven H., and Rajiv Nath Rimal. 1996. 'Time of Voting Decision and Openness to Persuasion.' In *Political Persuasion and Attitude Change*, edited by Diana C. Mutz, Paul Sniderman, and Richard Brody, 267–91. Ann Arbor: University of Michigan Press.

Chong, Dennis, and James Druckman. 2007a. 'Framing Public Opinion in Competitive Democracies.' *American Political Science Review* 101, no. 4: 637–55.

– 2007b. 'Framing Theory.' *Annual Review of Political Science* 10, no. 1: 103–26.

– 2007c. 'A Theory of Framing and Opinion Formation in Competitive Elite Environments.' *Journal of Communication* 57, no. 1: 99–118.

Christin, Thomas, Simon Hug, and Pascal Sciarini. 2002. 'Interests and Information in Referendum Voting: An Analysis of Swiss Voters.' *European Journal of Political Research* 41, no. 6: 759–76.

Cigler, Allan J., and Russell Getter. 1977. 'Conflict Resolution in the Post-Election Period: A Test of the Depolarization Thesis.' *Western Political Quarterly* 30, no. 3: 363–76.

Clarke, Harold D., and Allan Kornberg. 1994. 'The Politics and Economics of Constitutional Choice: Voting in Canada's 1992 National Referendum.' *Journal of Politics* 56, no. 4: 940–62.

– 1996. 'Choosing Canada? The 1995 Quebec Sovereignty Referendum.' *PS: Political Science and Politics* 29, no. 4: 676–82.

Clarke, Harold D., Matthew Goodwin, and Paul Whiteley. 2017. *Brexit: Why Britain Voted to Leave the European Union*. Cambridge: Cambridge University Press.

Closa, Carlos. 2007. 'Why Convene Referendums? Explaining Choices in EU Constitutional Politics.' *Journal of European Public Policy* 14, no. 8: 1311–32.

Cobb, Michael, and James Kuklinski. 1997. 'Changing Minds: Political Arguments and Political Persuasion.' *American Journal of Political Science* 41, no. 1: 88–121.

Colantone, Italo, and Piero Stanig. 2018. 'Global Competition and Brexit.' *American Political Science Review* 112, no. 2: 201–18.

Coleman, William D. 1988. *Business and Politics: A Study in Collective Action*. Montreal: McGill-Queen's University Press.

Collard, Sharon, and Zoey Breuer. 2009. *Attitudes towards Investment Choice and Risk within the Personal Account Scheme: Report of a Qualitative Study*. Department for Work and Pensions, Research Report no. 565, Bristol: University of Bristol.

Craig, Stephen C., Michael D. Martinez, Jason Gainous, and James G. Kane. 2006. 'Winners, Losers, and Election Context: Voter Responses to the 2000 Presidential Election.' *Political Research Quarterly* 59, no. 4: 579–92.

Curini, Luigi, Willy Jou, and Vincenzo Memoli. 2011. 'Satisfaction with Democracy and the Winner/Loser Debate: The Role of Policy Preferences and Past Experience.' *British Journal of Political Science* 42, no. 2: 241–61.

Curtice, John. 2015. *How Deeply Does Britain's Euroscepticism Run?* London: NatCen Social Research.

Curtice, John, and Geoffrey Evans. 2015. 'Britain and Europe: Are We All Eurosceptics Now?' In *British Social Attitudes: The 32nd Report*, edited by John Curtice and Rachel Ormston. London: NatCen Social Research.

Dahl, Robert. 1989. *Democracy and Its Critics*. New Haven: Yale University Press.

d'Ancona, Matthew. 2017. *Post Truth: The New War on Truth and How to Fight Back*. London: Ebury Press.

Darcy, R., and Michael Laver. 1990. 'Referendum Dynamics and the Irish Divorce Amendment.' *Public Opinion Quarterly* 54, no. 1: 1–20.

Delli Carpini, Michael X., and Scott Keeter. 1996. *What Americans Know about Politics and Why It Matters*. New Haven: Yale University Press.

Denver, David. 2002. 'Voting in the 1997 Scottish and Welsh Devolution Referendums: Information, Interests and Opinions.' *European Journal of Political Research* 41, no. 6: 827–43.

de Vreese, Claes. 2007. *The Dynamics of Referendum Campaigns: An International Perspective*. Basingstoke: Palgrave Macmillan.

de Vreese, Claes, and Hajo Boomgaarden. 2007. 'Immigration, Identity, Economy and the Government: Understanding Variation in Explanations for Outcomes of EU-Related Referendums.' In *The Dynamics of Referendum Campaigns: An International Perspective*, edited by C. de Vreese. Basingstoke: Palgrave Macmillan.

de Vreese, Claes, and Holli Semetko. 2004. *Political Campaigning in Referendums: Framing the Referendum Issue*. Abingdon: Routledge.

De Vries, Catherine. 2009. 'Taking Europe to Its Extremes: Extremist Parties and Public Euroscepticism.' *Party Politics* 15, no, 1: 5–28.

Dinan, Desmond. 2012. 'Governance and Institutions: Impact of the Escalating Crisis.' *Journal of Common Market Studies* 50, no. 2: 85–98.

DR's Investigative Research Team. 2016. 'Europe Has Grown More Eurosceptic.' https://www.dr.dk/nyheder/udland/brexit/europe-has-grown-more-eurosceptic.

Druckman, James. 2001. 'On the Limits of Framing Effects: Who Can Frame?' *Journal of Politics* 63, no. 4: 1041–66.

Druckman, James, and Rose McDermott. 2008. 'Emotion and the Framing of Risky Choice.' *Political Behavior* 30, no. 3: 297–321.

Edelman, Murray. 1985. 'Political Language and Political Reality.' *PS: Political Science and Politics* 18, no. 1: 10–19.

Ehrlich, Sean, and Cherie Maestas. 2010. 'Risk Orientation, Risk Exposure, and Policy Opinions: The Case of Free Trade.' *Political Psychology* 31, no. 5: 657–83.

Bibliography

Elkink, Johan, and Richard Sinnott. 2015. 'Political Knowledge and Campaign Effects in the 2008 Irish Referendum on the Lisbon Treaty.' *Electoral Studies* 38, no. 2: 217–25.

Entman, Robert M. 2004. *Projections of Power: Framing News, Public Opinion, and U.S. Foreign Policy*. Chicago: University of Chicago Press.

Erikson, Robert S., and Christopher Wlezien. 2012. *The Timeline of Presidential Elections: How Campaigns Do (and Do Not) Matter*. Chicago: University of Chicago Press.

Esaiasson, Peter. 2011. 'Electoral Losers Revisited: How Citizens React to Defeat at the Ballot Box.' *Electoral Studies* 30, no. 1: 102–13.

Evans, Geoffrey. 2003. 'Will We Ever Vote for the Euro?' In *British Social Attitudes: The 20th Report*, edited by Alison Park, John Curtice, Katarina Thomson, Lindsey Jarvis, and Catherine Bromley. London: Sage.

Evans, Geoffrey, and Sarah Butt. 2007. 'Explaining Change in British Public Opinion on the European Union: Top Down or Bottom Up?' *Acta Politica* 42, nos. 2–3: 173–90.

Evans, Geoffrey, and Pippa Norris, eds. 1999. *Critical Elections: British Parties and Voters in Long-Term Perspective*. London: Sage.

Evans, Jocelyn A. J., and Gilles Ivaldi. 2005. 'An Extremist Autarky: The Systemic Segregation of the French Extreme Right.' *South European Society and Politics* 10, no. 2: 351–66.

Ezrow, Lawrence, and Georgios Xezonakis. 2011. 'Citizen Satisfaction with Democracy and Party Policy Offerings.' *Comparative Political Studies* 44, no. 9: 1152–78.

Feinberg, Matthew, and Robb Willer. 2011. 'Apocalypse Soon? Dire Messages Reduce Belief in Global Warming by Contradicting Just World Beliefs.' *Psychological Science* 22, no. 1: 34–8.

Festinger, Leon. 1957. *A Theory of Cognitive Dissonance*. Stanford: Stanford University Press.

Figner, Bernd, and Elke U. Weber. 2011. 'Who Takes Risks and Why?: Determinants of Risk Taking.' *Current Directions in Psychological Sciences* 20, no. 4: 211–16.

Finkel, Steven E. 1993. 'Re-Examining the 'Minimal Effects' Model in Recent Presidential Elections.' *Journal of Politics* 55, no. 1: 1–21.

Fisher, Stephen, and Alan Renwick. 2016. 'Do People Tend to Vote against Change in Referendums?' *Elections Etc*, 22 June 2016.

Forster, Anthony. 2002. *Euroscepticism in Contemporary British Politics: Opposition to Europe in the British Conservative and Labour Parties since 1945*. London: Routledge.

Fournier, Patrick, Richard Nadeau, André Blais, Elisabeth Gidengil and Neil Nevitte. 2001. 'Validation of Time of Voting Decision Recall.' *Public Opinion Quarterly* 65, no 1: 95–107.

Fournier, Patrick, Richard Nadeau, André Blais, Elisabeth Gidengil, and Neil Nevitte. 2004. 'Time-of-Voting Decision and Susceptibility to Campaign Effects.' *Electoral Studies* 23, no. 4: 661–81.

Fox, Stuart, and Sioned Pearce. 2018. 'The Generational Decay of Euroscepticism in the UK and the EU Referendum.' *Journal of Elections, Public Opinion and Parties* 28, no. 1: 19–37.

Franklin, Mark, Cees van der Eijk, and Michael Marsh. 1995. 'Referendum Outcomes and Trust in Government: Public Support for Europe in the Wake of Maastricht.' *West European Politics* 18, no. 3: 101–17.

Frenkel, Oden, and Anthony Doob. 1976. 'Postdecision Dissonance at the Polling Booth.' *Canadian Journal of Behavioral Science* 8, no. 4: 347–50.

Funder, David C., and C. Randall Colvin. 1991. 'Explorations in Behavioral Consistency: Properties of Persons, Situations, and Behaviors.' *Journal of Personality and Social Psychology* 60, no. 5: 773–94.

Gabel, Matthew. 1998. *Interest and Integration: Market Liberalization, Public Opinion and European Union.* Ann Arbor: University of Michigan Press

Gabel, Matthew, and Harvey Palmer. 1995. 'Understanding Variation in Public Support for European Integration.' *European Journal of Political Research* 27, no. 1: 3–19.

Gamson, William. 1988. 'Political Discourse and Collective Action.' In *International Social Movement Research*, vol. 1, edited by B. Klandermans, H. Kriesi, and S. Tarrow. Greenwich: JAI Press.

Garry, John. 2013. 'Direct Democracy and Regional Integration: Citizens' Perceptions of Treaty Implications and the Irish Reversal on Lisbon.' *European Journal of Political Research* 52, no. 1: 94–118.

– 2014. 'Emotions and Voting in EU Referendums.' *European Union Politics* 15, no. 2: 235–54.

Garry, John, Michael Marsh, and Richard Sinnott. 2005. '"Second-Order" versus "Issue-Voting" Effects in EU Referendums: Evidence from the Irish Nice Treaty Referendums.' *European Union Politics* 6, no. 2: 201–21.

Geddes, Andrew. 2013. *Britain and the European Union.* Basingstoke: Palgrave Macmillan.

Gifford, Chris. 2014. *The Making of Eurosceptic Britain*. 2nd ed. London: Routledge.

Gleissner, Martin, and Claes de Vreese. 2005. 'News about the EU Constitution: Journalistic Challenges and Media Portrayal of the European Union Constitution.' *Journalism* 6, no. 2: 221–42.

Glencross, Andrew. 2016. *Why the UK Voted for Brexit: David Cameron's Great Miscalculation*. London: Palgrave Macmillan.

Goffman, Erving. 1974. *Frame Analysis: An Essay on the Organization of Experience*. New York: Harper & Row.

Goldsmith, Arthur. 2005. 'Plebiscites, Fiscal Policy and the Poor: Learning from US Experience with Direct Democracy.' *Development Policy Review* 23, no. 5: 553–66.

Goodwin, Matthew, and Oliver Heath. 2016. 'The 2016 Referendum, Brexit and the Left Behind: An Aggregate-Level Analysis of the Result.' *Political Quarterly* 87, no. 3: 323–32.

Goodwin, Matthew, Simon Hix, and Mark Pickup. 2018. 'For and against Brexit: A Survey Experiment of the Impact of Campaign Effects on Public Attitudes toward EU Membership.' Published online, *British Journal of Political Science*, February. doi:10.1017/S0007123417 000667.

Gopian, David J., and Sissie Hadjiharalambous. 1994. 'Late-Deciding in Presidential Election.' *Political Behavior* 16, no. 1: 55–78.

Granberg, Donald. 1993. 'Political Perception.' In *Explorations in Political Psychology*, edited by Shanto Iyengar and William J. McGuire. Durham: Duke University Press.

Granberg, Donald, Jeff Kasmer, and Tim Nanneman. 1988. 'An Empirical Examination of Two Theories of Political Perception.' *Western Political Quarterly* 41, no. 1: 29–46.

Grand, Peter, and Guido Tiemann. 2013. 'Projection Effects and Specification Bias in Spatial Models of European Parliament Elections.' *European Union Politics* 14, no. 4: 497–521.

Greene, William H. 2003. *Econometric Analysis*. 5th ed. Upper Saddle River, NJ: Prentice-Hall.

Groenendyk, Eric. 2011. 'Current Emotion Research in Political Science: How Emotions Help Democracy Overcome Its Collective Action Problem.' *Emotion Review* 3, no. 4: 455–63.

Hafer, Carolyn, and Laurent Bègue. 2005. 'Experimental Research on Just-World Theory: Problems, Developments, and Future Challenges.' *Psychological Bulletin* 131, no. 1: 128–67.

Hannan, Daniel. 2016. *Why Vote Leave*. London: Head of Zeus.

Harley, Nicola. 2016. 'Brexit: Government Rejects Petition Signed by Four Million Calling for Second EU Referendum.' *Telegraph* (London), 9 July 2016.

Henderson, Ailsa, James Mitchell, Rob Johns, and Chris Carman. 2015. 'The Scottish Question, Six Months On.' Paper presented at the Transatlantic Seminar Series, Politics and International Relations, University of Edinburgh.

Highhouse, Scott, Christopher D. Nye, Doc C. Chang, and Thaddeus B. Rada. 2017. 'Structure of the Dospert: Is There Evidence of a General Risk Factor?' *Journal of Behavioral Decision Making* 30, no. 2: 400–6.

Highley, John, and Ian McAllister. 2002. 'Elite Division and Voter Confusion: Australia's Republic Referendum in 1999.' *European Journal of Political Research* 41, no. 6: 845–61.

Hobolt, Sara. 2005. 'When Europe Matters: The Impact of Political Information on Voting Behaviour in EU Referendums.' *Journal of Elections, Public Opinion and Parties* 15, no. 1: 85–109.

– 2006a. 'Direct Democracy and European Integration.' *Journal of European Public Policy* 13, no. 1: 153–66.

– 2006b. 'How Parties Affect Vote Choice in European Integration Referendums.' *Party Politics* 12, no. 5: 623–47.

– 2009. *Europe in Question: Referendums on European Integration.* New York: Oxford University Press.

– 2016. 'The Brexit Vote: A Divided Nation, a Divided Continent.' *Journal of European Public Policy* 23, no. 9: 1259–77.

Hobolt, Sara, and Sylvain Brouard. 2011. 'Contesting the European Union? Why the Dutch and the French Rejected the European Constitution.' *Political Research Quarterly* 64, no. 2: 309–22.

Hobolt, Sara, and Christopher Wratil. 2015. 'Which Arguments Will Win the Referendum? Immigration or the Economy?' *LSE Brexit.* LSEblogs.lse.ac.uk/brexit/2016/06/21/which-argument-will-win-the-referendum-immigraton-or-the-economy/.

Holbrook, Thomas M. 1996. *Do Campaigns Matter?* Thousand Oaks, CA: Sage.

Holmes, Michael. 2008. 'The Referendum on the Treaty of Lisbon in the Republic of Ireland, 12 June 2008.' European Parties Elections and Referendums Network, Referendum Briefing Paper no. 16, 1–9.

Hooghe, Liesbet, and Gary Marks. 2004. 'Does Identity or Economic Rationality Drive Public Opinion on European Integration?' *PS: Political Science and Politics* 37, no. 3: 415–20.

Hopkin, Jonathan, and Ben Rosamond. 2017. 'Post-Truth Politics, Bullshit and Bad Ideas: "Deficit Fetishism" in the UK.' *New Political Economy* 23, no. 6: 641–55.

Howell, Patrick, and Florian Justwan. 2013. 'Nail-Biters and No-Contests: The Effect of Electoral Margins on Satisfaction with Democracy in Winners and Losers.' *Electoral Studies* 32, no. 2: 334–43.

Huddy, Leonie, and Anna Gunnthorsdottir. 2000. 'The Persuasive Effects of Emotive Visual Imagery: Superficial Manipulation or the Product of Passionate Reason?' *Political Psychology* 21, no. 4: 745–78.

Hyink, Bernard. 1969. 'California Revises Its Constitution.' *Western Political Quarterly* 22, no. 3: 637–54.

Iyengar, Shanto. 1993. 'Agenda Setting and Beyond: Television News and the Strength of Political Issues.' In *Agenda Formation*, edited by W. Riker. Ann Arbor: University of Michigan Press.

Jackson, Daniel, Einar Thorsen, and Dominic Wring, eds. 2016. *EU Referendum Analysis 2016: Media, Voters and the Campaign.* Loughborough, UK: Loughborough University, Centre for Research in Communication and Culture.

Jennings, Will, and Stephen Fisher. 2016. *Expert Predictions of the 2016 EU Referendum.* London: Political Studies Association.

Jerit, Jennifer. 2004. 'Survival of the Fittest: Rhetoric during the Course of an Election Campaign.' *Political Psychology* 25, no. 4: 563–75.

Jerit, Jennifer, and Jason Barabas. 2006. 'Bankrupt Rhetoric: How Misleading Information Affects Knowledge about Social Security.' *Public Opinion Quarterly* 70, no. 3: 278–303.

Johns, Rob. 2014. 'Why Scotland Voted "No".' Paper presented at the Department of Politics and International Relations, Royal Holloway, University of London.

Johnston, Richard, André Blais, Elisabeth Gidengil, and Neil Nevitte. 1996. *The Challenge of Direct Democracy: The 1992 Canadian Referendum.* Montreal: McGill-Queen's University Press.

Joslyn, Mark R. 1998. 'Opinion Change after the Election.' Paper presented at the annual meeting of the American Political Science Association, Boston, September.

Kahneman, Daniel. 2011. *Thinking Fast and Slow.* London: Penguin Books.

Kahneman, Daniel, and Amos Tversky. 1979. 'Prospect Theory: An Analysis of Decision under Risk.' *Econometrica* 47, no. 2: 263–92.

– 1984. 'Choices, Values, and Frames.' *American Psychologist* 39, no. 4: 341–50.

228 Bibliography

Kam, Cindy D., and Elizabeth N. Simas. 2010. 'Risk Orientations and Policy Frames.' *Journal of Politics* 72, no. 2: 381–96.

– 2012. 'Risk Attitudes, Candidate Characteristics, and Vote Choice.' *Public Opinion Quarterly* 76, no. 4: 747–60.

Keating, Michael. 2009. *The Independence of Scotland: Self-Government and the Shifting Politics of Union.* Oxford: Oxford University Press.

Kim, Myunghee. 2009. 'Cross-National Analyses of Satisfaction with Democracy and Ideological Congruence.' *Journal of Elections, Public Opinion and Parties* 19, no. 1: 49–72.

King, Anthony. 1977. *The 1975 Referendum on the Common Market.* Washington, DC: American Enterprise Institute.

Kritzinger, Sylvia, Eva Zeglovits, Michael Lewis-Beck, and Richard Nadeau. 2013. *The Austrian Voter.* Vienna: University of Vienna Press.

Kuklinski, James H., and Paul J. Quirk. 2000. 'Reconsidering the Rational Public: Cognition, Heuristics, and Mass Opinion.' In *Elements of Reason: Cognition, and the Bounds of Rationality*, edited by Arthur Lupia, Mathew D. McCubbins, and Samuel L. Popkin. Cambridge: Cambridge University Press.

Lau, Richard. 1985. 'Two Explanations for Negativity Effects in Political Behavior.' *American Journal of Political Science* 29, no. 1: 119–38.

Lavine, Howard. 2001. 'The Electoral Consequences of Ambivalence toward Presidential Candidates.' *American Journal of Political Science* 45, no. 4: 915–29.

Laycock, Samantha. 2013. 'Is Referendum Voting Distinctive? Evidence from Three UK Cases.' *Electoral Studies* 32, no. 2: 236–52.

Lecheler, Sophie, and Claes de Vreese. 2012. 'What a Difference a Day Makes?: The Effects of Repetitive and Competitive News Framing over Time.' *Communication Research* 40, no. 2: 147–75.

LeDuc, Lawrence. 2002. 'Opinion Change and Voting Behaviour in Referendums.' *European Journal of Political Research* 41, no. 6: 711–32.

– 2003. *The Politics of Direct Democracy: Referendums in Global Perspective.* New York: Broadview Press.

– 2005. 'Saving the Pound or Voting for Europe? Expectations for Referendums on the Constitution and the Euro.' *Journal of Elections, Public Opinion and Parties* 15, no. 2: 169–96.

LeDuc, Lawrence, and Jon Pammett. 1995. 'Referendum Voting: Attitudes and Behaviour in the 1992 Constitutional Referendum.' *Canadian Journal of Political Science* 28, no. 1: 3–33.

Bibliography

Lerner, Jennifer S., and Dachner Keltner. 2001. 'Fear, Anger and Risk.' *Journal of Personality and Social Psychology* 81, no. 1: 146–59.

Lewis-Beck, Michael S., William Jacoby, Helmut Norpoth, and Herbert Weisberg. 2008. *The American Voter Revisited*. Ann Arbor: University of Michigan Press.

Lewis-Beck, Michael S., Richard Nadeau, and Martial Foucault. 2013. 'The Compleat Economic Voter: New Theory and British Evidence.' *British Journal of Political Science* 43, no. 2: 241–61.

Liñeira, Robert, Ailsa Henderson, and Liam Delaney. 2017. 'Voters' Response to the Referendum Campaign.' In *Debating Scotland*, edited by Michael Keating, 165–90. Oxford: Oxford University Press.

Lipset, Seymour M. 1960. *Political Man: The Social Bases of Politics*. New York: Doubleday.

Loewen, Peter, and André Blais. 2006. 'Testing Publius' Federalism: Losers' Consent, Winners' Lament?' Paper prepared for the Conference on the Comparative Study of Electoral Systems, Seville, Spain.

Lupia, Arthur, and Mathew D. McCubbins. 1998. *The Democratic Dilemma: Can Citizens Learn What They Need to Know?* Cambridge: Cambridge University Press.

Lupia, Arthur, and Jesse O. Menning. 2009. 'When Can Politicians Scare Citizens into Supporting Bad Policies?' *American Journal of Political Science* 53, no. 1: 90–106.

Magleby, David. 1984. *Direct Legislation: Voting on Ballot Propositions in the United States*. Baltimore: Johns Hopkins University Press.

Magleby, David, and Kelly Patterson. 1998. 'Consultants and Direct Democracy.' *PS: Political Science and Politics* 31, no. 2: 160–9.

Marcus, George E. 2000. 'Emotions in Politics.' In *Annual Review of Political Science* 3, no. 1: 221–50.

Marcus, George E., and Michael B. MacKuen. 1993. 'Anxiety, Enthusiasm, and the Vote: The Emotional Underpinnings of Learning and Involvement during Presidential Campaigns.' *American Political Science Review* 87, no. 3: 672–85.

Marcus, George E., W. Russell Neuman, and Michael MacKuen. 2000. *Affective Intelligence and Political Judgment*. Chicago: University of Chicago Press.

Martin, Pierre, and Richard Nadeau. 2001. 'Understanding Opinion Formation on Quebec Sovereignty.' In *Citizen Politics: Research and Theory in Canadian Political Behaviour*, edited by Joanna Everitt and Brenda O'Neill, 142–58. Don Mills: Oxford University Press.

Matti, Joshua, and Yang Zhou. 2017. 'The Political Economy of Brexit: Explaining the Vote.' *Applied Economics Letters* 24, no. 16: 1131–4.

McAllister, Ian. 2001. 'Elections without Cues: The 1999 Australian Republic Referendum.' *Australian Journal of Political Science* 36, no. 2: 247–69.

McAllister, Ian, and Donley Studlar. 1991. 'Bandwagon, Underdog, or Projection? Opinion Polls and Electoral Choice in Britain, 1979–1987.' *Journal of Politics* 53, no. 3: 720–41.

McClelland, David C. 1987. *Human Motivation*. New York: Cambridge University Press.

McGuire, William J. 1968. 'Theory of the Structure of Human Thought.' In *Theories of Cognitive Consistency: A Sourcebook*, edited by Robert P. Abelson. Chicago: Rand McNally.

McLaren, Lauren. 2002. 'Public Support for the European Union: Cost/Benefit Analysis or Perceived Cultural Threat?' *Journal of Politics* 64, no. 2: 551–66.

– 2006. *Identity, Interests and Attitudes to European Integration*. Basingstoke: Palgrave Macmillan.

Meadwell, Hudson. 1993. 'The Politics of Nationalism in Quebec.' *World Politics* 45, no. 2: 203–41.

– 1995. 'Breaking the Mould?: Quebec Independence and Secession in the Developed West.' In *Notions of Nationalism*, edited by S. Periwal. Budapest: Central European University Press.

Mendez, Fernando, Mario Mendez, and Vasiliki Triga. 2016. *Referendums and the European Union: A Comparative Inquiry*. Cambridge: Cambridge University Press.

Meyer, Christoph. 1999. 'Political Legitimacy and the Invisibility of Politics: Exploring the European Union's Communication Deficit.' *Journal of Common Market Studies* 37, no. 4: 617–39.

Mitchell, James. 2016. 'The Referendum Campaign.' In *The Scottish Independence Referendum: Constitutional and Political Implications*, edited by A. McHarg, T. Mullen, A. Page, and N. Walker. Oxford: Oxford University Press.

Moehler, Devra C. 2009. 'Critical Citizens and Submissive Subjects: Elections Losers and Winners in Africa.' *British Journal of Political Science* 39, no. 2: 345–66.

Moore, Martin, and Gordon Ramsay. 2017. *UK Media Coverage of the 2016 EU Referendum Campaign*. King's College London: Centre for the Study of Media, Communication and Power.

Morgenstern, Scott, and Elizabeth Zechmeister. 2001. 'Better the Devil You Know Than the Saint You Don't? Risk Propensity and Vote Choice in Mexico.' *Journal of Politics* 63, no. 1: 93–119.

Morel, Laurence, and Matt Qvortrup. 2018. *The Routledge Handbook to Referendums and Direct Democracy*. London: Routledge.

Morisi, Davide. 2018. 'Choosing the Risky Option: Information and Risk Propensity in Referendum Campaigns.' *Public Opinion Quarterly* 82, no. 3: 447–69.

Mosbacher, Michael, and Oliver Wiseman. 2016. *Brexit Revolt: How the UK Voted to Leave the EU*. London: New Culture Forum.

Mullen, Tom. 2014. 'The Scottish Independence Referendum.' *Journal of Law and Society* 41, no. 4: 627–40.

– 2016. Introduction to *The Scottish Independence Referendum: Constitutional and Political Implications*, edited by A. McHarg, T. Mullen, A. Page, and N. Walker. Oxford: Oxford University Press.

Nadeau, Richard. 1992. 'Le virage souverainiste des Québécois.' *Recherches sociographiques* 33, no 1: 9–28.

Nadeau, Richard, Éric Bélanger, and Ece Özlem Atikcan. 2018. 'Are Political Risks Domain-Specific?' Unpublished manuscript.

Nadeau, Richard, Éric Bélanger, Michael S. Lewis-Beck, Bruno Cautrès, and Martial Foucault. 2012. *Les élections présidentielles: Le vote des Français de Mitterrand à Sarkozy*. Paris: Presses de Sciences Po.

Nadeau, Richard, Éric Bélanger, Michael S. Lewis-Beck, Mathieu Turgeon, and François Gélineau. 2017. *Latin American Elections: Choice and Change*. Ann Arbor: University of Michigan Press.

Nadeau, Richard, and André Blais. 1993. 'The Effect of Participation on Losers' Consent.' *British Journal of Political Science* 23, no. 4: 553–63.

Nadeau, Richard, Ruth Dassonneville, Michael S. Lewis-Beck, and Philippe Mongrain. 2019. 'Are Election Results More Unpredictable? A Forecasting Test.' *Political Science Research and Methods*. DOI: https://doi.org/10.1017/psrm.2019.24.

Nadeau, Richard, and Christopher Fleury. 1995. 'Gains linguistiques anticipés et appui à la souveraineté du Québec.' *Canadian Journal of Political Science* 28, no. 1: 35–50.

Nadeau, Richard, and Michael S. Lewis-Beck. 2012. 'Does a Presidential Candidate's Campaign Affect the Election Outcome?' *Foresight* 24: 15–19.

Nadeau, Richard, Pierre Martin, and André Blais. 1999. 'Attitude towards Risk-Taking and Individual Choice in the Quebec Referendum on Sovereignty.' *British Journal of Political Science* 29, no. 3: 523–39.

Nadeau, Richard, Neil Nevitte, Elisabeth Gidengil, and André Blais. 2008. 'Election Campaigns as Information Campaigns: Who Learns What and Does It Matter?' *Political Communication* 25, no. 3: 229–48.

Nadeau, Richard, and Richard Niemi. 1995. 'Educated Guesses: The Process of Answering Factual Knowledge Questions in Surveys.' *Public Opinion Quarterly* 59, no. 3: 323–46.

Nadeau, Richard, Richard Niemi, and Timothy Amato. 1994. 'Expectations and Preferences in British General Elections.' *American Political Science Review* 88, no. 2: 371–83.

– 1995. 'Emotions, Issue Importance and Political Learning.' *American Journal of Political Science* 39, no. 3: 558–74.

Nadeau, Richard, François Pétry, and Éric Bélanger. 2010. 'Strategic Issue Framing in Election Campaigns: The Case of Health Care in the 2000 Canadian Federal Election.' *Political Communication* 27, no. 4: 367–88.

Neuman, Russell, George Marcus, Ann Crigler, and Michael MacKuen. 2007. *The Affect Effect: Dynamics of Emotion in Political Thinking and Behavior*. Chicago: University of Chicago Press.

Norris, Pippa, John Curtice, David Sanders, Margaret Scammell, and Holli Semetko. 1999. *On Message: Communicating the Campaign*. London: Sage.

Oliver, Craig. 2016. *Unleashing Demons: The Inside Story of Brexit*. London: Hodder & Stoughton.

Oppermann, Kai. 2013. 'The Politics of Discretionary Government Commitments to European Integration Referendums.' *Journal of European Public Policy* 20, no. 5, 684–701.

Pammett, Jon, and Lawrence LeDuc. 2001. 'Sovereignty, Leadership and Voting in the Quebec Referendums.' Electoral Studies 20, no. 2: 265–80.

Pennebaker, James. 1993. 'Putting Stress into Words: Health, Linguistic, and Therapeutic Implications.' *Behaviour Research and Therapy* 31, no. 6: 539–48.

Pennebaker, James, and Martha Francis. 1996. 'Cognitive, Emotional, and Language Processes in Disclosure.' *Cognition and Emotion* 10, no. 6: 601–26.

Petty, Richard E., and John T. Cacioppo. 1986. *Communication and Persuasion: Central and Peripheral Routes to Attitude Change*. New York: Springer-Verlag.

Pfau, Michael, and Henry Kenski. 1990. *Attack Politics: Strategy and Defense*. New York: Praeger.

Piketty, Thomas, and Emmanuel Saez. 2003. 'Income Inequality in the United States, 1913–1998.' *Quarterly Journal of Economics* 118, no. 1: 1–39.

Price, Vincent, and John R. Zaller. 1993. 'Who Gets the News? Alternative Measures of News Receptions and Their Implications for Research.' *Public Opinion Quarterly* 57, no. 2: 133–64.

Przeworski, Adam. 1991. *Democracy and the Market: Political and Economic Reforms in Eastern Europe and Latin America*. Cambridge: Cambridge University Press.

Qvortrup, Matt. 2013. *Direct Democracy: A Comparative Study of the Theory and Practice of Government by the People*. Manchester: Manchester University Press.

Rasinski, Kenneth. 1989. 'The Effect of Question Wording on Public Support for Government Spending.' *Public Opinion Quarterly* 53, no. 3: 388–94.

Rasmussen, Jorgen. 1997. '"What Kind of Vision Is That?": British Public Attitudes towards the European Community during the Thatcher Era.' *British Journal of Political Science* 27, no, 1: 111–18.

Ray, Leonard. 2003. 'Reconsidering the Link between Incumbent Support and Pro-EU Opinion.' *European Union Politics* 4, no. 3: 259–79.

Regan, Dennis T., and Martin Kilduff. 1988. 'Optimism after Elections: Dissonance Reduction at the Ballot Box.' *Political Psychology* 9, no. 1: 101–7.

Reif, Karlheinz, and Hermann Schmitt. 1980. 'Nine Second-Order National Elections: A Conceptual Framework for the Analysis of European Election Results.' *European Journal of Political Research* 8, no. 1: 3–44.

Renwick, Alan. 2014. 'Don't Trust Your Poll Lead: How Public Opinion Changes during Referendum Campaigns.' In *Sex, Lies and the Ballot Box: 50 Things You Need to Know about British Elections*, edited by P. Cowley and R. Ford. London: Biteback.

Renwick, Alan, Matthew Flinders, and Will Jennings. 2016. 'Calming the Storm: Fighting Falsehoods, Fig Leaves and Fairy Tales.' In *EU Referendum Analysis 2016: Media, Voters and the Campaign*, edited by Daniel Jackson, Einar Thorsen, and Dominic Wring, 31–2. Loughborough, UK: The Centre for the Study of Journalism, Culture and Community.

Rich, Timothy S. 2015. 'Losers' Consent or Non-Voter Consent? Satisfaction with Democracy in East Asia.' *Asian Journal of Political Science* 23, no. 3: 243–59.

Rich, Timothy S., and Mallory Treece. 2018. 'Losers' and Non-Voters' Consent: Democratic Satisfaction in the 2009 and 2013 Elections in Germany.' *Government and Opposition* 53, no. 3: 416–36.

Ridout, Travis, and Michael Franz. 2011. *The Persuasive Power of Campaign Advertising*. Philadelphia: Temple University Press.

Ridout, Travis, and Kathleen Searles. 2011. 'It's My Campaign I'll Cry If I Want To: How and When Campaigns Use Emotional Appeals.' *Political Psychology* 32, no. 3: 439–58.

Bibliography

Riker, Wiliam, ed. 1993. *Agenda Formation*. Ann Arbor: University of Michigan Press.

Rose, Richard, and Gabriela Borz. 2013. 'What Determines Demand for European Union Referendums?' *Journal of European Integration* 35, no. 5: 619–33.

Samuelson, William, and Richard Zeckhauser. 1988. 'Status Quo Bias in Decision Making.' *Journal of Risk and Uncertainty* 1, no. 1: 7–59.

Schwarz, Norbert. 2000. 'Emotion, Cognition, and Decision Making.' *Cognition and Emotion* 14: 433–40.

Scott, Andrew. 2016. 'Economics and National Autonomy.' In *The Scottish Independence Referendum: Comstitutional and Political Implications*, edited by A. McHarg, T. Mullen, A. Page, and N. Walker. Oxford: Oxford University Press.

Shipman, Tim. 2016. *All Out War: The Full Story of How Brexit Sank Britain's Political Class*. London: William Collins.

– 2017. *Fall Out: A Year of Political Mayhem*. London: William Collins.

Singh, Shane, Ekrem Karakoç, and André Blais. 2012. 'Differentiating Winners: How Elections Affect Satisfaction with Democracy.' *Electoral Studies* 31, no. 1: 201–11.

Singh, Shane, Ignacio Lago, and André Blais. 2011. 'Winning and Competitiveness as Determinants of Political Support.' *Social Science Quarterly* 92, no. 3: 695–709.

Sinnott, Richard, and Johan Elkink. 2010. 'Attitudes and Behaviour in the Second Referendum on the Treaty of Lisbon.' Report for the UK Department of Foreign Affairs.

Sinnott, Richard, Johan Elkink, Kevin O'Rourke, and James McBride. 2009. 'Attitudes and Behaviour in the Referendum on the Treaty of Lisbon.' Report for the UK Department of Foreign Affairs.

Siune, Karen, Palle Svensson, and Ole Tonsgaard. 1994. 'The European Union: The Danes Said "No" in 1992, but "Yes" in 1993: How and Why?' *Electoral Studies* 13, no. 2: 107–16.

Sniderman, Paul, Richard A. Brody, and Philip Tetlock. 1991. *Reasoning and Choice: Explorations in Political Psychology*. Cambridge: Cambridge University Press.

Sniderman, Paul, and Sean Theriault. 2004. 'The Structure of Political Argument and the Logic of Issue Framing.' In *Studies in Public Opinion: Attitudes, Nonattitudes, Measurement Error, and Change*, edited by W. Saris and P. Sniderman. Princeton: Princeton University Press.

Snow, David, Burke Rochford Jr, Steven Worden, and Robert Benford. 1986. 'Frame Alignment Processes, Micromobilization, and Movement Participation.' *American Sociological Review* 51, no. 4: 464–81.

Soroka, Stuart. 2002. *Agenda-Setting Dynamics in Canada*. Vancouver: UBC Press.

– 2014. *Negativity in Democratic Politics: Causes and Consequences*. Cambridge: Cambridge University Press.

Spanier, Bernd. 2012. *Europe, Anyone? The 'Communication Deficit' of the European Union Revisited*. Germany: Nomos.

Startin, Nicholas. 2015. 'Have We Reached a Tipping Point? The Mainstreaming of Euroscepticism in the UK.' *International Political Science Review* 36, no. 3: 311–23.

Statham, Paul. 2010. 'Media Performance and Europe's "Communication Deficit": A Study of Journalists' Perceptions.' In *Mapping the European Public Sphere: Institutions, Media and Civil Society*, edited by C. Bee and E. Bozzini. Farnham: Ashgate.

Steenbergen, Marco R., and Tomasz Siczek. 2017. 'Better the Devil You Know? Risk-Taking, Globalization and Populism in Great Britain.' *European Union Politics* 18, no. 1: 119–36.

Stephenson, Laura B., and Jean Crête. 2011. 'Studying Political Behavior: A Comparison of Telephone and Internet Surveys.' *International Journal of Public Opinion Research* 23, no. 1: 24–55.

Swales, Kirby. 2016. *Understanding the Leave Vote*. London: NatCen Social Research.

Taggart, Paul. 1998. 'A Touchstone of Dissent: Euroscepticism in Contemporary Western European Party Systems.' *European Journal of Political Research* 33, no. 3: 363–88.

Taggart, Paul, and Aleks Szczerbiak. 2013. 'Coming In from the Cold? Euroscepticism, Government Participation and Party Positions on Europe.' *Journal of Common Market Studies* 51, no. 1: 17–37.

Tarrow, Sidney. 1998. *Power in Movement: Social Movements and Contentious Politics*. Cambridge: Cambridge University Press.

Thaler, Richard. 1980. 'Toward a Positive Theory of Consumer Choice.' *Journal of Economic Behavior and Organization* 1, no. 1: 39–60.

– 1994. *The Winner's Curse: Paradoxes and Anomalies of Economic Life*. Princeton: Princeton University Press.

Tversky, Amos, and Daniel Kahneman. 1990. 'Rational Choice and the Framing of Decisions.' In *The Limits of Rationality*, edited by K. Cook and M. Levi. Chicago: University of Chicago Press.

Usherwood, Simon, and Nick Startin. 2013. 'Euroscepticism as a Persistent Phenomenon.' *Journal of Common Market Studies* 51, no. 1: 1–16.

Usherwood, Simon, and Katharine A.M. Wright. 2017. 'Sticks and Stones: Comparing Twitter Campaigning Strategies in the EU Referendum.' *British Journal of Politics and International Relations* 19, no. 2: 371–88.

Van Ingelgom, Virginie. 2014. *Integrating Indifference: A Comparative, Qualitative and Quantitative Approach to the Legitimacy of European Integration*. Colchester: ECPR Press.

Vasilopoulou, Sofia. 2016. 'UK Euroscepticism and the Brexit Referendum.' *Political Quarterly* 87, no. 2: 219–27.

Vavreck, Lynn. 2009. *The Message Matters: The Economy and Presidential Campaigns*. Princeton: Princeton University Press.

Wagner, Markus, and Sofia Vasilopoulou. 2016. 'Emotions and Brexit: How Did They Affect the Result?' *History of Emotions Blog*. www.qmul.ca.uk/emotions. Posted 7 July by Helen Sark.

Weber, Elke U., Ann-Renée Blais, and Nancy E. Betz. 2002. 'A Domain-Specific Risk-Attitude Scale: Measuring Risk Perceptions and Risk Behaviours.' *Journal of Behavioural Decision Making* 15, no. 4: 263–90.

Weber, Elke U., and Christopher Hsee. 1998. 'Cross-Cultural Differences in Risk Perception, but Cross-Cultural Similarities in Attitudes towards Perceived Risks.' *Management Science* 44, no. 9: 1205–17.

Willocq, Simon. 2019. 'Explaining Time of Vote Decision: The Socio-Structural, Attitudinal, and Contextual Determinants of Late Deciding.' *Political Studies Review* 17, no. 1: 53–64.

Witte, Kim, and Mike Allen. 2000. 'A Meta-Analysis of Fear Appeals: Implications for Effective Public Health Campaigns.' *Health Education and Behavior* 27, no. 5: 591–615.

Yale, François, and Claire Durand. 2011. 'What did Quebeckers Want? Impact of Question Wording, Constitutional Proposal and Context on Support for Sovereignty, 1976–2008.' *American Review of Canadian Studies* 41, no. 3: 242–58.

Young, Robert. 1998. *The Secession of Quebec and the Future of Canada*. Montreal and Kingston: McGill-Queen's University Press.

Zaller, John R. 1992. *The Nature and Origins and Mass Opinion*. Cambridge: Cambridge University Press.

Index

Page references in *italics* indicate a figure; page references in **bold** indicate a table.

Ahern, Bertie, 42
'alternative facts,' 19, 180
Anderson, Christopher J., 97, 154, 160
Anderton, Phil, 59, 62, 65, 66–7
attitude: definition of, 15
Australian referendum on monarchy (1999), 10

Banks, Aaron, 20
Baron Crespo, Enrique, 47
Better Together campaign: core message, 56, 58–9; cost-benefit approach, 65–6; democracy and fairness arguments, 61; economic considerations, 59–60, 61; emotional appeal, 65; outreach of soft voters, 57–9; posters, *58,* 59; as 'Project Fear,' 20, 62, 63, 148; *vs.* Remain campaign, 59–60, 62–3, 170; slogans, 66–7; supporters, 56
Biltgen, François, 47
Blais, André, 12, 54, 178, 213n5
Bommel, Harry van, 47
Bone, Peter, 20
Brexit campaign: *vs.* 2015 election campaign, 90; anti-EU agenda, 41,

49, 68, 83–6; borders issue, 179–80, 182–3; characteristics of, 83, 173–4; economic arguments, 20, 28, 32, 47, 50, 55, 59–60, 76–7, 78, 136, 169–70; emotional appeal, 176–7; immigration issue, 60, 80–1, 83–4, 171; media coverage of, 64, 75, 89–93, *91, 93*; misleading information, 179, 180; outreach of undecided voters, 59–60, 76–7, 112, 123, 169; posters, 22–5; as 'Project Fear,' 71, 82, 92, 171; public knowledge of the EU, 86–8; resonance of arguments among electorate, 88–9, 129–33; in social media, 209n57; sovereignty issue, 77, 80, 180–1; strategies, 31, 40, 67–8, **69,** 70, **72,** 72–3, 93–4. *See also* individual strategies; Leave side; Remain side
Brexit negotiations, 31, 49, 63, 86, 166
Brexit referendum: abstainers, 214n8; announcement of, 3, 20; call for second, 151, 166, 172–3; *vs.* EU referendums, 4, 5, 31, 34, 35–41, 169, 181–2, 203n3; framing the

choice in, 51–2, 65–6, 67, 179; *vs.* independence referendums, 52–67, 131–2; initial goal of, 125; late voting decisions, 161–2; legitimacy of, 172–3; media content analyses, 29–30; public-opinion survey, 30, 31–2, 171; *vs.* Quebec referendum, 27, 131–2; reason for holding, 6; risk assessment, 5, 7; *vs.* Scottish referendum, 8, 27, 55, 59–60, 62–3, 66, 68, 70, 169–70; spending on, 20; studies of, 5, 6–7, 8, 28–30, 170; typology of, 21, 173–5; undecided voters, 27, 28, 32, 33, 44

Brexit referendum results: emotional reactions to, 162–3; 'graceful' and 'sore' losers, 152, 154; legitimacy of, 152; non-binding character of, 213n6; predictions about, 3–4, 21, 67–8; reaction to, 151–2, 157, 158; voters' acceptance of, 33, 157, 172–3, 177–8, 213n7. *See also* graceful losers; sore losers; winners

Brinkhorst, Laurens-Jan, 46
Britain Stronger in Europe: leader, 20; posters, 22–3
British Political Studies Association, 3
British public opinion: on attachment toward the EU, 105, 106; on attachment toward the UK, 106; on benefits of EU membership, 106–7, 107; on Cameron's deal with the EU, 125–6; on degree of EU intervention, 105–6, 106; on European integration, 107–8, 108; Euroscepticism in, 97; long-term trends in, 6; on performance of the EU in various issues, 107–9, 109, 210n8
British Social Attitudes Survey (BSA), 97

Brown, Anthony, 49
Brown, Gordon, 54
Búrca, Déirdre de, 43
Butt, Sarah, 210n8

Cameron, David: Brexit referendum and, 3, 20, 83, 122, 171; on British democracy, 151, 152; deal with the EU, 49, 125, 126, 182; popularity rating, 140–1, 141; voter perception of, 125–6, 127, 127, 130
Canadian constitutional referendum (1992), 10, 13
Canadian 'free trade election' (1988), 12, 213n5, 213n7
Chong, Dennis, 19
Christin, Thomas, 203n4
Churchill, Winston, 168, 179
Clarke, Harold D., 7, 100
Clement, Nico, 42
Clinton, Hillary, 18
Coetzee, Ryan, 76, 78, 81, 83
Cóir (Irish Catholic fundamentalists), 45
Coleman, William D., 152
Conway, Kellyanne, 18–19
Corbyn, Jeremy: popularity rating, 149; voter perception of, 127, 129, 130
Coughlan, Anthony, 43
Cox, Pat, 43, 50
Creighton, Lucinda, 48
Crespo, Enrique Baron, 47
Cummings, Dominic, 77, 89
Curtice, John, 97, 122

Danish referendum on common currency (2000), 12
Debons, Claude, 42
democracy, 33, 155, 178, 213n3
de-risking strategy, 28, 72, 75–88
Dinan, Desmond, 37
Donk, Wim van de, 46

Donner, Piet-Hein, 46
Druckman, James, 19
Dupont-Aignan, Nicolas, 42
Dutch referendum on European Constitution, 10, 43–4, 46, 50

Eickhout, Bas, 44
elections: *vs.* referendums, 9–10, 11, 43; truisms of, 3–4
Ellery, Matthew, 80, 82, 84, 87
Elliott, Matthew: on anti-EU attitudes, 74; on appeal for swing voters, 76–7; on Brexit referendum, 124; on lack of exit plan, 63, 85; on overcoming status quo bias, 78; on sovereignty issue, 77; on Vote Leave campaign, 21, 63, 82, 84, 95
emotions: impact on voting behaviour, 141–3, **143**, 204n9, 204n10; in referendum campaigns, 36, 176–7; in shaping public opinion, 16–18; study of, 141–2; types of, 176
Esaiasson, Peter, 213n2
EU referendums: anti-EU campaigns, 41–3, 44–5, 47–9; *vs.* Brexit referendum, 4, 5, 31, 34, 35–41, 169, 181–2, 203n3; campaign information, 36; campaign strategies, 39–40, **40**, 41–4, 68, **69**; economic considerations, 4–5; emotional appeal, 17, 36–7; framing the choice in, 36, 51–2, 67; losers' consent in, 155; negative outcomes, 37; as opinion formation referendums, 35; pro-EU campaigns, 38, 41–2, 49–50; risk card in, 44–7; scapegoating the EU, 50–1; status quo bias, 44–7; studies of, 7, 35–7, 39–40; treaty ratification referendums, 37, 38; on Turkish membership in the EU, 37, 47, 48; voter behaviour, 36

Eurobarometer surveys, 97, 209n4
European Constitution: referendums on, 10, 17, 36–7, 42, 43–5, 46, 47, 50, 51
Euroscepticism: in British politics, 7, 89, 99; in the EU referendums, 41–2; impact on Brexit, 51, 75; in Scotland, 60
Evans, Geoffrey, 97, 210n8

Farage, Nigel: anti-immigrant message, 21, 84; in Brexit campaign, 20, 44, 76, 83; popularity rating, 140–1, **141**, 149; voter perception of, 127, 129, **130**
Fayot, Ben, 50
Feinberg, Matthew, 204n10
Fiscal Compact Treaty referendum, 5, 37, 38, 40, 49
Fisher, Stephen, 13
Forster, Anthony, 96
Fox, Stuart, 210n7
framing, 15, 16–17, 18, 19, 204n8
framing the choice: in EU referendums, 36, 51–2; in independence referendums, 65–7; in referendum campaigns, 12, 13–19
French referendum on European Constitution, 10, 17, 36–7, 42, 44–5, 51

Ganley, Declan, 42, 43, 44, 77
Garry, John, 36
Gerbrandy, Gerben Jan, 44
Gifford, Chris, 96
'gift of oratory,' 168
Giménez Villahoz, Marc, 42
Goerens, Charles, 47
going beyond 50 per cent strategy: in Brexit referendum, **69**, **72**, 76–7; in EU referendums, 11, 41–4; in Scottish referendum, **69**
Goodwin, Matthew, 6, 7, 8, 100, 103

Gove, Michael, 20, 77, 79
graceful losers: attitudinal variables, 163; behavioural variables, 163; as cross-pressured voters, 164; decision-making process, 160; descriptive statistics for, **164**; emotional reaction of, 164; level of sophistication, 156, 164, 166; marginal effects of anchor variables, *165*; multinomial regression model of, **202**; profile of, 160, 178; satisfaction with democracy, 157, **159**, 160, 166; socio-demographic attributes, 163; socioeconomic attributes, 160; *vs.* sore losers, 156–60, 162, 163, 214n14; *vs.* winners, 159–60
Grassroots Out campaign, 20, 21

Hannan, Daniel, 20, 46
Heath, Oliver, 6, 100, 103
Hecht, Jason D., 97
Henderson, Ailsa, 55
Hobolt, Sara, 7, 36, 100
Horan, Blair, 43
House of Commons Treasury Select Committee, 179
Hug, Simon, 203n4

independence referendums: categories of, 52; cost-benefit considerations, 53, 56; economic arguments, 52–3; fear factor, 60–1; framing the choice in, 65–7; main issue of, 52; status quo bias in, 54–5; strategies, 53, 55; undecided voters, 54, 56; as uphill struggle, 52, 55
interview data: collection of, 34–5; keywords, **41**; list of interviewees, 188–94; questionnaire, 29, 187–8; structure of, 28–9, 40–1, 71–2, 170
Irish referendums: on divorce, 10; on the Senate, 13. *See also* Lisbon Treaty referendums

Jenkins, Blair: on anti-EU attitudes, 74; on fear factor, 60–1, 62, 63, 71, 92; on immigration issue, 182; on power of slogans, 67; on risk-based arguments, 64; view of undecided voters, 59; on Yes Scotland campaign, 57
Jerit, Jennifer, 12
Johnson, Alan: on anti-EU attitudes, 74–5; criticism of Leave side, 82, 84; on economic argument, 79; on immigration issue, 80–1; on media portrayal of campaign messages, 89–90; on public knowledge about the EU, 87; on Remain side arguments, 88; on sovereignty issue, 180–1; on Take Back Control slogan, 183
Johnson, Boris: Brexit referendum campaign, 20, 77, 79, 82; emotional appeal, 176; exit deal of, 70, 166, 170; popularity rating, 140–1, **141**, 149; voter perception of, 127, 128–9, **130**

Kanuty, Pierre, 47
Keating, Michael, 52
Keltner, Dachner, 177
Kiely, Brendan, 48

Laffan, Brigid, 48
Laffeber, Marije, 47
Leave.EU, 20, 60, 63, 83
Leave side: de-risking strategy, 73, 94, 124–5, 148, 149, 170, 171, 172; economic arguments, 79, 80, 132–3, 169; emotional appeal, 176–7; faulty promises of, 80; framing choices, 169; going beyond 50% strategy, **72**; impact of campaign arguments on vote choice, 133–4, **135**, 136; main weakness of, 80; messages on

immigration and health care, 49, 172; outreach of moderate voters, 112; performance of leaders, 128–9, 149; 'Project Fear,' 171; reaction to Brexit referendum result, 157, 158; scapegoating the EU strategy, 72, 95–6, 165, 171; sovereignty argument, 93; status quo bias, 72; supporters' profile, 100–1, 103, 111, 112, 157; supportive emotions toward the victory of, 142–3, 143; 'Two Futures' strategy, 132; voter perception of, 126–8, 128. *See also* Vote Leave campaign

Leave vote: logistic regression models of, *116*, 116–18, *117*, *139*, *142*, *144*, *147*, *148*, 200–1; satisfaction with democracy and, **158**, **159**

LeDuc, Lawrence: on types of referendums, 21, 35, 52, 73, 204n7; on voting behaviour in referendum campaigns, 9–10, 11, 12, 13

Lerner, Jennifer, 177

Libertas Ireland, 42, 43, 44

Lisbon Treaty referendums: anti-EU campaign, 44, 45, 48; economic argument, 42, 45; pro-EU campaign, 45, 49, 50; repeat voting, 5, 37, 38, 181; sovereignty issue, 77

losers' consent: attitudinal variables, 160, 163; behavioural variables, 160, 163; in Brexit referendum, 152, 155, 165–6; democratic theory and, 178; emotional factor, 160–1; in EU referendums, 155; individual-level factors of, 154–5; measures of, 154; motivations of voters and, 153–4, 173; phenomenon of, 151–2; scapegoating the EU and, 165; studies of, 152–5, 166–7

Luxembourg referendum on European Constitution, 42, 47, 50

Maastricht Treaty referendum (1992), 5, 37–8, 39, 49, 98, 181

Maaten, Jules, 46

Major, John, 179

Maltese referendum on divorce (2011), 204n5

Martin, Pierre, 12, 54

May, Theresa, 31, 49, 70, 86, 166, 170

McDonald, Mary Lou, 42

McGrory, James: on anti-EU campaign, 75; on elections, 3; on immigration issue, 81; on Leave side campaign, 83, 84, 85; on Remain campaign, 79, 86–7; on slogans, 181; on sovereignty, 180

McGuirk, John, 42

Meadwell, Hudson, 53

Mendes, Silvia M., 154

Morisi, Davide, 8

Mosar, Laurent, 42, 47

Mullen, Tom, 54

Nadeau, Richard, 12, 54, 178, 213n5

National Health Service (NHS): in Brexit referendum campaign, 28, 79, 80, 86, 88

New Zealand referendum on electoral system, 11

Nice Treaty referendums, 5, 37, 38, 39, 45, 49, 181

Nicolaï, Atzo, 46, 50, 51

Nunn, Naoise, 43, 48

Obama, Barack, 18, 81, 82

Osborne, George, 64, 65, 82, 90

Pearce, Sioned, 210n7

political communication strategies, 174–5

post-truth politics, 178–9

Pringle, Kevin: on arguments on democracy and fairness, 61;

criticism of Leave campaign, 63–4;
on currency of independent
Scotland, 64–5; de-risking pitch
in Scottish referendum, 61; outreach of middle-ground voters,
57–8; on Scottish 'Project Fear,' 34,
62–3; on slogans, 66–7; view of
undecided voters, 59
Przeworski, Adam, 155
public opinion: bias towards negative
information, 18; emotions in shaping, 16–18; in referendum campaigns, 10–11, 12, 14; theoretical
framework, 15; volatility of, 10

Quebec sovereignty referendum: vs.
Brexit referendum, 27, 131–2; economic risks, 52, 53; OUI campaign, 211n3; questions used in,
53; roots of, 215n4; sovereignty
issue, 212n7; status quo bias,
54–5; voters' mobilization, 11, 177

referendums: vs. elections, 9–10;
framing the choice in, 13–19;
images and music in, 204n9; opinion change patterns, 10–11, 12,
14, 35; strategies, 9, 11, 13; studies
of, 9, 13; types of, 10, 204n7; voting behaviour, 9–10. See also independence referendums; individual
referendums
Remain side: vs. Better Together campaign, 59–60, 66, 170; campaign
strategies, 5, 72, 72–3, 74, 93–4,
148, 149–50; cost-benefit
approach of, 65; criticism of, 65,
74, 80, 81–2; economic arguments,
20, 28, 32, 38, 79, 82, 129, 137,
149, 169, 170; Eurosceptic arguments, 83; immigration issue, 60,
80–1; impact of campaign arguments on vote choice, 134, 135,

136; lack of understanding of the
EU, 50, 166; leaders of, 149; media
portrayal of, 89–92; neutralization
of opponents' arguments, 138,
139–40; outreach of undecided voters, 27, 44, 136; posters, 20, 22–3;
'Project Fear' of, 20, 62–3, 148; risk
attitudes, 147; scapegoating the EU
and, 27–8, 74, 95–6; slogans, 89;
status quo bias, 78; strength of,
88–9; weakness of, 122, 136
Renwick, Alan, 13
Ricard-Nihoul, Gaëtane, 51
Rich, Timothy S., 154, 213n3
risk attitudes, 146–7
risk aversion effect, 38, 53, 131, 137,
175–6, 203n4
Roche, Dick, 48
Rose, Stuart, Lord: as chair of Britain
Stronger, 20; criticism of Remain
campaign, 80, 81–2; on economy
arguments, 76, 79; on lack of exit
plan, 85; on public knowledge
about the EU, 87; on "Take Back
Control' slogan, 89

Salmond, Alex, 62
satisfaction with democracy: explanatory model of, 159; and Leave
vote, 158, 159; linear regression
models for, 161, 162; measurement
of, 214n9; socio-demographic
characteristics and, 158
scapegoating the EU: in Brexit campaign, 31–2, 51, 72, 74–5, 109–15,
170–1, 172; in EU referendums,
50–1; impact on vote choice, 95;
tradition in British politics, 27–8,
32, 73–4, 95–100
Schengen agreement, 98
Sciarini, Pascal, 203n4
Scottish devolution referendum
(1997), 11, 204n7

Scottish independence referendum (2014): actors, 56; announcement of, 56; arguments, 56; *vs.* Brexit, 8, 27, 55, 59–60, 62–4, 66, 68, 70, 169–70; *vs.* EU referendums, 21; framing the choice in, 65–6; question of Scottish currency, 63–4; risk attitudes, 8; risks and benefits assessment, 52–3, 54; sovereignty issue, 177, 212n7; strategies, **69**; undecided voters, 44; voting behaviour, 13, 57–60. *See also* Better Together campaign; Yes Scotland campaign

Scottish National Party (SNP), 54

Shorthouse, Rob, 58, 59, 60, 61–2, 65

Socialist Coalition, 20

Socialist Party (Netherlands), 43

sore losers: descriptive statistics for, **164**; *vs.* graceful losers, 156–60, 162, 163; marginal effects of anchor variables, *165*; regression model of, **202**; satisfaction with democracy and, **159**; *vs.* winners, 157, 160, 163–4, 214n14

Spanish referendum on European Constitution, 42

status quo bias: in Brexit referendum, **69, 72**, 77–83; characteristics of, 11–13, 203n4; emotions and, 175–7; in EU referendums, 44–7, **69**; in independence referendums, 54–5, 60–3; perspectives on, 12, 175–8; rational arguments and, 177; in Scottish referendum, **69**

Stuart, Gisela, 63, 77, 78, 82, 85, 87, 89

Survation (polling firm), 30, 101

Swales, Kirby, 100

Swedish referendum: on common European currency, 12; on EU membership, 11

Thatcher, Margaret, 96

Tice, Richard, 63, 78, 83, 85, 87–8, 90

Toland, Ciarán, 45

Trump, Donald, 18, 85, 181

Ubéda, Olivier, 48

undecided voters: in Brexit campaign, 27, 44, 59, 76–7, 112, 123, 136, 169, 213n16; in independence referendums, 44, 54, 56

United Kingdom: 2015 general elections, 44, 48, 74, 76, 79; attitudes toward the EU, 74, 97–9, 99, 122–3; electoral reform referendum, 13, 21; 'European' identity trends, 97, 98; Euroscepticism, 96, 210n7; Exchange Rate Mechanism crisis, 96; feelings of national identity, 105; idea of sovereignty, 180

United Kingdom Independence Party (UKIP), 6

Usherwood, Simon, 209n57

Van Heijningen, Hans, 43

Vavreck, Lynn, 211n3

Vote Leave campaign: control and sovereignty issues, 84; de-risking strategy, 28, 31, 62, 76, 81–3; emotional appeal, 27, 28, 66–7; foundations of, 74, 203n3; immigration issue, 31, 32, 60, 83–4; lack of concrete exit plan, 49, 64, 85–6; leaflet of, 21, 26; media coverage, 91–2; National Health Service issue, 31, 32; outreach of undecided voters, 123; political associations, 44; posters of, 20–1, 24–5; risk card, 46; slogans, 20, 28, 66, 77, 85, 122, 169; 'Two Futures' theme, 46, 78; *vs.* Yes Scotland campaign, 62–3 voter perceptions: of Brexit campaign arguments, 129–33; of Cameron's deal with the EU, 125–6, 127; of the consequences of a Leave vote, 131, 132; of economic arguments, 131–2; of immigration issue, 133, 134; of leaders' performance, 127, 128, 130; of performance of Leave and Remain campaigns, 126–7, 128; of UK's financial contribution to the EU, 138–9

voting behaviour: in elections, 169; in referendums, 9–10, 169

voting decision in Brexit campaign: age factor, 100, 101, 102, 116, 196; attachment toward the UK and, 110, 111; attitude toward the EU and, 96, 104–9, 110, 111, 119, 120, 122, 209n2; dependent variables, 195; early and late deciders, 118–19, 121, 130, 143–6, 145, 172; education factor, 100, 101–2, 103, 119; emotional factor, 141–3; Eurosceptic bias and, 96–7, 99, 121–2; gender factor, 100, 101, 102, 196; ideology effect, 116, 119, 196; impact of campaign arguments on, 133–40; issue variable, 198; leader popularity and, 140–1, 199, 212n10; multivariate models of, 115–16, 116, 121; NHS funding issue, 134, 135, 136, 137, 138, 172; opinion and attitude variables, 197–8; opinion of European free trade and, 113–14, 114; opinion of European immigration and, 114, 114–15, 134, 172; opinion of the degree of EU intervention and, 110–11, 112; opinion of the EU interference into British affairs and, 117–18; opinion on degree of European integration and, 112, 112–14; opinion on the EU membership and, 112, 113; overview, 147–50; risk attitudes and, 146–7, 196, 212n15; scapegoating of the EU and, 109–15, 171–2; socioeconomic factors, 100–4, 119, 121, 196; support for campaign arguments and, 137–8, 138; wealth factor, 100, 102–3, 104, 116, 196

White, Karen, 48
Whiteley, Paul, 7, 100
Why Vote Leave (Hannan), 46
Willer, Robb, 204n10
winners: decision making, 214n14; descriptive statistics for, 164; *vs.* graceful losers, 159–60; marginal effects of anchor variables, 165; multinomial regression model of, 202; profile, 152, 154; satisfaction with democracy, 158, 159; *vs.* sore losers, 157, 160, 163–4, 214n14
Wright, Katharine, 209n57

Yes Scotland campaign: actors, 56; criticism of, 62–3; economic arguments, 61–2; emotional appeal, 65, 66; idea of 'Devolution Max,' 148–9; outreach of soft voters, 57–9; posters, 57, 61; slogans, 56, 66–7; themes, 56, 133; *vs.* Vote Leave campaign, 62–3; weakness of, 62; White Paper, 62, 63